D1738565

REFLEC

REFLECTIONS

The Piano Music of Maurice Ravel

Paul Roberts

AMADEUS
PRESS

AN IMPRINT OF HAL LEONARD CORPORATION

Published in 2012 by Amadeus Press
An Imprint of Hal Leonard Corporation
7777 West Bluemound Road
Milwaukee, WI 53213

Trade Book Division Editorial Offices
33 Plymouth St., Montclair, NJ 07042

The author gratefully acknowledges Éditions Gallimard for permission to reprint
the poem 'La petite gare aux ombres courtes' and excerpts from 'Dans la rue qui
monte au soleil', 'La rampe s'allume', and 'La mer phosphorescente perle entre
les arbres', which are taken from *Poèmes; suivi de 'Pour la musique'*, by Léon-Paul
Fargue © Éditions Gallimard, Paris, 1919.

Every reasonable effort has been made to contact copyright holders and secure
permission. Any omissions brought to our attention will be remedied in future
editions.

Printed in the United States of America

Book design by Mark Lerner

Library of Congress Cataloging-in-Publication Data

Roberts, Paul, 1949-
  Reflections : the piano music of Maurice Ravel / Paul Roberts.
      p. cm.
  Includes bibliographical references and index.
    ISBN 978-1-57467-202-2 (alk. paper)
  1. Ravel, Maurice, 1875-1937. Piano music. 2. Piano music--20th century--History and
criticism. 3. Piano music--19th century--History and criticism. I. Title.
  ML410.R23R63 2012
  786.2092--dc23
                        2012001832

www.amadeuspress.com

*To all my colleagues, friends and students in
Portland, Oregon, who have given me such support and
inspiration over many years, and especially to Harold Gray*

Sonatine p 124

Contents

CONTENTS

Preface

At the beginning of the twentieth century Maurice Ravel refused to be daunted by the shadow of the mighty Claude Debussy. At the beginning of the twenty-first Ravel's voice sounds more distinctive than ever. I came late to the younger man's music, intoxicated as I was by Debussy and the rich outpouring of scholarship that coincided with my student days and that heady period around 1968, the fiftieth anniversary of Debussy's death. My late arrival is responsible, perhaps, for the fact that now I am unable to leave Ravel alone. I have needed to make up lost time. I do, however, have a clear memory of being overcome, as a student at the University of York, by the discovery of *Le tombeau de Couperin*, introduced to me by a friend who was a philosophy student, who in those days knew far more about music than I. The seed had been planted. I also learnt at that point that non-musicians experience music as richly as practitioners, indeed, often with greater insight, unencumbered as they are by the stresses that are part of the profession – a lesson that has remained with me ever since. I counsel my students that they underestimate their audience at their peril. Part of my intention in this present book is to address this audience. (I have assembled Appendix A, 'Details for Performance', in order to spare the general reader some rather detailed and abstruse advice for pianists working on the scores. I trust my students, from whom I have learnt so much, will not take this opportunity to turn to this first and then skip the rest.)

Another Debussy anniversary falls in 2012, but it is certain Ravel will remain obstinately undaunted. To treat him in this way, as if he were still alive, is the curious prerogative of those of us who live constantly in the presence of his art. Debussy the man is, for me, shadowy, mysterious. I am uneasy about him, as he himself was uneasy, private, troubled, morally compromised. Ravel too was famously reserved, which was endlessly frustrating for his friends, but his presence in my mind is distinctly clearer, harder – the impeccably dressed, diminutive man who was fiercely sure of the strength and purpose of his art, disconcertingly direct and honest in his opinions, with a deep vein of compassion and an unwavering moral compass.

I could not have written this book without Arbie Orenstein's *A Ravel Reader* by my side (and its French equivalent, *Lettres, écrits, entretiens*, which has been my preferred source); nor Roger Nichols's inestimable editions of the piano works, with detailed background notes, for Peters. I am only sorry not to have been able to draw on Nichols's new biography of Ravel, which arrived just as I had delivered my manuscript; but his collection of contemporary memoirs, *Ravel Remembered*, has been invaluable (and I am grateful to him for permission to quote from it), as has his early monograph, *Ravel*. I much regret not having been able to read Steven Huebner's essay 'Ravel's Poetics: Literary Currents, Classical Takes' (in *Unmasking Ravel: New Perspectives on the Music*, edited by Peter Kaminsky), as I see that he covers similar ground to my own interests in Ravel's literary connections. This book too appeared after my own was completed. As ever Roy Howat has been unfailingly generous in sharing background material. I have also benefited from the timely publication of his book *The Art of French Piano Music*. I am grateful to Arbie Orenstein for allowing me to quote from a private letter in his collection (and to Roger Nichols for drawing my attention to it), in which Ravel reflects on the meaning of the title 'Alborada del gracioso'. I thank a host of other scholars, past and present, whose work is listed in my bibliography.

I would like to thank my editors at Amadeus Press, especially Jessica Burr, for her unfailing courtesy and support, and Barbara Norton for her painstaking attention to detail. My son Ned cast a meticulously critical eye over the final stages of this project that went far beyond filial loyalty, and in large measure my ability to bring *Reflections* to completion I owe to him.

I would like to thank all my students, friends and colleagues who have professed an abiding interest in the progress of this book over a number of years for their patience. This companion volume to my *Images: The Piano Music of Claude Debussy* has been a long time in coming, always promised but delivered only in small morsels on those many occasions when I have given lecture-recitals and performances of Ravel's music. The positive result of this delay, however, has been that in the course of the journey my understanding of Ravel, the man as well as the music, has deepened immeasurably.

Paul Roberts, East Sussex, England, December 2011

Chronological List of Ravel's Piano Music

Title	Date of composition/publication	First performance/by
Sérénade grotesque	c.1892/1975	1975/Arbie Orenstein
Menuet antique	1895/1898	1898/Ricardo Viñes
Sites auriculaires (for two pianos)	1895–7/1975	1898/Martha Dron and Ricardo Viñes
Pavane pour une infante défunte	1899/1900	1902/Ricardo Viñes
Jeux d'eau	1901/1902	1902/Ricardo Viñes
Sonatine	1903–5/1905	1906/Paul de Lestang
Minuet in C-sharp Minor	1904/2007	
Miroirs	1904–5/1906	1906/Ricardo Viñes
Gaspard de la nuit	1908/1908	1909/Ricardo Viñes
Ma mère l'oye (for four hands)	1908–10/1910	1910/Jeanne Leleu and Geneviève Durony
Menuet sur le nom d'Haydn	1909/1909	1911/Ennemond Trillat
Valses nobles et sentimentales	1911/1911	1911/Louis Aubert
Prélude	1913/1913	1913/Jeanne Leleu
Le tombeau de Couperin	1914–17/1918	1919/Marguerite Long
À la manière de Borodine/Chabrier	1913/1914	1913/Alfredo Casella
Frontispice (for two pianos five hands)	1918/1919	

I don't ask for my music to be interpreted, only to be played.

Maurice Ravel, composer

*If there is any trouble with interpretation, it is mainly due to
the fact that interpreters are trying too hard to suppress their
own imagination in rendering music.*

Ernst Krenek, composer and theorist

There are no interpretations, only misinterpretations.

Harold Bloom, literary critic

*European music is founded on the artificial sound of a note
and of a scale; in this it is the opposite of the objective sound of
the world. Since its beginnings, Western music is bound, by an
insurmountable convention, to the need to express subjectivity.
It stands against the harsh sound of the outside world just
as the sensitive soul stands against the insensibility of the
universe.*

Milan Kundera, novelist, literary critic, and music critic

REFLECTIONS

Introduction

The piano music of Maurice Ravel is among the most thrilling, the most colourful, the most subtle and, for pianists, the most challenging of the repertoire. This book is about this music, how we might relate to it as listeners and performers, what it sounds like (if ever that can be put into words), what it feels like under our fingers and what we might do with it. But this book is also, inescapably, about the man who created the music. To write about one's own experience of the piano music, to explore the impulses behind the great works in the hope that clues may be found to a deeper understanding for practitioners and listeners alike, is to find oneself engaged in a form of biography. To marvel at the delicate arabesques of *Jeux d'eau*, the exotic tone painting of *Miroirs*, the astounding virtuosity of *Gaspard de la nuit*, the jewel-like perfection of *Valses nobles et sentimentales* and the controlled emotional intensity of *Le tombeau de Couperin* is finally to ask the question, 'Who was the extraordinary person who created this?'

Ravel's biography will emerge only indirectly in the following pages. It is the great piano works that are central to this study – but in examining their genesis, their character and the derivations and intentions behind their titles, the composer himself will inevitably appear in the foreground, and he will always be part of the background hum. This is not to say that biography can 'explain' the music – just that it is bound to be part of any account that is not directly and formally analytical. The inspiration that he drew from, for example, Louis Bertrand's book of prose poems, *Gaspard de la nuit*, published under his pen name, Aloysius Bertrand – the subject of chapter 4 – is essentially part of his biography; by examining these poems, which he read at the most formative stage of his development as an artist and which provided him with the imaginative core of his greatest piano work, we are touching on central aspects of the man as well as the music. What is more, the history of Ravel's discovery of *Gaspard de la nuit* is bound up with his close friendship with Ricardo Viñes, who was to become one of the most important pianists of the age, who introduced almost all of Ravel's (and Debussy's) piano works to the world and who, it might be argued, provided Ravel (and Debussy) with the crucial impetus for writing piano works in the first place.

My title, *Reflections*, comes from Ravel's major set of piano pieces, *Miroirs*. At the end of his life Ravel noted that his own title was inspired by some lines from Shakespeare's *Julius Caesar*: 'The eye sees not itself / But by reflection, by some other things' – lines which Ravel, having no English, knew only in French translation ('La vue ne se connaît pas elle-même avant d'avoir voyagé et rencontré un miroir où elle peut se connaître'). The translation dilutes the aphoristic concentration of Shakespeare's thought (and the French cannot contain the play on 'eye'/'I'), but it preserves the insight into the nature of self-knowledge: we cannot see ourselves other than by way of 'some other things,' those objects from the external world through which, by engaging with them, we recognise and make sense of ourselves.

It is characteristic of Shakespeare that such a simple idea as looking into a mirror should involve so much more than self-reflection. It is characteristic of Ravel that, in being so reticent about his music, he should raise far more questions than he answers. In this regard it is appropriate that in French Shakespeare's lines express the idea as a journey of discovery and an encounter with the self ('d'avoir voyagé et rencontré un miroir'): it is possible that the source of the title *Miroirs* came to Ravel not at the time he wrote the work, in 1904–5, but after a lifetime, some twenty-five years later. As far as we know he had never mentioned it before.

To engage with and experience great music incontrovertibly shapes our awareness of ourselves. My intention in this book, apart from wanting to write about piano music that I am passionate about – and so to provide, as a teacher and performer, a context for my students and my public – has been to address this wider aspect of the phenomenon of music, to explore those many questions that arise when we attempt to go beyond the notes, the construction, the demonstrable material of the music that is its melody, harmony and rhythm. I wanted to reflect upon (the double meaning of my title) the way we listen to and receive Ravel's music, how and why we perform it as we do – and thus how we might do it better – and how this might be related to the enigma of the composer's own creative process.

I have not offered here any formal musical analysis of Ravel's piano works, though there will be occasional illustrative musical quotations for those readers, especially pianists, who are familiar with the scores. But this book is not only for performers of Ravel. I hope my readers will include those drawn by the seductions of the music as experienced in recordings or the concert hall, as well as those intrigued by the enigma of the man.

So if not through analysis, the science of music, how else can one reflect on music and make any sense of it? Historical and biographical methods have been tried and tested, although how far they, any more than analysis, can take us into the actual *experience* of music, what Ernst Krenek called 'the inmost essence of music itself,' is a moot point. My own approach develops from my experience as a performer – an interpreter – and behind it lies a question not often asked: what is it like playing Ravel's piano works? This is a question closely followed by another: what is it like listening to them? 'The interpreter,' observed Krenek, in a valuable and necessary statement of the obvious, 'is the first with whom the composition has registered; as its first recipient, the interpreter has had an experience akin to that of the listener, only many times more intense.' I would add, as a warning to my students, that the intensity of the listener's experience is in direct proportion to the intensity of the performer's. Intensity is all.

Ravel's piano music is notoriously difficult, but not only because of technique – and anyway, many pianists today surmount 'Scarbo' with apparent ease. The music is difficult because of the breadth and quality of its sophistication and the unerring precision with which the composer constructs an object so perfectly honed that the performer is fearful of damaging it. This is of course a challenge at a technical level, applying as much to the minimalist *Ma mère l'oye* as to the maximalist *Gaspard de la nuit*. But difficulties of execution are nothing compared to the nature of Ravel's musical thought – what he communicates. In a rare confession of faith, Ravel told Jules Renard (who provided the text for the composer's song cycle *Histoires naturelles*) that he wanted music to communicate in the same way as Renard's poetry: 'I think and I feel in music and I would like to think and feel the same things as you.'

Musical thought – often equated, as here by Ravel, with feeling – is a concept notoriously difficult to isolate for discussion. But for many musicians it certainly exists, or at least some entity is palpably present when we summon in our minds our experience of music in order to talk about it. In the case of Ravel, we only have to think of *Ma mère l'oye* – or the second movement of the G Major Piano Concerto, or the cadenzas from both piano concertos, or the first movement of the Sonatine, or the opening theme of the Piano Trio – to recall at once the intimate tenderness (which, astonishingly, many of Ravel's early critics complained he did not have) and those extraordinary subtleties of sensual pleasure that his music characteristically offers. But Ravel was not only a composer of exquisite proportions. Pianists might recall the orchestral evocation of dawn in *Daphnis et Chloé* and congratulate themselves that the breathtaking scale of its emotional landscape is also to be found, again and again, in the piano literature (and even in *Ma mère l'oye*).

Ravel found it almost impossible to talk about his music; indeed, he often denied the concepts of thought and feeling altogether. 'I don't have ideas,' he once said. 'To begin with, nothing forces itself on me. . . . [I begin by writing down] a note at random, then a second one and, sometimes, a third. I then see what results by contrasting, combining and separating them. . . . As you see there's nothing mysterious or secret in all this.' Yet, as his comment to Renard shows, he was fully aware that the creative mind works at a far deeper level than this (and as for there being 'nothing . . . secret' in the compositional process, in reality Ravel never allowed anyone to witness him composing). There is strong evidence for G. W. Hopkins's view that 'the mysterious, whether seen as inspiration or as alchemy, was clearly understood [by Ravel] to have a leading role in the process of composition.' That Ravel was compelled to mask the process is part of the enigma of the man that will emerge in the course of this book.

Readers who are not pianists will, I hope, find much to interest them regarding Ravel's case – his exceptionally private, often re-pressed, but immensely attractive personality – and how this might be manifested in his art. As I did in my book on Debussy, *Images*, I have set out to illuminate the background to this art, to lead all curious performers and listeners towards, for example, the literary origins of the night-dweller Gaspard and the seductive Ondine, and of that nightmare vision of the gibbet in the reddening sunset; and towards the literary friends that spurred Ravel's imagination in *Jeux d'eau*, *Miroirs* and *Valses nobles et sentimentales*. I also discuss *Valses nobles* in relation to Ravel's sense of irony, and *Le tombeau de*

Couperin in relation to the impact of the First World War on his psyche and the problematic response to the war that he revealed (or perhaps concealed) in this elegantly turned French suite.

My subject is the solo piano music, so I have not attempted to deal with piano concertos or the chamber music with piano. Neither have I covered the piano versions of what are really orchestral works, so I have not discussed *Rapsodie espagnole* and *La valse*, though I have included *Ma mère l'oye*, as its first version was written unequivocally for piano (albeit piano duet), and it is the single great work of Ravel that nearly all aspiring pianists have played.

My recurring reference points include the looming and catalytic presence of Debussy in Ravel's life; the Catalan pianist Ricardo Viñes, the closest friend of Ravel's early years, whose diary recounts fascinating details of the cultural life of the time; and the less well-known figure of Henriette Faure, who left a remarkably insightful account of the music and the man, and of her intensive series of piano lessons with him, in her memoir *Mon maître Maurice Ravel* (1978). I have found her record a more interesting and lively account than the better-known one by her compatriot Vlado Perlemuter (published in 1953 as *Ravel d'après Ravel* and translated into English in 1970 as *Ravel According to Ravel*). Faure was the first pianist to give an all-Ravel piano recital (in Paris in 1923, at the age of nineteen), followed a few years later by the twenty-three-year-old Perlemuter, who similarly had an intensive series of lessons with the composer. I have also drawn on the memoirs of Ravel's intimate friend, the writer Léon-Paul Fargue, whose poetry had a major influence on the genesis of *Miroirs*.

Influence, inspiration, the poetry of Fargue – the phenomenon of a composer's creative process and how one might understand it – brings me back to Ernst Krenek, and especially to his essay 'Basic Principles of a New Theory of Musical Aesthetics'. My exploration of the context and derivation of Ravel's piano works illustrates

Krenek's theory concerning the idea that exists prior to composition – the total, informing idea from which the composer draws
the impulse, as well as the material, for his creation.

I discovered Krenek's theory only after the main portion of this
book was written, and I am grateful to Jeremy Cox for introducing
me to it. My reflections on Ravel's art he encouraged me to view
as having a valid connection to a theoretical framework. 'It is the
thought's inherent need to present itself which creates the language,'
wrote Krenek. 'It would not exist without thoughts. On the other
hand without language the thought is not only incommunicable but
in the strictly literal sense, unthinkable.' In this context, 'language',
of course, means musical language.

One of the most striking features of Krenek's theory is his insistence that the whole exists *before* the parts, that although the process
might be as Ravel insouciantly described it – the writing down of
one note, then a second, then a third – the fundamental creative
impulse is a perception, all at once, of the whole. Moreover (and this
is of great relevance to the performer), 'there cannot be any doubt
that it is the totality of the thought that we grasp in listening, not the
sum of a number of individual notes, nor the concrete presentation
of a key-consciousness, nor the absence of it.'

The musical thought is subordinate to the idea, which can 'more
or less be identified with the total conception of the work, which
contains factors relating to both form and content. . .'. The idea
is, so to speak, the top layer of the creative process, the one near-
est to extramusical matter, from which it receives impulses of the
most varied kinds. These impulses are then transmuted into the
thought (or what Krenek called the 'thought-gestalt'), from which
the musical language emerges. But so as not to run away with the
idea that the resulting music is simply 'about' the extramusical
matter, Krenek insists that we are dealing with 'the *musical* thought,
that is, a thought that belongs exclusively to the sphere of music
and can only be expressed with musical means, which is identical

with its realisation in music material and cannot be separated from it. It cannot be encountered, described, defined or even named in verbal language.'

This crucial observation remains true even when the music is expressly referential. 'Your fountains are sad,' Ravel told Henriette Faure when she first played *Jeux d'eau* to him. 'Anyone would think you hadn't read the subtitle [*sous-titre*] by Henri de Régnier, "Laughing river god tickled by the water".' In Krenek's terms this is a clear reference to the idea that gives birth to the thought-gestalt. It is inconceivable that Ravel would make such a reference if the poetic tag he added to the piece were not deeply implicated in some way with its creation. We might argue that Ravel wrote the piece and dreamed up the title in an idle moment afterwards (and hence the subtitle too – *sous-titre*, which is stronger than 'quotation' or 'epigraph', is the word Faure recalls Ravel using for his Régnier quotation); but to accept this argument would be to ignore not only his remark to Faure, but the seriousness of his intentions as a composer.

So where does this leave Krenek's argument that the musical thought cannot be 'named in verbal language'? It leaves it intact. It is the *musical* thought that cannot be named. The piano piece *Jeux d'eau* is that thought, the extramusical idea realised in purely musical terms. The piece does its work only in the realm of musical language; it can only be perceived as music, and the more familiar we are with it, the more we relate to its musical totality, its musical essence. This does not mean we are forbidden to talk about it. But for the performer the music itself, in performance, is the final word.

Ravel held strong views on the art of performance. 'Performers must not be slaves,' the pianist Paul Wittgenstein complained when defending his own rewritings of passages in the Concerto for the Left Hand – to which Ravel retorted, 'Performers *are* slaves.' We do not have to accept such a strict definition of the performer's art to recognise that our task is always to make manifest the integrity of the music and to communicate the composer's intentions in the clearest possible way. But the preparation towards this end takes the performer far beyond the letter of the score, and also far beyond questions of technical dexterity – though without meticulous attention to both we cannot even make a start. Beyond lies the element of imagination, of imaginative identification with the sounds as they come off the page, which the performer has to relate to the wider context of narrative and image, if these are present (in *Gaspard*, for example, or 'La vallée des cloches'), and to style (the appropriate manner or character of a waltz rhythm or the feel of a folk idiom). Context and style provide the touchstones for the exploration of Ravel's piano music in the pages that follow, in which we will also have a frequent glimpse of the man himself, guiding our hand, warning us by his scrupulous example to be ever-scrupulous ourselves in the 'interpretation' of his art.

1

Maurice Ravel, 1875–1937

Ravel's concern with perfecting his craft, for satisfying the deepest needs of his constantly seeking spirit, gave him a certain hardness, made him seem unapproachable, over-meticulous, cold. What an error! Beneath the exterior neatness and precision . . . was a loving heart, simple, gentle and tormented.
Léon-Paul Fargue, 'Autour de Ravel' (1939)

In the 1920s, when Ravel had become one of the most celebrated composers in Europe and one of the most courted by the press, he showed himself fully aware of the nature of biography in relation to the public thirst for explanations of his music. In 1927, just before his four-month tour of America the following year, he told a journalist:

In my childhood I had a great interest in mechanical things. Machines fascinated me. As a small boy I often visited factories with my brother, very often. It was these machines, their clanking and roaring, and the Spanish folk songs sung by my mother in the evenings to rock me to sleep, which formed my first musical education.

This is especially interesting because, although these remarks – simply a polite exposition given in order to satisfy an American public eager for anecdote – pre-date *Boléro* by a year, in them lies the dual heart of Ravel's most celebrated orchestral work: the machine-like precision and monotony of the snare-drum rhythm and the ambience imparted by what Ravel referred to later as 'folk tunes of the usual Spanish-Arabian kind.' We might easily assume that he designed these remarks as an explanation, for the newspapers, of his new composition. But *Boléro* had not yet been written or even consciously thought out. The commission that led to it, a ballet for Ida Rubinstein, was an event still to come, and even then Ravel's initial idea was to orchestrate some of the piano pieces from Albéniz's *Iberia*. He hit on the idea of *Boléro* only when copyright laws prevented him from carrying out those plans.

Yet in the light of Ravel's remarks to the American journalist, we might see the genesis of *Boléro* not only as the result of an alignment of circumstances, of commissions and laws of copyright, but as a work waiting to be written, one Ravel had carried within him all his life, a work intimately bound up with the facts of his childhood, with his father and mother. So there is a Freudian interpretation asking to be made, underlined by Ravel's subsequent awareness of, as he described it, the 'musico-sexual' nature of *Boléro* (the ingredient, he said, which made it so popular).

Such questions carry over into our exploration of the piano music: identifying, for example, by way of their literary sources, the sexual impulses behind such pieces as 'Alborada del gracioso' and 'Scarbo' might illuminate our interpretation of these works and, completing the circle, lead back to the man and to a legitimate curiosity about his own sexuality, a staple of biographical enquiry. There is actually no evidence of any sexual relationships in Ravel's life, though there has been much speculation on the likelihood of his homosexuality. (This is plausibly argued by Benjamin Ivry in his biography of Ravel.) What *is* evident is a concealment of outward emotion, of human warmth, behind the façade of an obsessively neat and elegant personal appearance and a coolly formal manner. A contemporary observer of Ravel in later life noted 'a tiny man, delicate, with a matte complexion and hair almost entirely white; nervous, and hiding his nerves with difficulty; detached and unostentatiously elegant; more sensitive than he liked to appear.' His appearance and manner were partly designed to enable him to cope with his physical stature – *petit Ravel* was an appellation, the pianist Marguerite Long recalled, which caused him to 'shut himself up in sad, stolid silence.'

If Ravel's biography has some bearing on the nature of his art, then what is especially interesting is the way in which the music might be seen to reveal aspects of experience, emotion, feeling, that seem to be absent from the outer life – the life as recorded in the recollections of friends – and from what we learn of Ravel from his letters and interviews. This is contentious ground for musicology, especially in Ravel's case, as Steven Huebner has pointed out: 'Ravel exhibited a well-honed distinction between his public and private persona, and of the place of his creative work in that dichotomy. Most conspicuously, he generally denied the role of self-expression in his music.' But self-expression is far too simple a term for what I have in mind regarding the connection between biography and creativity (as indeed it is for Huebner, for whom biography includes 'the emotional world of the subject'). I am suggesting that while, on the one hand, the exquisite and refined elements of Ravel's music appear to fit with what we know of his tastes and manners, on the other hand its emotional charge, its bursts of passion and unbridled energy, do not. And then there is the curious fact, attested to many times by his friends, that when the effort of creation had passed, he appeared serenely detached from the result. 'His music only occupied him insofar as it was something to do – to do well,' recalled his close friend and biographer Alexis Roland-Manuel. 'Once the work was done, the game over, he thought out a new exercise.' Roland-Manuel was echoing another of Ravel's closest friends, Léon-Paul Fargue:

One of the most striking characteristics of this fascinating Pyrenean was his concern for perfection. This man of extreme intelligence, diversity, precision, whose knowledge was prodigious and whose facility proverbial, had the character and qualities of an artisan. No comparison pleased him more. He liked making, and making well.

This attitude was not without its contradictions. Ravel was most certainly not detached from the way his music was *performed*: he famously refused to acknowledge Toscanini's public salute after a performance of *Boléro* that had incensed him because the maestro had taken the piece too fast; and he was annoyed with Ricardo Viñes when he refused to take 'Le gibet' at the slow tempo indicated because, Viñes told him, 'it would bore the public.' Ravel's self-image as a maker of fine objects meant that he expected them to exist in performance exactly as he had intended – to the letter. 'I don't ask for my music to be interpreted, only to be played,' he proclaimed. As we will see, this has led to an essential misunderstanding of the nature of Ravel's art, and above all to a misconception of its emotional scope.

According to Artur Rubinstein, who witnessed Ravel's haughty formality with those who tried to get close to him, he showed 'a complete indifference for everybody around him'. Rubinstein claimed close friendship with the composer, but he was not in fact one of his loyal inner circle (though he was one of the finest interpreters of the music). But as Roland-Manuel recalled, even Ravel's

best friends could not help feeling secretly aggrieved that he did not show them a deeper intimacy. The most devoted feelings and the closest of friendships hardly affected his manner of greeting in the slightest. Affection, with him, was something he was almost incapable of expressing other than in unexpected kindnesses of attention. He seemed to suffer from the deepest embarrassment, almost like a physical impediment, when he had to put his feelings into words.

So it seems Ravel's was a repressed existence, emotionally and most probably sexually, which he counteracted and corrected through his music (and the huge consumption of his beloved *caporal bleu* cigarettes). Yet even in his music, as Roland-Manuel observed, 'a curious discretion always pushed Ravel to grant more of a heart to clocks than to clockmakers, more of a soul to trees than to humans.' In marked contrast to Debussy's outpourings, Ravel wrote few love songs, and overt erotic suggestion is largely absent from his music. (In *Gaspard* an erotic shimmer can safely be ascribed to the female Ondine, because she is a creature of the elements, not human.) Yet there is a formidable power in his music that, it could be argued, can only come from an awareness of passions more usually denied: the act of denial makes their expression, when it comes, all the more intense. By the processes of meticulously controlled artistic creation, through the scrupulous disciplines of compositional technique – on which he was imperiously insistent with the few pupils he agreed to teach – Ravel was able to expose these deep veins of his consciousness. The results include the climax of 'Ondine' and the romantic agony of 'Scarbo'; the thrilling unleashing of power in *La valse*, *Boléro* and the Concerto for the Left Hand; the sublime evocation of dawn in *Daphnis et Chloé*; the momentum and climax of the Toccata from *Le tombeau de Couperin*; the vastness of the sea in 'Une barque sur l'océan'; and the hair-raising exploits of the clown in 'Alborada del gracioso'.

Equally, the 'knowingness' displayed in such works as *Shéhérazade*, *La valse* and *L'heure espagnole*, as well as in those works influenced by jazz and popular music, is all the more astonishing if Ravel really did not 'know': his music, surely, manifests an acute understanding of the impulses and attractions of decadence, an easy acquaintance with the louche and the bohemian, which was completely at variance with his dapper and controlled exterior manner. Looking a little closer, we find that Ravel was in fact a keen observer of the foibles of life, that he took a delighted interest in the unconventional, the untamed. This explains his friendly acquaintance with *les filles* of a local brasserie, the prostitutes with whom he was on such friendly terms. His friend and pupil Manuel Rosenthal claimed that this camaraderie, which he witnessed, proved Ravel's heterosexuality. However, it does no such thing. Politically Ravel was left leaning, and it would have been highly characteristic of him to have had no moral scruples with regard to prostitutes, to have considered them as equals. It does not follow that he employed their services. And even if he did, as the critic Hans-Heinz Stuckenschmidt believed to be the case, this proves nothing about the focus of his sexuality.

On occasion, at home and among friends (and as long as he could be in control of mixing the cocktails), he could be untamed himself, as the soprano Marcelle Gerar recalled:

> Ravel was in a very gay, carefree mood, borrowed Mme Gil-Marchex's cloak and Hélène Jourdan-Morhange's hat and did a dance in drag. . . . Ravel then took the hard core of the party to a cabaret and, through a deafening din of jazz, launched on a closely reasoned discussion with Léon-Paul Fargue about the nature of Art, full of surprises and paradoxes, till four o'clock in the morning.

One of the most acute analyses of Ravel's personality was made by Viñes. 'He has in him a mixture of medieval Catholicism and satanic impiety,' Viñes noted in his diary for November 1896, when Ravel was twenty-one. And more than forty years later, the year after Ravel's death, Viñes wrote: 'His complex, even contradictory character makes nonsense of attempts to classify it. Even so, I think one can sum it up impartially by saying that the tastes and natural propensities of this extraordinary artist has almost nothing in common with what he thought he was or what he *wanted* to be.'

What did he want to be? Ravel once observed how lucky he was to have been a composer, because he was good at nothing else. At the same time, although he knew he was an artist, it seems he had a fear of being one. His extreme elegance of clothing, a friend from his youth noted, was a manifestation of his desire to 'lose himself in the anonymity of a bourgeois correctness and thus avoid the appearance of being an "artist", which was then all the rage.' Later Ravel developed a profound fear of being regarded as a seer, a grand representative of feeling and insight, a proponent of *sincerity* – the vogue word of his age, which he refused to accept had anything to do with artistic creativity. Had he known it, he would surely have subscribed to T. S. Eliot's view (most famously espoused in his essay 'Tradition and the Individual Talent', published in 1919) on the impersonality of the artist. For Eliot, the artist creates his art in a state of detachment, unaffected by the subjective processes of personal emotion. 'Poetry is not a turning loose of emotion,' Eliot wrote, 'but an escape from emotion; it is not the expression of personality, but an escape from personality.' Both Eliot and Ravel drew from their own deeply introverted personalities a working philosophy of art.

What Ravel wanted to be was an artist detached from the *angst* popularly associated with being one; he wanted to be an artisan. To his pupils he suggested that he was no more talented than anyone else; 'each one of you, if you worked as I work, could do as I do.' He described *Boléro* as simply 'a little thing [for] Ida Rubinstein'; and at a festival of his music in Paris, to cries of 'Bravo Ravel, a triumph!' he responded, 'Oh no, just the fashion.' Such statements, by themselves, might reveal little more than a highly defensive modesty. But overall it does seem that Ravel achieved an essential objectivity with regard to his art that came close to Eliot's dictum that 'the more perfect the artist, the more completely separate in him will be the man who suffers and the mind which creates.' Eliot's formula dismisses the cliché of the tormented artist – an archetypal romantic image – while acknowledging its truth. The artist *does* suffer, but it is not the suffering that makes the art: this seems to be the position that Ravel took such immense care to demonstrate, while hiding the suffering – he knew precisely what it took to be an artist, but he rarely spoke of it. (Though he once confessed that the artist 'is obsessed by his creative work and by the problems which it poses. He lives a little like an awakened dreamer.') And he composed in the greatest secret. 'Everything must be done, or appear to be done, as if by a miracle,' wrote Roland-Manuel. 'There was not a trace of his work on the piano or on his work-table, no sketches to be seen. Nothing in his hands, nothing in his pockets, the conjuror had even conjured away the evidence of his tricks.' Such concealment of the act of creation is essentially, in Eliot's sense, a concealment of the self.

Early critics of Ravel detected a coolness in the music as well as in the man. A frequent complaint was that Ravel's music appeared 'artificial'. 'But does the idea never occur to these people that I might be "artificial" by nature?' the composer observed to Michel Calvocoressi. It is a revealing paradox – naturally artificial – and takes us to the heart of Ravel's deeply held convictions on the nature of art. 'I know that a *conscious* artist is always right,' Ravel said. 'I say *conscious* and not *sincere*, because in the latter word there is something humiliating. An artist *cannot* be sincere. Falsehood, taken as the power of illusion, is the only superiority of man over animals.' This most controlled of artists then related the humiliations of sincerity to the dangers of spontaneity: 'When one allows oneself spontaneity, one babbles and that's all.' And he concluded:

> The truth is, one can never have enough control. Moreover, since we cannot express ourselves without exploiting and thus transforming our emotions, isn't it better at least to be fully aware and acknowledge that art is the supreme imposture? What is sometimes called my insensibility is simply a scruple not to write just anything.

The emotions are not denied as a source of art, but the artist has to know that emotion itself is not art – or he will merely 'babble'.

Being overwhelmed by the emotional power of the Prelude of Wagner's *Tristan und Isolde* (as Ravel was in his youth when, according to Viñes's diary, he 'trembled convulsively and cried like a child') does not make one an artist, however sincere the emotional response may be. Ravel told the composer Frank Martin that 'the greatest of all dangers for an artist is sincerity. Had we been sincere we should have written nothing but Wagnerian music.'

It seems that Ravel shared with Eliot a deep, instinctive fear of emotion, of its destructive power – a fear of being unmanned by overwhelming feeling. (His objective, he said, was 'technical perfection – I can strive ceaselessly for this, since I know I can never attain it.') Both shielded themselves behind a façade of elegant correctness – Eliot too was known for his neat sartorial manner, though Ravel's was more scrupulously fashionable – but each in his own different way betrayed deep internal contradictions. In an uncomfortably confessional insight, Eliot revealed that the process of depersonalisation was achieved at a huge cost: 'The creation of a work of art is like some other forms of creation; it is a painful and unpleasant business; it is a sacrifice of the man to the work; it is a kind of death.' Ravel did not speak in these stark terms, though the obsessive secrecy of his composing, his bachelor existence, and his inability to show emotional warmth to his friends point to a similar experience.

Such, then, is the portrait of the extraordinary man whom we know as Maurice Ravel, composer. Performers see the man ever-present behind the music, even as we simultaneously recognise the compositions as separate entities, obeying their own laws and communicating through their purely musical processes of harmony, melody and rhythm. For the performer, the expression 'playing Ravel', a convenient short-hand, takes on a wider meaning the more we explore the enigma of his personality and the manner in which he led his life.

2

Impressions:
Ravel and Liszt – *Jeux d'eau*

The butterfly wings of this piece can't support the weight – or
the pedalling, whichever – of a virtuoso.

Claude Debussy, letter to Jacques Durand, 27 September 1917

Claude Debussy had a great admiration for Ravel's early masterpiece
Jeux d'eau. In a letter dated from near the end of his life, Debussy
both criticises and praises a recital he had just attended by the
legendary French pianist Francis Planté: 'The man is prodigious –
and yet at the same time a little frightening: at the first concert he
broke a hammer, and at his age (he's 78) that's quite something! He
played – very well – the Toccata (*Pour le piano*: C Debussy); and he
was marvellous also in Liszt's 'Feux-follets'. Less good in Ravel's
Jeux d'eau.' Then comes his typically perceptive and concise critique
as to why, quoted in the epigraph to this chapter.

Much is revealed here about the different performance styles
required for Debussy's Toccata and Ravel's *Jeux d'eau*, which are
virtually contemporary with each other. The keyboard style of *Jeux
d'eau*, while echoing Liszt, was essentially new: for all the leggiero
markings in Liszt's 'Feux-follets', the touch required is hardly that
of a butterfly's wings. It seems likely that Planté, steeped as he was

in the pianism of the nineteenth century (he was a close friend of Liszt's), failed to respond to the needs of Ravel's first masterpiece, whereas he found in Debussy's *Pour le piano* a style more suited to a robust nineteenth-century manner. *Jeux d'eau* had a marked influence on Debussy, challenging him to break away from the more conventional keyboard style – although he employed it with considerable brilliance and flare – of *Pour le piano*. Ravel, in his turn a great admirer of Debussy, knew what he was talking about when he said that 'from a *purely pianistic* point of view, [*Pour le piano*] contained nothing very new.'

Jeux d'eau was given its first public performance on 5 April 1902 by Viñes, who in the same concert premiered what was to become one of the most popular pieces of the Ravel repertoire, *Pavane pour une infante défunte*. The *Pavane* had been written three years earlier, and Ravel soon became embarrassed by the popularity of a piece that he considered to have been both poorly structured and overly influenced by Emmanuel Chabrier. Surprisingly, Ravel was at first unsure of the worth of *Jeux d'eau* as well, though he later came to see that it was 'the origin of all the pianistic innovations which have been noticed in my works.'

The technical and imaginative challenges of *Jeux d'eau* are considerable, though they are frequently underestimated by performers. Perhaps Planté himself underestimated them in 1917. Ravel, on the other hand, continued to feel that as a composition *Jeux d'eau* was in fact overestimated. It gave him a certain fame when it first appeared – critics largely dismissed is as cacophonic, though it quickly became popular with audiences, principally through the indefatigable Viñes – but he felt its reputation prevented him from moving on. 'I very much want to write something that will free me from *Jeux d'eau*,' he said a few years later. The work which finally liberated him, *Miroirs*, will be the subject of the next chapter.

In his early monograph on Ravel, Roger Nichols made the point that 'to hear *Jeux d'eau* well played is a life-enhancing experience.'

So how do we begin building a performance of this remarkable and difficult piece? What merit is there in the traditional view of Ravel as a cool classicist, whose music requires strict adherence to certain precise and controlled performance techniques? This attitude has a long history, for which Ravel himself, as we saw in chapter 1, was partly responsible. It was promulgated by his early disciples, who sought to embalm the teaching and practice of his music. Thus the writer and critic Émile Vuillermoz, one of the early group of Ravel's friends from the first decade of the century, could write in 1925: 'The Debussyan manner calls for the collaboration of an active sensibility. Ravel's only asks for an attentive respect. There are several ways of playing Debussy. There is only one way of playing Ravel.' So began the restrictive attitude which echoes to this day in the teaching of Ravel.

Vuillermoz's words were quoted with approval by Roland-Manuel in his biography of 1938, to which he added: 'One cannot expect a pianist's confession from the piano of Ravel.' Roland-Manuel, a close friend and pupil of Ravel's, was a sympathetic and often perceptive observer. His biography of the composer, *À la gloire de Ravel*, translated into English in 1947, remains a staple resource. But it seems his objective judgement of the music was sometimes hindered by an unconscious acceptance of contemporary attitudes towards Ravel, above all concerning his apparently restricted emotional landscape – *le petit Ravel*. In defending his friend against this charge, he never quite managed to avoid its imprint: 'One must not expect from Ravel works in which feeling is continually exaggerated by the violence of its expression. One must not ask Ravel to stir the dark waters of desire or willingly to reveal the gulfs of despair.' In other words, Ravel was not Liszt, towards whom, in his implied reference, Roland-Manuel shows the characteristically ambivalent attitude of the post-romantic age.

In Britain a similar attitude towards Ravel's stature was displayed in Norman Demuth's *Ravel*, published in 1947, part of the influential

Master Musicians Serics (reprinted in the United States as The Great Composers), and the first book on Ravel by an English author. Demuth, part of the English musical establishment of the mid-twentieth century, was a composer and professor of composition at the Royal Academy of Music. Ravel had died only ten years earlier, and almost at once Europe, and the world, had been put on hold by the war. We learn from Demuth that Ravel's Sonatine and Debussy's 'La cathédrale engloutie' were at that time the best-known works of modernism among piano students. *Gaspard* was rarely played in its entirety, he tells us, though 'worthy to rank with the finest music' and 'the highest pinnacle in contemporary music.' Yet, despite his largely laudatory account, Demuth manages to hand down from his own pinnacle a view that only underlines Ravel's status as a *petit maître.* Notwithstanding the date, one is still left gaping at the assertion in the final chapter (which in the American edition is turned into a proclamation on the first page) that Ravel could not be 'in any way comparable' to such figures as Beethoven, Brahms, Berlioz, Wagner, Elgar and Sibelius:

> In his own country he could not be considered in the same category as [Vincent] D'Indy, [Albert] Roussel or [Paul] Dukas – and for the same reason Debussy must be excluded from the list of those who can be called great. However, it may be argued that the French goût [taste] does not run along these lines and that if a composer reflects the characteristics and temper of his own country in a faithful manner, then the substance of his music, provided that the quality is adequate, may credit him with a kind of national greatness.

Nevertheless it is clear that Demuth was attracted to Ravel's especially French *goût*, despite his discomfort that the composer shows no interest in the apocalyptic, or in 'vast frescoes and sym-phonies.' (His remark on Ravel's 'Noctuelles' is typical of this often startling ambivalence: the piece is 'not very appealing musically,' amounting to 'very little from the listener's point of view, but the player finds every bar a joy.') And as for there being only one way to play Ravel, for Demuth this way 'is not an extra specialized one. . . . He requires tidy playing and impeccable workmanship.' So Ravel was inevitably reduced, and largely remained so during the second half of the twentieth century. To use Roger Nichols's terminology, 'it was the ways in which Ravel [was] thought to fall short of the canonic' that dominated discourse, even among those who views were largely laudatory.

'Tidy playing and impeccable workmanship' are indeed prerequisites for performing *Jeux d'eau,* but as a comment on the nature of Ravel's art (and the performer's art too), it is destructively inadequate. The vividly colouristic effects of *Jeux d'eau,* high in the upper register, the precision and lightness of touch these require (Debussy's 'butterfly wings') and all the demands for sculptural grace and dramatic structure make it a piece which can in no sense be thought to play itself. So, to return to the original question, how is an interpretation to be arrived at, and if we accept that there is indeed more than one way of playing Ravel, what justification might there be for choosing one interpretation over another? The pianist needs to take a position, to build an interpretation that grows from within (the imagination, in relation to the title), as well as without (style and technique).

When Ravel was asked how his piece should be played, he was supposed to have replied, 'Why, like Liszt of course', a typically mischievous remark which should perhaps not be taken at face value (considering the experience of Francis Planté with which we began), but one which betrays an awareness on Ravel's part of comparisons that were bound to be made. He perhaps found the piece *too* Lisztian, one reason that he at first did not want it published. The title provided a hostage to fortune. He would have been thinking of Liszt's own fountains, the magnificent 'Les jeux d'eaux à la Villa d'Este' of 1877, and so of course would everyone

else. By this interpretation, his remark can be seen as characteristically self-deprecating, an attempt to acknowledge a debt and also
to deflect criticism before it is made. Indeed, in comparison to 'Les
jeux d'eaux à la Villa d'Este', Ravel's piece is slight – but then Liszt's
is a masterwork by an aged colossus, imbued with spiritual insight
and a lifetime's experience. Ravel's piece is the first fruit of genius, a
work by a composer who, at twenty-six years old, was still a student
at the Paris Conservatoire. In fact the dissimilarities between the
two pieces are more striking than their resemblances. The two make
an ideal pairing in concert, for the listener hears, in addition to
similarities of detail and context, precisely what Ravel's *Jeux d'eau*
is not – what it does not achieve or attempt to achieve – and yet is
left with a strong impression of its originality.

Even the differences between Liszt's and Ravel's chosen epigraphs are instructive. On the manuscript of Liszt's piece (though
not usually in the published score) he wrote a biblical quotation, in
Latin, from John 4:14: 'But the water that I shall give him shall be in
him a well of water springing up into everlasting life' – a metaphor
for spiritual growth. Liszt saw his fountains (in the courtyard of the
Villa d'Este at Tivoli, near Rome, where he spent much of his time
in later life) as aspiring heavenwards, a symbol of the nourishment
to be drawn from the deep wells of spiritual contemplation. Such
spirituality was far from Ravel's mind in his own *Jeux d'eau*. On
his own manuscript he placed a quotation by the poet and novelist
Henri de Régnier: 'Dieu fluvial riant de l'eau qui le chatouille' –
laughing river god tickled by the water. The image conveyed is strong
and audacious, though translation does little justice to the musical
quality of the words. Régnier, as a follower of Stéphane Mallarmé
and Paul Verlaine, was renowned for the musicality of his verse, and
his line captures in the rhythms and tones of the French language a
palpable tinkling and chuckling, image and sound effortlessly fused.

Ravel was very up to date in his choice of epigraph, for when he
wrote it at the head of his new piece in November 1901 the collection

of poems from which it came had not yet been published. Régnier's *La cité des eaux* came out in 1902, so clearly Ravel already knew the manuscript (and had possibly heard it read aloud by Régnier, who was a friend) – an interesting glimpse into his literary interests and connections. The title of Régnier's collection refers specifically to the fountains in the gardens of Versailles (known as the Grandes Eaux de Versailles). The quotation – which appears not only in Ravel's hand above the first stave of the autograph of 1901, but also in Régnier's hand on the title page, and signed by him – is from 'Fête d'eau', a poem inspired by the multiple fountains of the Bassin de Latone (see Appendix C). The sculptures from which the water gushes depict the demigoddess Leto, mother of Apollo and Artemis, presiding over a circle of spouting turtles and frogs – so the laughing god of Régnier's line is actually female, which should add another dimension to a performer's sense of the easeful grace and sensuousness at the heart of *Jeux d'eau*. As Roger Nichols has pointed out, in his complete edition of Ravel's piano works, the 'god' of the epigraph should be understood in the sense of divinity or godhead, not as a male god.

These are small details, but far from insignificant. Ravel expected not only faithfulness to his score but meticulous attention to his epigraphs too – hence his admonishment to Faure insisting that she pay attention to the Régnier quotation placed at the beginning of the score. So important did the composer consider it that he wanted it published in the programme of the first performance, given by Viñes.

The extramusical contexts, then, of the two pieces by Liszt and Ravel are markedly different, the one devoutly Christian, the other mischievously pagan, with the two epigraphs presenting a clear contrast between the spiritual and the sensuous. Ravel replaces Liszt's spirituality with a conception of water as sensation, at once tactile, aural and visual. Liszt's piece conveys sound as sensation too, heard most obviously at the opening, where the spray and tumble of fountains are symbolised by rapidly ascending and descending arpeggios and brilliant-sounding tremolandos (Liszt's vivace marking at the beginning is significant and often overlooked). But once the exultant mood is established, the religious contemplation begins, and the piece develops into a series of heartfelt meditations on an Italian cantilena: song, prayer, melodic incantation, these are fully in the foreground of this music, but swathed in water-like tone painting, above, below and within. Indeed, with the biblical quotation in mind, it is the 'within' that Liszt captures so unerringly. The decorative figurations now nourish and support a melodic line, and the tremolandos themselves become infused with melody. Liszt symbolises in this music the very presence of the wellspring that gives life to all around it (see example 1).

The impression left by Ravel's *Jeux d'eau* is not of such ardent melodic expressiveness (that would come later, in 'Ondine') – the piece moves altogether faster, in rapidly repeating and circular motifs that dart, dazzle and intoxicate. Ravel makes very little use of the ubiquitous Lisztian tremolando, though he does turn Liszt's triple-note trills from the opening of 'Villa d'Este' (bar 22; see example 2) into a breathtaking cluster-note trill high on the keyboard (bar 48; see example 3). Ravel's climax here is an audacious display

Example 1. Liszt, 'Les jeux d'eaux à la Villa d'Este', bars 40–52.

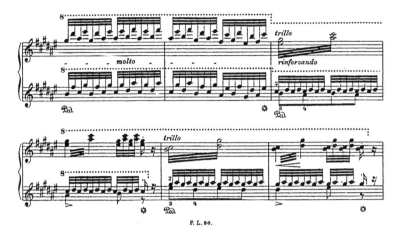

Example 2. Liszt, 'Les jeux d'eaux à la Villa d'Este', bars 20–5.

of virtuoso pianism, of Lisztian elan, that holds the listener transfixed before the plunging glissando dissipates the tension and the mood becomes darker. Yet this climax has little of the grandeur and emotional charge of Liszt's – which is cast as a massive fortissimo re-orchestration of the opening theme – and does not attempt it. The principal pianistic characteristic of *Jeux d'eau* is that diagnosed by Debussy in his image of 'butterfly wings', requiring a delicacy of touch that Ravel was to explore further in 'Noctuelles'.

So, despite the echoes, *Jeux d'eau* did not aspire to be 'Les jeux d'eaux à la Villa d'Este'. Ravel's ambitions at this stage were avowedly more modest – and, with characteristic detachment, he could not understand what all the fuss was about when his piano piece became so popular. As a genre piece *Jeux d'eau* is actually far closer

Example 3. Ravel, *Jeux d'eau*, bar 48.

29

to Liszt's much earlier 'Au bord d'une source' (Beside a Spring): it is similar in mood, it shares a similarly colouristic use of dissonance to evoke the sparkle and touch of water droplets (broadly, Liszt's piece employs clashing seconds; Ravel's, sevenths), and the cross-handed melodic arrangement at the opening of the Liszt is strongly echoed in bars 29–32 of the Ravel (see examples 4 and 5). Even the epigraphs suggest a common imagery. Liszt quotes a line from Schiller, 'The games of young Nature begin in murmuring coolness', which might equally apply to the opening of Ravel's *Jeux d'eau* (the literal translation of which is 'games of water'; an only slightly less literal translation would be 'the play of water').

The special sound of *Jeux d'eau* comes from its harmonic language and texture, the way in which Ravel uses Lisztian figurations – the crystalline multi-fingered passagework, itself strongly influenced by Chopin, that Liszt had exploited for such evocatively descriptive purposes – to highlight a plethora of dissonances, largely in the upper register of the piano. Such high-pitched figurations allow the harmonic resonance to be undamped – pedalled – for long periods, adding to the build-up of colour. Ricardo Viñes claimed he discovered this pedal technique from Ravel himself, 'who recommended using pedal in high registers, so as to create, rather than

Example 4. Ravel, *Jeux d'eau*, bars 29–32.

Example 5. Liszt, 'Au bord d'une source', bars 1–4.

clarity, the blurred impression of vibrations in the air.' This, he said, is particularly appropriate for the final passage, 'where the melody sings against the misty figuration of the right hand.' But it seems to me that the piece can hardly be played in any other way. Such a technique would have been an essential aspect of nineteenth-century piano playing, as Viñes, an ardent Lisztian, would have known. The performer also needs to exploit in *Jeux d'eau* (and similarly in 'Noctuelles', 'Une barque sur l'océan' and 'Ondine', to give only the most obvious examples) a considerable use of half pedals and flutter pedals, as well as moments of clean, unpedalled sound (all techniques required for performing Liszt) in order to highlight the full range of sonorities and textures the music offers. If Ravel created a new piano style in *Jeux d'eau*, it was because he divined some of the secrets of Liszt's methods and exploited them for his own ends. He renewed the Lisztian style, suffering from the assault of Beethoven, whose music held sway at the Paris Conservatoire during Ravel's student years there, and brought it into the twentieth century.

It was Viñes who made *Jeux d'eau* famous (Ravel inscribed in Viñes's copy of *Jeux d'eau* 'Au gardien de la clé des eaux' [to the keeper of the key to the waters]); but it was Ravel who played the piece first, in Fauré's composition class at the Paris Conservatoire (it is dedicated 'To my dear teacher Gabriel Fauré'), and then to his Apaches friends. Many decades later Fargue recalled the effect the music had on them:

> One evening Maurice Ravel allowed us to hear the first rendering of the *Pavane pour une infante défunte* and *Jeux d'eau*, to which we listened with the silence of conspirators. The irony, the colour and the novelty of these pieces were for us a revelation, steeped as we were body and soul in the 'impressionism' of Claude Debussy. Ravel, with the first strike of his rapier, positioned himself as an independent force of the first order, a grand master of an œuvre at once personal, singular [*isolé*], secretive.... The charm of these two pieces, the first notes of Ravel that echo in my memory, stayed with all of us for days afterwards. Here, for us, was a strange fire, a precious object we had just discovered, arrayed in resonances and refinements that belonged to no one else.

In those days Ravel could play the piano; indeed, like Debussy, he enrolled as a piano student at the Paris Conservatoire and in 1891, at the age of sixteen, he won a first prize in a competition, ahead of Alfred Cortot. Later he dropped his piano studies and rarely practised, and in the 1920s his frequent performances of his own music, the simpler pieces, became an embarrassment to himself and to others. (Roger Woodley has shown that many of the early piano-roll recordings in the 1920s which Ravel was supposed to have made were in fact played by Robert Casadesus.) He was no better at conducting. 'His long, narrow, bony hands made awkward gestures in the air,' recalled Fargue. 'And neither were they a pianist's hands, which explains his somewhat stiff manner at the keyboard, and consequently his fear of making an exhibition of himself.' This was in the early 1930s, not long after Ravel, upon being asked to perform *Jeux d'eau*, declared that he had 'never played it in his life.' He certainly had played it, and when he first composed it he certainly could. We will see later that even in the 1920s there were aspects of his playing that were uniquely impressive, especially when he was demonstrating his wishes to Faure. We get some idea of this from his recordings on piano roll, although we also hear his limitations.

We can assume that Fargue's 'strange fire' refers to *Jeux d'eau*, rather than the *Pavane*, suggesting, perhaps, an appropriately Lisztian manner in Ravel's early rendering, in keeping with his remark that is should played like Liszt. There *is* 'a strange fire' about *Jeux d'eau*. At the fast tempo at which I believe this piece should be taken, it has a dramatic tension that qualifies, but does not overrule, the insubstantiality implied by Debussy's comparison to 'butterfly wings'. Roger Woodley has drawn attention to just this manner of playing in Cortot's 1923 recording: 'The sense of an extended improvisation with obvious links back to the Lisztian tradition . . . is rarely matched by later pianists.'

Fargue's recollections of Ravel, and his early manner of playing his own music, have an air of authenticity, capturing in their imprecise way – in the way of memory – an historical moment, the first awed reactions to what was to mark a turning point in French piano music. And *Jeux d'eau* can still elicit this reaction, over a hundred years later – indeed, it is the performer's task that it should. A fast tempo is essential to this end (the first edition has the eighth note at 144; Cortot begins at 168 and gets faster; Casadesus, who worked closely with Ravel, is also above 160), enhancing the sparkle, capturing the inherent fire and energy, enabling the continuously repeated and sequential motifs to cohere, to metamorphose into 'the sound of water, the musical sounds of fountains, waterfalls and streams,' as Ravel, at the end of his life, described his intentions for the piece. This is an interesting shift away from the image of the title and suggests that the later Ravel, like Faure, had not been paying attention to the epigraph at the head of the score.

Whatever improvisatory freedom the performer seeks in *Jeux d'eau* cannot come at the expense of the overall pulse – at least not in the sense of rubato. The rhythmic precision of *Jeux d'eau* is integral to its effect, for two reasons. The germinating structure of the piece, what propels it, is motivic repetition, and almost everywhere the motifs are underpinned by an ostinato-like eighth-note rhythm. Both these characteristics, along with the bell-like sounds of the upper reaches of the keyboard, give to the music the character of Indonesian gamelans. The gamelan will forever be associated with Debussy, but Ravel too knew the exotic sounds of the gongs and metallophones of Java, heard for the first time in Europe at the 1889 Exposition Universelle in Paris. Ravel heard them there too (he was fourteen years old) and no doubt subsequently. Although he never made the comparison, it is distinctly possible that part of the originality of *Jeux d'eau* stems from his exposure to the repetitive and percussive style of gamelan music, with its strict pulse, intricate counterpoint and delicate, as well as brilliant, sonorities. Debussy's 'Pagodes', with its deliberate allusions to the gamelan, was written a year after *Jeux d'eau* and shows the strong influence of Ravel's new piece. Debussy may have divined the relationship, whether Ravel was conscious of it himself or not. 'Pagodes' is even more obviously related to the gamelan because of the piece's pervasive pentatonic scale – a musical cliché used to impart an oriental ambience. But it was surely the particular sonority of *Jeux d'eau* that showed Debussy what could be achieved on the piano, one that, in the real world as opposed to the symbolic, is incontestably closer to the sound of a gamelan than to the sound of water.

The gamelan appears again in Ravel's piano music, surely this time in deliberate guise, at the opening and close of 'La vallée des cloches' a few years later. And where he did acknowledge its influence was in a movement from his suite for piano duet, *Ma mère l'oye*: 'I consider the music of Java the most sophisticated music of the Far East,' he said in 1931, 'and I frequently derive themes from it: "Laideronnette" in *Ma mère l'oye*, with its temple bells, was derived from Java, both harmonically and melodically.'

The second reason for a strict pulse in *Jeux d'eau*, which makes further sense of the repetitive rhythms, comes from Ravel's lifelong interest in mechanical objects. We saw in chapter 1 how he became captivated by the machines in the factories he visited as a child, and how 'their clanking and roaring' formed part, as he said, of his 'first musical education.' At his home, Le Belvédère, where he lived after the First World War, he became an eager collector of clever clockwork objects and mechanical toys. Fountains are mechanical objects, man-made waterspouts, in which the water is channelled into repeated, uniform patterns. 'The musical sounds of fountains' actually seems more apposite to *Jeux d'eau* than Ravel's other image, 'waterfalls and streams', a qualification made nearly thirty years after the music was composed. His original idea was more distinct, associated with Régnier's stylized fountains, at once energetic and graceful, constantly at play in a highly controlled environment. In Régnier's imagination the sounds of the fountains metamorphose into the laughter of the goddess of the sculpture, bringing it to life. Ravel, in his turn, responds to the imaginative conceit of the poem but at the same time imagines the fountain's underlying mechanism. There is a direct line from *Jeux d'eau*, which disguises its mechanical rigour with Lisztian elan (and the colours of musical impression-ism), to *Boléro*, in which there is no disguise at all.

3

Reflections: Ravel, Debussy, Léon-Paul Fargue – *Miroirs*

*We had more or less the same tastes in art, which was very
fortunate for people as fanatical as we were, because, as
someone has said, one can only discuss things with like-minded
people, especially questions of subtle distinction. Ravel shared
our predilections, our weakness, our manias, for Chinese art,
Mallarmé and Verlaine, Rimbaud and Corbière, Cézanne
and Van Gogh, Rameau and Chopin, Whistler and Valéry, the
Russians and Debussy.*

Léon-Paul Fargue, *Maurice Ravel* (1949)

Ravel and his friends, the group of young artists, writers poets,
and musicians who called themselves, not entirely ironically, the
Apaches (the hooligans), were ardent Debussyists. Debussy was
thirteen years older than Ravel and by the time of the premiere of
Pelléas et Mélisande in 1902 had become the leading composer of the
avant-garde. The Apaches, according to Léon-Paul Fargue, one of
the group's founders, missed not a single performance of Debussy's
opera during its first run of twenty-nine performances. During the
early performances, which were subject to the usual Parisian tumult,

they undoubtedly made their support noisily apparent – though it is difficult to see the neat and aloof Ravel taking part in the rowdiness.

The two composers could hardly have failed to become acquainted with each other in the small musical world centred on the Conservatoire and the various concert venues and music societies that promoted new music. Ravel was alert to every move of Debussy's during the late 1890s, swapping scores and sight-reading whatever he could with Ricardo Viñes (who in the next decade was to give the first performances of nearly all the new piano works of both composers, and who provided the conduit through which the two engaged in artistic combat). In a revealing recollection of this period, the singer Jane Bathori, another great early interpreter of Ravel, wrote: 'I met Ravel in 1898. He was then a pupil in Fauré's class and, before speaking to me of what he was writing himself, he talked about Claude Debussy, for whom he professed a deep admiration.'

Debussy, in his turn, was interested in the younger composer's early compositions. After the first performance, in 1898, of Ravel's two-piano work *Sites auriculaires*, he asked to borrow the score. Following Debussy's marriage the next year, Ravel became an occasional visitor to his tiny apartment on the rue Cardinet, where he was invited to hear the as-yet-unperformed *Pelléas et Mélisande* played (and sung) by Debussy at the piano. Then, in 1901, Ravel sought permission to arrange Debussy's new orchestral work *Nocturnes* for two pianos. Debussy presented him with a signed copy of *Nocturnes* and, a year later, a copy of *Pour le piano*, with the gracious inscription, 'To Maurice Ravel, in friendship, and in homage to "Jeux d'eau"'.

Several short, friendly missives from Debussy survive from the two men's correspondence. Their growing intimacy is revealed in a letter from Debussy of June 1901, on the day Ravel returns to Paris with the shared second prize in the Prix de Rome: 'Welcome home! my dear friend, and I trust you are happy. Kind regards'. But the most interesting letter contains Debussy's celebrated opinion of Ravel's String Quartet, which until recently was known only anecdotally and considered of doubtful provenance. His String Quartet was the first extended masterpiece of Ravel's early years and, along with *Shéhérazade*, the composition that most clearly showed Debussy's influence. Fauré, the quartet's dedicatee, had had several criticisms, and so Ravel planned to alter it just before its premiere. Debussy too had seen the score. Here is the full text of his letter to Ravel – published in 2005 in the complete definitive edition of Debussy's correspondence – dated 4 March 1904, the day before the premiere:

> Dear friend,
> I have just heard from Bardac [Ravel's friend and a composition pupil of Debussy's] about what you are intending to do with your quartet, above all that you are to make the Andante less weighted. In the name of all the Gods, and in mine, do not do this. Just think how different things sound in a hall with and without an audience. Yes, the viola might stand out a bit, but couldn't you ask him to play quieter? Otherwise don't touch a thing, and you will see everything will be fine.
>
> My affectionate regards,
> Claude Debussy

The story was first related by Maurice Delage, a composition pupil and close friend of Ravel's, whose misquotation of the original letter – 'In the name of the gods of music, and in mine, change nothing in your String Quartet' – has been repeated in most commentaries ever since.

So for a few years at the beginning of the century the two composers, Ravel and Debussy, were on friendly terms. They had similar tastes, they trod the same artistic ground, they moved in the same milieu. (Viñes's diary for November 1901 records a visit to Debussy's apartment and notes that 'Ravel was there, and we left together.') This is remarkably evident in Fargue's recollection, quoted in the epigraph to this chapter: the list of Ravel's tastes, and those of his fellow Apaches, reads like a list of Debussy's from his great formative decade of the 1890s. They certainly should have been friends. But their warm relationship was not to last, partly because of the inevitable rivalry between them, and partly because of the circumstances of the break-up of Debussy's first marriage in 1904, a period when Debussy felt under siege and knew Ravel to be in the camp who supported his abandoned wife. The estrangement between the two composers was also exacerbated by the value judgements of critics, who either lauded Ravel as a stick with which to beat Debussy or dismissed Ravel as a mere imitator.

There is a parallel to be drawn with Chopin and Liszt some eighty years earlier, different personalities who occupied similar ground as artists – and in their case, rival pianists as well as composers. They should have been allies, but instead, like Ravel and Debussy, they became competitors, and were similarly urged on in their rivalry by friends and commentators. Debussy became particularly touchy, especially as he was, independently, suffering his own denigration from critics; Ravel is supposed to have been a rare example of an artist unaffected by criticism, though the truth, as we shall see, seems to have been that he was as affected as anyone.

After *Jeux d'eau* Ravel needed to move on. *Miroirs*, begun in the autumn of 1904, represents this deliberate departure, an ambitious set of five pieces that he intended would offer a far wider range of pianistic possibilities and a canvas on which he could explore a new harmonic idiom. He always drew musical inspiration from the piano, whether composing at it or writing directly for it. Manuel Rosenthal, a pupil and close friend of Ravel's after the First World War, noted: 'Like Debussy, to whom he often referred, he claimed that "the piano is the composer's harmonic treatise. It's there one finds everything."'

If Debussy was aware of *Jeux d'eau*, Ravel, just prior to planning *Miroirs*, was certainly aware of the new piano works of Debussy: his *Estampes* was first performed in January 1904 by Viñes, and the lovely, still infrequently played *D'un cahier d'esquisses* (From a Sketchbook) was completed in the same month. It was Viñes who brought this piece to Ravel's attention, having played it one evening for Debussy. Immediately afterwards, that same evening, he related to Ravel everything he had heard Debussy say about his own new approach to composition. 'Debussy told him', wrote Roland-Manuel, 'that he dreamed of composing a kind of music whose form was so free as to seem improvised; to produce works [that] would appear to be torn from the pages of a sketchbook [*d'un cahier d'esquisses*].' There is more to this story than would have been apparent to Viñes at the time. The music Debussy was referring to, in addition to the small piano piece, was almost certainly *La mer*, on which he was then working. *D'un cahier d'esquisses* has strong resemblances to *La mer* and is clearly a spin-off from it, a discarded sketch or a necessary recreation from the major creative effort of this period. What is more, *La mer* manifests an extraordinarily original formal structure, indeed one 'so free as to seem improvised'.

Ravel approved of Debussy's pronouncement and, according to Roland-Manuel, 'admitted that the music he was then working on had similar concerns.' (It was at this point he was supposed to have voiced his desire to be 'freed' from *Jeux d'eau*.) The music was 'Oiseaux tristes', the first of the *Miroirs* to be written. Ravel later claimed this piece to be 'the most typical' of his new style, without elucidating. It is more harmonically adventurous than *Jeux d'eau*, and indeed, following Debussy, it is freer in form. It was Debussy's idea of form, we note, that struck Ravel. But to what greater extent does Debussy's influence lie behind *Miroirs*? According to Roland-Manuel's story, Ravel was already in the process of developing a freer form – independently, it seems, of Debussy (though he never achieved the kind of free forms manifested in

La mer). There is little in the harmonic language of *Miroirs* that resembles Debussy, beyond a superficial similarity in their use of added ninths. But this was enough for contemporary critics to accuse Ravel of imitation, as attested by Ravel's friend, champion and fellow Apache Michel Dmitri Calvocoressi: '[When] a listener hears a succession of perfect dominant-tonic chords, [he] never thinks of associating them with one composer or another; [yet] he thinks of M. Debussy whenever he hears a chord of the ninth or the slightest suspicion of a second.'

But the influence of example, the catalytic challenge provided by another artist's work, is more significant (which operated on Debussy too, keenly aware as he was of the younger composer's growing reputation). As a title, *Miroirs* (Mirrors, or Reflections) invites pictorial associations in the same way as Debussy's *Estampes* (Prints). Debussy was also working on the first set of his *Images* (Pictures) at this time, though the three pieces would not be published until October 1905, a year later. Ravel would certainly have been aware of them, however, through Viñes, who had already heard Debussy demonstrate early versions of the pieces. Viñes would surely have related details to his friend, just as he had with *D'un cahier d'esquisses*. Equally, Debussy was well acquainted with *Miroirs*. As Viñes wrote in his diary for 3 February 1906:

> At 3 in the afternoon I went to Debussy's so he could hear his *Images* [book 1], which I have already played several times, and to him too. He was clearly very happy with my playing, for afterwards he asked his current wife [Emma] to come in and listen. They wanted to get to know Ravel's *Miroirs* which they hadn't heard before, and I played it to them. I left their house at six.

The birth of *Miroirs* was witnessed with fascination by the Apaches, as Maurice Delage recalled:

Ravel arrives one evening with a thin roll of paper, somewhat crumpled from his walk. He carefully unfolds it, smoothing the creases carefully with a gentle hand, and plays, in the calm of the night, 'Oiseaux tristes'. It is the first of the five piano pieces which will become *Miroirs*, and which he will continue to bring us slowly, one by one, at intervals directly in proportion to their number of pages.

Viñes's diary records the event as having taken place on Tuesday evening, 11 October 1904: 'Ravel revealed his new piano piece to us. It pleased only me' – the others, it seems, were at first mystified by Ravel's new idiom. 'Only once in those early days did a work of his bewilder us for a time,' wrote Calvocoressi. 'It was "Oiseaux tristes", which he played to us again and again without our being able to understand what he was after. He was rather disconcerted to find us indifferent to a piece into which he had put so much of himself.'
As for Ravel's own view:

> The title *Miroirs*, five piano pieces composed in 1905, has authorized my critics to consider this collection as being among those works which belong to the impressionist movement. I do not contradict this at all, if one understands the terms by analogy. A rather fleeting analogy, moreover, since impressionism does not seem to have any precise meaning outside the domain of painting. In any case, the word Mirror should not lead one to assume that I wish to affirm a subjectivist theory of art. A sentence by Shakespeare helped me to formulate a completely opposite position: 'The eye sees not itself / But by reflection, by some other things.'

So Ravel accepted, reluctantly, the judgement that *Miroirs* belonged to musical impressionism. He was being disingenuous in denying that the term had any 'precise meaning outside the domain of painting,' for in music impressionism had a very clear meaning, denoting pieces that set out to convey an impression of a given image signaled in a title or in a tag of poetry. The five pieces of *Miroirs* do just this; the eight pieces of *Valses nobles et sentimentales* do not. And as for understanding the term as an analogy, Ravel could not reasonably expect it to be understood in any other way. Just as Debussy hated the term ('impressionism, symbolism . . . useful terms of abuse'), so was Ravel also at pains to distance himself from a limiting label. Nevertheless, both of them, following a tradition that goes back at least to the keyboard suites of François Couperin and Jean-Philippe Rameau – and which was revived in the descriptively titled music of Robert Schumann and Franz Liszt, music that they both knew well – gave highly evocative titles to their piano music and did so for over a decade. What is more, they succeeded in creating a match between sound and image of such believable accuracy that a new term had to be coined (or at least borrowed) to distinguish the new style.

Ravel's quotation from Shakespeare is particularly apt, for it underlines the nature of metaphor: as the eye cannot actually see itself, it understands, 'sees', in reference to something else. We understand ourselves by what we see reflected back from the world around us. Baudelaire, whose influence on late nineteenth-century artists (including Debussy and Ravel) was considerable, made a similar point when he wrote that 'the universe is nothing but a storehouse of images and signs . . . it is a kind of pasture for the imagination [of the artist] to digest and transform.' This has considerable relevance to Debussy's use of the term *image*. It is in Baudelaire's sense that Ravel's 'mirror' is similar to Debussy's 'picture': an allusion to the raw material, as it were, of the external world that informs the creative act. And it is this which makes Ravel, at this phase of his life, an impressionist.

Whatever the precise nature of the influence Debussy and Ravel exerted on each other, the titles of their respective piano works in the first decade of the twentieth century show the two working within the same descriptive genre: Ravel's musical mirror reflected fountains, moths, a ship on the ocean and a valley of bells (as well as, a few years later, a water sprite, a hanged man on a gallows and a diabolical dwarf), while Debussy made musical prints and images of Chinese pagodas, Spanish evenings, gardens in the rain, reflections in water and bells heard through the leaves of a forest. Although these two highly independent artists, with completely distinct visions of what they wished to achieve, wished to remain aloof from any suggestion of competition, for the public and the critics the contest was obvious. And it was carried into the public arena by Viñes – who, for example, on 6 January 1906 gave the premiere of *Miroirs*, followed just one month later, on 6 February, by the premiere of Debussy's *Images*, book 1. Commentators had already noticed that in Debussy's 'Soirée dans Grenade' from *Estampes* (given its first performance by Viñes in January 1904) there were strong echoes of the 'Habanera' from Ravel's *Sites auriculaires*, amounting to virtual quotation (indeed, Debussy was accused of plagiarism), the manuscript of which, as we have seen, Debussy had borrowed after the first performance. There are also distinct signs of *Jeux d'eau* in Debussy's 'Pagodes'; Ravel, for his part, echoes the gamelan-inspired patterns and sonorities of 'Pagodes' in his 'Vallée des cloches' (refining and returning the compliment that 'Pagodes' paid to his own gamelan allusions in *Jeux d'eau*); and there is almost a complete quotation of a bar from Debussy's 'Hommage à Rameau' in Ravel's 'Le gibet' (see examples 6 and 7).

But these details remain, in the end, mere details. In substance, the differences between these two composers could not be greater. Ravel became irritated, understandably, by being constantly in Debussy's shadow – not by reason of the shadow itself, which he revered, but because many commentators refused to accept his music as existing in a light of its own. Ravel was especially stung, after the premiere of *Miroirs*, by the claim that it was Debussy who had invented the 'new manner of writing for the piano, a special style

Example 6. Debussy, 'Hommage à Rameau', bars 31–3.

of particular virtuosity', as the critic Pierre Lalo wrote in *Le temps* in January 1906: 'Today one hardly hears any pieces which do not contain the arabesques, passagework and arpeggios discovered by M. Debussy.' Ravel wrote a dignified letter of reply:

> You dwell upon the fact that Debussy invented a rather special kind of pianistic writing. Now, *Jeux d'eau* was published at the beginning of 1902, when nothing more than Debussy's three pieces, *Pour le piano*, were extant. I don't have to tell you of my deep admiration for these pieces, but from a purely pianistic point of view, they contained nothing new.

Ravel underlined 'purely pianistic' to reinforce his point. It is one of the curiosities of Debussy's development that, despite a number of piano works from around the 1890s (including the *Arabesques* and the *Suite bergamasque*, as well as a number of pieces with generic titles such as Ballade, Mazurka, and Nocturne, written largely to earn money), the piano as a solo instrument did not draw his full creative interest until the descriptively conceived *Estampes* of 1903, followed closely by *Images*, book 1 (1903–5). He was at the time over forty years old. *Pour le piano* from 1901, as Ravel recognised, is hardly an exception, as magnificent as it is. *Estampes* seems like a new start for Debussy, with traces of Ravel

Example 7. Ravel, 'Le gibet', bars 12–14.

shading its surface. But in staking his prior claim to the 'new style', Ravel was intent only on establishing his independence from Debussy. He did not wish to claim that he had had any influence on the older composer.

From our historical distance, the charge made against Ravel, that he was a follower of Debussy, is easy to refute – and Ravel himself was calmly assured in his rejection of it. 'I was influenced by Debussy, but voluntarily so,' he told a journalist in 1931, near the end of his creative life. 'I never accepted Debussyan principles; I believe this to be so obvious that no one can doubt it.'

'Noctuelles'

As a student I came across the first piece of *Miroirs*, for some reason, long after *Gaspard de la nuit* and *Jeux d'eau* – even, I recall, after *Le tombeau de Couperin*. I allow little significance to this personal history except for my recollection of the impact 'Noctuelles' made on me. I remember exactly where I was, and what I was doing when I heard it – it was a performance on the radio – and how thrilled I was to discover new Ravel. It was a kind of awakening that I recall to this day whenever I hear or perform this piece. Wrestling at that time with the execution of 'Noctuelles' – which requires a far greater sophistication and agility of touch than *Jeux d'eau*, and a different kind of refinement from *Gaspard* – became for mc yet one more lesson in the painstaking process of trying to acquire a Ravelian technique that would illuminate the inimitable Ravelian imagination. I am reminded of some further comments by Fargue, to whom 'Noctuelles' is dedicated: 'The piano for us, during this wonderful period, took on a new significance. Maurice Ravel was in the process, in front of us, of transforming the technique of piano playing.'

The dedication to Fargue is highly significant. He remained one of Ravel's closest friends throughout his life and was of considerable influence on the composer's early imaginative development. Some fifty years after the creation of the original group of Apaches, Émile Vuillermoz, one of their number at the beginning of the century, observed that 'through the imaginative influence [*l'influence spiri-tuel*] that he exerted on Ravel in particular, Fargue has his place in the history of the music of this period.' Vuillermoz is using the language of the *fin de siècle* in order to recall the climate in which Ravel was nurtured. That a poet could influence the course of music history would have been a familiar enough proposition in Symbolist circles, and the very existence of the Apaches is practical proof of connectivity – cross-fertilisation – in action.

'I got to know Ravel around 1902,' Fargue recalled, in his account of the early Apaches gatherings in Montmartre. 'It was at the home of the unassuming Paul Sordes, a painter of refinement, an ardent lover of music. . . . We would gather there once or twice a week, and each of us would read or play what we had just written or composed, in the friendliest atmosphere you could imagine.' (It was at one of these earliest gatherings that Fargue first heard the *Pavane pour une infante défunte* and *Jeux d'eau*, as we saw in the previous chapter.) Of Fargue himself at that time, his fellow Apache Calvocoressi recalled:

> He was then known to very few people, owing to his extreme re-luctance to appear in print. He used to read to us from very scrappy

manuscripts (bits of paper such as the Montmartre 'Chansonniers' draw from their pocketbook before starting to sing) his exquisitely wrought prose poems. He was very simple and lovable, despite many peculiarities, of which the most striking was an almost incurable incapacity to make up his mind about the things of everyday life.

Influenced by the musical sonorities and rhythms of Verlaine and Mallarmé, Fargue's early poetry provided a bridge between the nineteenth century and modernism, between Symbolism and the Surrealists. His images capture the loneliness of the city, the streets of Paris at night, cobbled alleyways, the city's railways inhabiting a semi-pastoral world in the heart of the metropolis, the mournful sounds of the locomotives; his themes are unrequited desire, memories of childhood, unease and longing, caught in his reactions to the night and its emptiness. His language, verging on the fragile unrealities of Surrealism, is interwoven with references to Parisian songs, to 'melodies lurking in the air [*des musiques diffuse rôdent*]', to moments of dreamlike stillness in which 'a piano slowly ponders [*un piano pense avec lenteur*].' Jean Cocteau remembered Fargue as 'one of those friends with whom one walks the streets until one drops. A thousand times I would walk with him, or he would walk with me, following those evenings when Ravel and Satie would play their music to us. He was gentle and ferocious. A night bird and a creature of the light.'

Not only was 'Noctuelles' dedicated to Fargue, but according to Vuillermoz it appears to have been inspired by 'the memory of one of his poems. . . . *Les noctuelles des hangars partent, d'un vol gauche, cravater des autres pouters* (In the sheds the night moths take off, in awkward flight, and circle around other beams).' Vuillermoz is the only source for this oft-repeated assertion; neither Fargue nor Ravel ever mentioned it. So let us weigh the evidence.

Vuillermoz's quotation is not in fact the first line of the poem, but a line from an untitled poem beginning 'La petite gare aux ombres courtes' (The little station of fleeting shadows) from Fargue's *Poèmes* of 1912 – published, then, many years after Ravel's 'Noctuelles' was written. But we will see that Fargue had written the poem at least seven years earlier, and that Ravel would certainly have known it. Vuillermoz goes on to discuss the importance of Fargue's influence on the Apaches and particularly on Ravel:

> With a few precise words, dense with startlingly rich imagery, he enveloped us in his kindly irony, affectionate mischief, lyrical imprecations, in language of such magnificence that we were spellbound.
>
> Ravel felt his influence very deeply. Fargue for him was unmatched as an arbiter of taste. The literary education of our composer was not very advanced. . . . Thanks to Fargue he heard constantly the true note, and he knew how to learn from it.

Fargue was certainly not the only arbiter of Ravel's literary tastes. The passionately literary Viñes guided him too, as we shall see in the next chapter. But Fargue was something different, a great poet in the line of Mallarmé, Verlaine, Bertrand and Charles Baudelaire, and there is no reason to doubt the general truth in Vuillermoz's vivid diagnosis.

The 'Noctuelles' poem evokes dreams and memories associated with an abandoned railway station, 'weary at five o'clock.' (See Appendix C for the full poem and its translation.) Fargue mingles scraps of memory, sounds, half-grasped images from childhood, with images of iron rails and blackened locomotives set in a pastoral wilderness:

> An engine, worn out with black, hollow coughing, stands silent. Everything stops and dreams. As before.
>
> Old things yawn, recognise the hour, and go back to sleep. In the sheds the night moths take off, in awkward flight, and circle around other beams.

In French the word *noctuelles* is unusual. The common term for moth is actually *un papillon de nuit* or *un papillon nocturne* – a nocturnal butterfly. The literal translation of *noctuelles*, 'owlet moth', is not only clumsy, but also irrelevant to the meaning of the poem. The purpose of the word for the poet is its musical frisson, and for the way its displacing strangeness fits the dreamlike qualities of the scene. In alighting on this word, Ravel showed again his taste for arresting titles, as in *Pavane pour une infante défunte* and *Sites auriculaires*. In *Miroirs* he would employ the archaic 'bark' in 'Une barque sur l'océan' and the mystifying 'Alborada del gracioso'; even the title 'Oiseaux tristes' – Sad Birds – is disconcerting. It seems, then, that the word *noctuelles* can connect only to Fargue – a connection underlined by Ravel's dedication.

A curious fact arises from Fargue's own dedications to the ten poems he collected together from his scraps of paper, sometime between 1905 and 1907, and to which at that time he gave the title 'Nocturnes'. As early as 1905 he planned to publish a volume, *Poèmes*, with his Nocturnes as the 'Premier cahier'. This first draft shows that five of the dedicatees were Apaches, but Ravel is not among them. Vuillermoz is there, and so is Calvocoressi. The 'Noctuelles' poem is dedicated to the composer Florent Schmitt, another of the early Apaches. This remains a remarkable oversight, considering Ravel and Fargue's close friendship and the deep respect they had for each other's art.

An explanation might lie in the characteristically Fargue-like disorganisation of this early publishing venture. For nearly a year, month by month, Fargue returned to his printer proofs covered in black-inked corrections, followed by numerous letters of explanation, until the exasperated Royer, of Nancy, wrote to say he had 'decided to avoid the horrors of the padded cell' and pulled out, sending back the manuscript and all Fargue's letters, unopened. It seems that Fargue took issue with 'several friends, the dedicatees', in his own words, for deciding his poems should be published without his being told, since he obviously considered they were not yet in their final form. In the eventual, expanded publication of 1912, the dedicatees' names are dropped. Perhaps, then, Ravel had good reasons for keeping out of it.

One further piece of evidence corroborates Vuillermoz's assertion, and it is easy to miss. In another memoir Maurice Delage, who became a composition pupil of Ravel's, writes of his first meeting with him at Paul Sordes's home, an introduction made by Fargue in late 1903. Delage gives brief cameos of the early Apaches, one by one, and finally he comes to Fargue:

> We call for a moment's silence. Fargue has allowed us to empty his pockets. (He knows perfectly in which one lies the image of 'the lime tree, swollen with shadow, and which already contains the whole of the evening.') With the profile of an Assyrian statue he raises his arms ready to read from his piece of paper. 'However,' he begins, 'this is not finished.' Then in a gaunt voice [*voix hâve*] he depicts for us 'The little station of fleeting shadows, weary at five o'clock.'

These are none other than quotations from the same 'Nocturne' in which the word *noctuelles* appears ('The little station . . .'). Delage's anecdote fits with Vuillermoz's recollection of Ravel's 'memory of a poem'. He would have known it first not from the printed page, but from a reading by the poet himself. The year Ravel's 'Noctuelles' was written, 1905, was exactly when Fargue was being urged to publish his 'Nocturnes' and was reading them to his friends.

The manner in which Ravel translates Fargue's moths into piano music might be seen as the kind of instance Debussy had in mind when he spoke of his knack of making 'flowers sprout out of chairs.' At the heart of Ravel's art here is the delightful paradox of sound symbolising silence – moths, of course, are soundless, yet we accept Ravel's evocation of them without protest. This is also the art of the poet, Fargue, who similarly, through the sound and rhythm of his language, manages to construct a faint but unmistakable aural evocation of the fluttering motion of the moths as they tumble around the beams: the phrase 'cravater d'autres poutres' has a kind of whispering sonority, entirely appropriate to the image Fargue wants to create in our minds (though it vanishes in translation). *Cravater* suggests encirclement, like a cravat; so the moths, having fluttered into the air from a beam in the old railway shed, circle around another beam. The sound of the poem would have been especially arresting, we can imagine, when read aloud by Fargue, 'a raconteur,' another friend recalled, 'whose voice could send shivers down your spine. Every word fell dead right, like the voice of a singer that never fails to reach its note.' This fits with Delage's recollection of Fargue's 'gaunt voice' when reading the 'Noctuelles' poem to the Apaches.

Ravel's music evokes both the movement and the following stillness. The unstable, dithering flight of the moths (*d'un vol gauche*) he captures by means of a pianissimo interplay of cross-rhythms and intense chromaticism that requires the lightest touch and the nimblest of finger work (appropriately, the very 'butterfly wings' of Debussy's admiring critique of *Jeux d'eau* that I quoted in chapter 2, but for the performer even more demanding). The texture and sonority of the piano writing creates a frisson of nervous energy, which is felt and controlled by the fingers, is experienced in the minds of the listeners, and translates into the image of the title. This refined alchemy is enhanced by the silence that follows in the ninth bar (see example 8), the way this silence is prepared and what it symbolises. We are in the presence of a parallel mode of reference, born from the musical language but separate from it, one that is so deeply fused with the way we receive and process musical argument that to isolate it for discussion is to risk destroying it through simplification. We can 'read' this passage as a fluttering of moths' wings, which then ceases as the moths land on the beam, not suddenly but in a gradual decaying of motion as each of the

Example 8. Ravel, 'Noctuelles', bars 1–9.

creatures comes to rest. From bar 6 Ravel obscures all feeling of the pulse which, up to this point, has anchored the shimmering textures with dance-like rhythmic repetitions; the movement accelerates and the pitch swoops upwards in two bursts (the onlooker seems to be gazing up at the beams), and the mind's eye envisages the moths settling one by one. Simultaneously the texture dissolves, articulated by a precisely indicated decrescendo from *p* to *ppp*, by widening gaps in the fabric of resonance and by the disintegration of the shimmering figurations. Ravel even indicates the manner of the final expiration of sound in the ninth bar: the last eighth note requires a minute lengthening (hence Ravel's tenuto marking) so that the sound itself decays, rather than being cut off abruptly by the dampers of the piano – there is nothing abrupt in the world of nocturnal moths. Silence reigns for two long quarter notes. It seems as if momentarily Ravel has transposed the moth into a butterfly, capturing that moment when it closes its wings and becomes almost invisible before again taking flight.

It was the perfection and apparent effortlessness of these kinds of details that led Hélène Jourdan-Morhange to talk of Ravel's 'straightforward painting [*peinture directe*]', though we can be sure the effort was actually considerable. We can be equally sure that the unification of sound and image was of such complexity as to have taken place unconsciously in Ravel's creative brain, in which the conscious activity was the manipulation of musical material.

The middle section of 'Noctuelles' also has affinities with the mood of Fargue's poem, its surreal images (such as 'The bus for the Hotel of Little Hell awaits'), its sense of dislocation and loss. Ravel employs here one of his signature devices: the slow repeated-note ostinato, found also in 'Oiseaux tristes' and 'La vallée des cloches' (and most famously in 'Le gibet' from *Gaspard de la nuit*). The motif seems to be associated in his mind with a certain dreamlike mood, with nostalgia and foreboding – 'sombre et expressif', as he marks it in 'Noctuelles'. If we place the 'Noctuelles' line in context, we can see how the poem defines this mood:

Everything stops and dreams. As before.

Old things yawn, recognise the hour, and go back to sleep. In the sheds the night moths take off, in awkward flight, and circle around other beams. A bird sings, in a questioning tone, from beside the track where night comes, near the water tank, over the tinkling flower-erbeds, over the listening flowers, in the tree swollen with shadow which already contains the whole of the evening.

Friend, you are sad. A lamp browns in a window opposite.

It is not only 'Noctuelles' that echoes from this passage, but 'Oiseaux tristes' too. Fargue's poetry, it seems, might have had a wider impact on *Miroirs* beyond the piece that Ravel dedicated to him.

'Oiseaux tristes'

At the end of his life Ravel spoke of the derivation of 'Oiseaux tristes' specifically in terms of 'birds lost in the torpor of a very dark forest during the hottest hours of summer.' For a composer who prided himself on being a maker, an artisan, one who wrote down 'a note at random, then a second one and, sometimes, a third' – in short an anti-romantic – this is a remarkable statement. Where had he heard such birds? According to Vuillermoz, the inspiration came from the famous forest of Fontainebleau, not far from Paris to the southeast, where Ravel was spending a weekend. 'One morning [he] was enchanted to hear the song of a blackbird, whose arabesque was at once elegant and melancholic. He had only faithfully to transcribe the theme, without changing a note, to achieve the poetic and limpid passage which spiritualises the nostalgic call of this French brother of the bird from *Siegfried*.' Vuillermoz's allusion is to Wagner's 'Forest Murmurs' in *Siegfried*, where the sounds and atmosphere of a forest are reproduced in tone painting that famously anticipates musical impressionism. But Wagner's orchestral interlude is luminous and joyful, distinctly different from Ravel's dark and perplexing musical miniature. The image of a sad bird is unusual – far removed from the warbling of a blackbird, which is rarely perceived as melancholy, despite Vuillermoz's assertion (his adjective is supplied in order to fit Ravel's music, not the blackbird). Birdsong is more usually associated, poetically, with the ecstasies of spring, hence the bubbling clarinets of Wagner. (We will see in chapter 6 that birdsong again caught Ravel's imagination when he was serving behind the lines during the First World War, and while he was writing *Le tombeau de Couperin*.)

It is possible that the birds of Fontainebleau influenced Ravel's musical imagination when he came to write 'Oiseaux tristes'. It is also possible that Fargue's 'Nocturnes' did too, poems in which we find implicit and explicit references to the arresting image of a sad bird. In the extract above, from 'The little station of fleeting shadows', the birdsong is expressly associated with torpor and darkness, and in the last line the word 'sadness' places the overall feeling of the scene. And this image is directly taken up in the last line of another poem, 'Dans la rue qui monte au soleil' (In the street climbing to the sun), one of the ten original 'Nocturnes' that would have been well-known to Ravel from Fargue's readings. What is more, the image is now associated with the sound of a piano. Again the poet is wandering the city streets at night:

A piano slowly ponders. There, at the dead end of the old streets, gaping wide like mutes wishing to speak, beats the strange light of troubled and humbled hearts. And all was gilded and dead in the window of the poor clockmaker.

But in a street named after a sad bird, there lives and smiles, day and night, the eternal Myrtis, fair of face.

We cannot, of course, know precisely how Fargue's influence was manifested in Ravel's creative imagination, but at the very least it seems clear that *Miroirs* arose in response to the stimuli he received from meetings of the Apaches, from the constant give-and-take of ideas and inspiration, from the receptive ears of like-minded artists, who provided, albeit in small number, the ideal public with which all artists crave a responsive and creative relationship. 'Fargue's every word carried authority,' recalled Vuillermoz. But if we accept that the fundamental impulse for a work of art comes partly from subconscious associations that feed into the disciplined workings of the conscious mind, then Ravel's *Miroirs* can be seen in part as a musical distillation of Fargue's imagery, or at least a response, a transposition into another medium. Where, after all, might these moths, birds, barks, and bells come from? ('Alborada del gracioso' stands apart, though, as we shall see, this title too has a literary derivation.) Ravel's alertness to the stimuli of the Apaches at this period would certainly have found in Fargue's imagery the perfect 'storehouse of images and signs,' which, in Baudelaire's phrase, as we saw earlier in this chapter, provided the material for his 'imagination to digest and transform.'

'Une barque sur l'océan'

'Une barque sur l'océan' exploits a wealth of arpeggiation, tremolandos and pedal effects in a sustained manner that is almost without precedent. (Liszt's 'Waldesrauschen' comes to mind as its precursor.) It is one of Ravel's great piano works, which fails to leap out as a landmark only because it rarely receives the performances it deserves. A dull performance of 'Scarbo', or even 'Ondine', leaves the potential of these works undisturbed – the music somehow survives. But in a dull performance of 'Une barque sur l'océan' the music doesn't survive – it can sound monotonous, repetitive, overlong. As we shall see, Ravel feared as much.

It is also one of Ravel's most completely impressionistic works, by which I mean the music seems at every moment to be impregnated by the image of the title. In fact the title is an absolute necessity for gauging interpretation. Not even 'Ondine' needs its narrative image as much as 'Une barque'. The music is imbued with the sea, the motion and the surge of waves, the booming and cascading of water against cliffs and rocks. If the pianist does not have a full imaginative grasp of these images, a sure sense of this music as metaphor, the piece will not come off the page. The most compelling metaphors of language find a fitting conjunction of previously unconnected images that suddenly illuminate meaning. 'Une barque sur l'océan' works in the same way, but in musical terms. With melody, harmony and rhythm, and with the fullest exploitation of the resources of the instrument, Ravel evokes his seascape, at once expansive and menacing, sparkling and storm torn, at its surge thrilling and at its ebb exquisitely reposeful. This is not a boat bobbing on the waves. The music tells us this without a doubt – or it should, if the performer has the imagination and resources to bring out what is there.

Henriette Faure misjudged her literary reference in her commentary on 'Une barque'. She suggests that one of Aloysius Bertrand's poems, 'Le soir sur l'eau', from *Gaspard de la nuit* (the whole of which Ravel had advised her to read before embarking on his own *Gaspard*), might have provided Ravel's initial inspiration. This is highly unlikely. The poem is a miniature Venetian intrigue, slightly comical, in which 'a black gondola glides by the marble palaces' while water laps around the steps. The poem has none of the sweep and terrifying majesty of Ravel's piece. Faure tells us she had not dared to ask him about the derivation of 'Une barque', 'knowing from experience the dangers involved in any conversation to do with ideas or serious feelings, of ever trying to break through his fierce reserve. The only serious dialogues, or at least serious monologues, that were ever possible were to do with the actual details of the work.'

'Une barque sur l'océan' is dedicated to the painter Paul Sordes, in whose house in Montmartre the first meeting of the Apaches took place. Sordes was also a fine amateur pianist, as another of the Apaches, Tristan Klingsor, recalled in one of the few records of the group to fill in Sordes's presence in any depth:

How seductive was this Paul Sordes! How unassuming and refined. He had studied piano from an early age. . . . He easily deciphered modern scores, sensitive to all the inflexions, ravished by the subtle harmonies that so pleased us all at that time. Like a painter he sought out the perfect nuance and rhythm; one could see he had adored Whistler; he was, perhaps, a kind of Ravel of the palette. But this blond dreamer was indolent, capricious, more interested in tasting the pleasures of art than in creating it.

So Sordes's career came to nothing, and he died penniless and unknown, not long before Ravel. But at the beginning of the century, full of optimism and idealism, he was, like Fargue, a highly significant figure in Ravel's formation. Vuillermoz tells us that in the company of 'the inspirational Fargue, at once down-to-earth and clairvoyant, and the painter Paul Sordes, whose refined sensuality was a constant example, Ravel developed the tools of his own critical sensibility.'

It would be nice to think that 'Une barque sur l'océan' was inspired by a painting by Sordes. Ravel owned a gouache by him which, according to Marcel Marnat, 'he carried around everywhere', but nothing more seems to be known of this painting. It is equally possible that, in dedicating the piece to Sordes, Ravel was paying homage to his pianism, and perhaps imagining what this 'Ravel of the palette' would do with it at the keyboard. However, against Klingsor's claims for Sordes's pianistic talent we can place Calvocoressi's comment that at the Apaches gatherings 'the reading [of scores] was done by Ravel and Ricardo Viñes, but occasionally by other, less expert, players, the worst of whom was certainly myself.' Ravel dedicated 'Alborada del gracioso', a work of notorious difficulty, to Calvocoressi – a Ravelian joke, perhaps. (He dedicated 'Oiseaux tristes', which makes few demands technically, to the true virtuoso Viñes, because, he told Calvocoressi, 'it was fun to inscribe to a pianist a piece that was not all "pianistic".')

Another thread in the fabric of influences behind 'Une barque sur l'océan' brings us again to Léon-Paul Fargue: there is an echo of Fargue's poetry in the title. The word *barque*, although not as rare as *noctuelle*, is not in everyday usage. Ravel employed it, in his characteristic way, for its poetic aura, so as to remove his image from the more prosaic 'boat' (*bâteau*). To translate the title as 'A Boat on the Ocean' is to diminish it, which is why the grander-sounding 'Ship' is better. But there are problems with this word too, for a 'bark' is usually taken to mean a small vessel, especially in French. However, in English (where the word can be spelled 'barque', showing its derivation from French) it can also mean a larger vessel with sails. My preferred title and spelling, in translation, would be 'A Barque on the Ocean', which leaves the question of size nicely balanced but preserves the archaism.

Small, or large, Ravel's *barque* is certainly not any ordinary boat, and neither can I see it, as Faure does, as Bertrand's gondola in which 'a cavalier and a lady are talking of love.' But here are some lines from Fargue's poem 'La rampe s'allume', one of the original ten 'Nocturnes'. We can be sure Ravel would have heard Fargue read it; and we can note at once the startling, surreal presence of a keyboard beside the sea:

> The stage is illuminated. A keyboard lights up beside the waves. The glow-worms of the sea form a chain. The slow rustling of sand creatures can be heard, seething and seeping.
>
> A laden barque is coming in through the darkness, where the glassy copes of slanting jellyfish break through the surface like first dreams on a warm night.
>
> Strangers loom like waves of the deep, hardly visible, obscured in soft darkness. Slow figures drag themselves from the ground, and displace the air like the broad leaves of a palm. The ghosts of a frail hour parade here, on this bank where music and thought, from the depths of time, come to an end. . . .
>
> The wind rises. The sea clamours and flames black, mingling her pathways.

The whole poem has an extraordinarily moving quality, combining within its surreal images, as is so often the case with Fargue, a sense of human isolation and a keen sensuousness. The landing stage is also a theatrical stage, illuminated by stage lights. This objectifies the scene and has the effect of increasing the poet's (and our) sense of isolation. What is the keyboard dong there? This startling and typically Farguian image belongs to the theatrical setting (a piano in the orchestra pit, or an instrument for accompanying silent movies), yet it is also a metaphor for the sounds of the sea and the sea creatures and the brilliance of the illumination (which is moonlit). As for the glow-worms, or iridescent algae – *noctiluques* – we are learning that Fargue had a taste for such obscurities. His listeners would very probably not have known the word any more than they knew the meaning of the word *noctuelle*.

The rising wind, the clamouring sea, flaming black – we are in the world of Ravel's 'Une barque sur l'océan'. And another sea poem by Fargue, 'La mer phosphorescente perle entre les arbres' (The Phosphorescent Sea Pearls Between the Trees) refers directly to *une petite barque*: 'It begins to rain over the bay. A cloud spreads its immense shadow over the heavy, muddied waters. A small barque paddles with all its heart. Lightning. A tree fern.' But this is no ordinary storm scene. On the cliffs 'a Monster' is watching, whose terrifying proportions would soon be captured for a mass audience by the new art of cinematography: 'Around the sharp edges of a circular abyss it carefully parts the carnivorous plants. It comes forth. It slowly places a huge webbed foot on the summit of the cliff, loosening a rain of splintered shale'. And it makes 'a deep sound that rolls and rumbles [*un bruit bien rond qui tourne et qui gronde*]' – the sound of the sea that, in 'Une barque sur l'océan', Ravel draws from the bass and pedals of the piano.

'Alborada del gracioso'

The title of this wonderful piece of musical exoticism is another example of Ravel's fascination with verbal intrigue. The obscure titles

Sites auriculaires and *Pavane pour une infante défunte* come to mind, but so too do all the titles of *Miroirs*, titles which suggest nothing is ever quite what it seems. This interest on Ravel's part was all of a piece with his dandyism, that cultivated Baudelarian manner that favoured obscurity and a certain aloofness, the depersonalising front that kept one's privacy intact by disguising it in elegant and mildly foppish clothing. Ravel, after all, was a child of the Symbolist movement. The dandyish air he assumed is captured perfectly in photos of this period. Later in life he was no less concerned with his appearance, though it became altogether quieter.

In a letter from 1907 answering a polite enquiry, Ravel had this to say:

> I understand your bafflement over how to translate the title 'Alborada del gracioso'. That is precisely why I decided not to translate it. The fact is that the gracioso of Spanish comedy is a rather special character and one which, so far as I know, is not found in any other theatrical tradition. We do have an equivalent, though, in the French theatre: Beaumarchais's Figaro. But he's more philosophical, less well-meaning than his Spanish ancestor. The simplest thing, I think, is to follow the title with the rough translation 'Aubade du bouffon' [Morning Song of the Clown]. That will be enough to explain the humoristic style of the piece.

This is as good as it gets from Ravel. It seems he was largely silent on the imaginative context of the piece when coaching Faure and Perlemuter, concentrating, as always, on minute details of articulation and rhythm. What stands out from his account, apart from the literary references, is the word 'humoristic' – in terms of characterisation, for the performer, it is the single, essential ingredient of the piece that should not be missed, yet so often is.

As Faure did for 'Une barque', Marcel Marnat offers a poem from Bertrand's *Gaspard de la nuit* as a possible source for 'Alborada'.

Again I am doubtful. The poem 'La sérénade' (from book 1 of *Le vieux Paris*), with its 'Goya-like vision', Marnat suggests, 'provided the exact canvas for "Alborada".' The poem is hilarious, witty, dangerous, all characteristics of 'Alborada', and reads (appropriately, as we shall see) like a stage farce in miniature. But it is not a Spanish scene, and it does not have a *gracioso* in a leading role, or in any role at all. And neither is a *sérénade* an *aubade* (Spanish: *alborada*), but in fact a piece of music from exactly the opposite end of the day.

So who and what was a *gracioso*? Ravel would have known precisely, the culture of Spain being such an important part of his inheritance. Faure remarked that 'Alborada del gracioso' 'was one of the most characteristic works of "le Ravel Français d'origine Espagnole."' It is of course a piece steeped in the traits of Spanish music, a mélange of allusions embracing flamenco, 'the scalding rhythms of Castille' (according to Faure), guitars, castanets and the *cante jondo* (deep song) of Andalusia. But there were precedents for this belonging to a long tradition within French music (including Chabrier's orchestral work *España* of 1883). But no other composer had entertained the idea of a *gracioso*, a specific literary reference with a very precise connotation.

The Spanish comedy that Ravel refers to is the *comedia* from what is known as the Golden Age (*Siglo de Oro*) of Spanish theatre, broadly contemporary with Shakespeare at the end of the sixteenth century but extending into the second half of the seventeenth. The prolific Lope de Vega (born in 1562, two years before Shakespeare) stood at its head, a playwright who created a hugely popular genre of fast-paced three-act dramas that fused the serious and the entertaining, the tragic and the comic, and in which the *gracioso* – an amoral and asocial free spirit, part clown, part subversive servant – took a leading thematic and structural role. The *gracioso* set the action in motion, controlled the multiple plots, and constantly commented on them, colluding with the spectators. The character subsequently became an important element in the plays of Lope's enthusiastic disciple, Tirso de Molina, and in the works of Pedro Calderón and Agustín Moreto y Cavana.

Ravel was only partly right to say the *gracioso* is not found in any other theatrical tradition. In French Renaissance drama there was a sharp-witted servant known as the *badin*, a character who took many forms, as rogue, simpleton, buffoon and dupe, and who had an equivalent in Spain called the *bobo*. Enid Welsford writes that the *gracioso* 'was a variant of the *bobo* who was represented as a rascally servant, who comments sarcastically on the other characters of the play and is often more than a match for his betters.' In developing his own drama, Lope de Vega was greatly influenced by the improvised comedy of the Italian theatre, the *commedia dell'arte*. Italian players travelled across Europe, into France, Spain and England, taking with them a lively, ribald comedy that, because it relied to a large extent on mime, was able to communicate irrespective of language barriers. This connects the *gracioso* to the highly subversive, black-masked Harlequin (Italian: Arlecchino) of the *commedia dell'arte*, whose comic antics were reinforced by a crack from his 'slapstick'. Harlequin was also an acrobat, and it seems the *gracioso* can be associated with a long tradition of theatrical clowning (as distinguished from the court clowns, in cap and bells, who were kept by monarchs) that included not only subversive parody – the servant aping the master with obscene language and gestures – but songs, dances, acrobatics and jigs (also a common and highly popular feature rounding off Elizabethan plays in England).

But the *gracioso* was not an improvised role, and was distinctly more central to the ethos and structure of the Spanish drama than Harlequin was for the *commedia dell'arte*. The *gracioso* was the chief instrument by which the playwright could 'hold up a mirror to nature,' which is how Lope de Vega described his own aims in his treatise on theatre from 1609, *The New Art of Writing Plays*. This is what made the *gracioso* unique, and which Ravel seems fully to have understood. It is the *gracioso*'s association with mirrors that explains the presence of 'Alborada del gracioso' – otherwise anomalous in a set of descriptive nature pieces – within *Miroirs*. 'Alborada' is central to Ravel's overall artistic conception. We can turn again to his comment on the title *Miroirs*, and his quotation from Shakespeare about the eye seeing only by reflection. It is clear that 'Alborada' was deeply connected to Ravel's identity as an artist, despite his claim that he was not affirming 'a subjectivist theory of art.' If the eye sees itself only by reflection, it is nevertheless seeking to see itself. Faure affirms (see Appendix A) that 'Alborada' was central to her lessons with Ravel. And Benjamin Ivry makes the point that 'a number of Ravel's friends believed that, in the "Alborada", Ravel drew a self-portrait as Gracioso, the antihero of romance, someone who looked at heterosexual love as an exterior observer or mirror-image antithesis.' (The mood of the piece can plausibly be interpreted as having a palpable sexual charge, which fits the *gracioso*'s role as go-between in love affairs.) Ivry adduces not Lope de Vega, but the later Golden Age drama of Tirso de Molina 'and others', as Ravel's source, in which the *gracioso* is altogether more obscenely ribald and Rabelaisian.

One such other, then, would be Moreto, who created one of the most memorable *gracioso*s in all of Spanish drama in the character Polilla from *El desdén con el desdén*. The word *polilla* means 'moth', an allusion to a flickering and ubiquitous presence, to changeability (in the play Polilla adopts the disguise of a doctor), but also to the *gracioso*'s role as a spoiler or destroyer. (It must surely be a coincidence, even if there were evidence of Ravel's knowledge of this play – as distinct from his certain knowledge of the stock type – that the image of a moth is twice present in *Miroirs*; but some kind of thought association cannot be ruled out.) This widens the context of 'Alborada' considerably, and by no means beyond what the extraordinarily cultured and astutely well-read Ravel might have had in mind. There is every reason to believe he was fully aware of the symbolic role of the *gracioso*, and that, as Janet Norden has said of Polilla, the character was closely associated with Carnival, the pre-Lent reversal of social and moral norms that annually gripped the cities of southern Europe (and still does). 'Polilla is a burlesque ruler of a courtly Carnestolendas [Shrovetide or Mardi Gras], the egoistic self-dubbed doctor, and the deceiver,' writes Norden. 'His burlesque quality is precisely an overflow of Carnival spirit into the restrained court scene. The *gracioso* communicates to the audience the ebullience which is experienced psychologically by the [other] characters, even though they cannot express it in the streets as the lower classes do.' In this sense the *gracioso*, as facilitator and go-between – not only in relation to his master's affairs, but also as director of the audience's response – can be understood as the presence of the author himself, much in the same way as Velázquez presents himself in such a painting as *Las meninas* (1656) through the contrivance of mirrors.

> Polilla's play transcends fantasy to confide in the audience, thus establishing a coexistence of Moreto's created art world and the natural spectator world, in both of which worlds Polilla is participant. Velásquez presented this same vision in his painting Las Meninas, which includes a self-portrait of the painter, who is in the act of painting the picture. The painter's self-portrait looks out at us as though from a mirror, and as though he were painting us. We are drawn into the world of artistic creation.

But it was not only the later Spanish Golden Age drama that presented this phenomenon. It was also central to Lope de Vega's original conception. The Spanish scholar Isabel Torres writes: 'The mirrors which dominate and deceive in Velásquez's painting disorientate the viewer, yet draw him into an artistic experience in which he confronts the artist himself. Lope's drama mirrors the confusion of pretence and reality and there at its centre . . . is the energetic and enigmatic Lope.'

It seems that the 'energetic and enigmatic' Ravel too is present at the centre of his own musical spectacle, the new creative departure that he labelled *Miroirs* and within which, in his Spanish mirror, he reflected himself dressed up as the *gracioso*. This is the same Ravel who later said, *gracioso*-like, 'Art is the supreme imposture.' The paradox at the centre of this remark is the very paradox at the centre of the concept of the clown, of Carnival, and of theatre itself. Writes Torres:

> Good theatre has no concept of the dramatic state as a limited space, but rather converts the entire auditorium into one staged experience. Actors and audience lose sense of a defining reality and become lost in an extended illusory moment. This is the 'art' which relates dramatists to actors to audience. Lope preaches it in his dramatic manual and he dramatizes it [in his plays].

I would suggest that Ravel does something similar in *Miroirs*. Torres's observations have a resonant parallel in the art of the performing musician, affirming our sense of *Miroirs* as a kind of theatre, a mini-opera without words, a series of imaginatively related aural cameos that have both visual and psychological dimensions which are open to a wide variety of interpretation and response. This surely is how the listener receives the complete work in performance – if, that is, the performer is imaginatively engaged. And each fine performance by a variety of pianists will reveal the work in a different light, with different emphases, different perspectives, exactly as a play will be revealed afresh under the hands of different directors. Ravel might have railed against 'interpretation', but he can only have meant imaginative misunderstanding.

Some detailed comments on performing 'Alborada' will be found in Appendix A. Here I will just mention the middle section, which I believe rarely gets the performance it needs. The Faure-like fright with which performers approach Ravel's scores often prevents a proper imaginative engagement with what is there, and with the context for why it is there. We are right in feeling trepidation, for Ravel's art is supremely sophisticated, and we are right to approach the score with the most vigilant respect; but wherein does this respect lie?

I would say that our attention in the middle section of 'Alborada' should be directed towards the nature of the Spanish idiom, the vocalisation, the freedom and timbre of folk singing, the hint of dark passions waiting to explode. But at the same time, so enigmatic is the Ravelian aesthetic that room should be left for a certain ironic detachment: how serious, how expressive after all (and expressive of what), is the passage beginning at bar 107, marked *le chant mf très expressif*? What is our *gracioso* up to here? Is Ravel facing two ways – is he offering darkness but actually parodying Spanish sentiment (as he so clearly does, without the darkness, in *L'heure espagnole*)? In 'Alborada del gracioso' there is no clear answer. I would prefer, in the act of performing, to remain open to all possibilities, which not only means the music is discovered afresh at each rendering, but allows the listener a role in the interpretation. In 'Alborada' there seems at times to be a menacing, brooding quality in this central section to which the performer should be faithful, but at the same time the melodic material is so extravagant, so potentially melodramatic and luscious, that we have an alternative interpretation through which it might all be viewed as a delightful confection.

Stuckenschmidt astutely observed that 'the fascination of this music, apart from its atmospheric magic, is that it makes the line between serious thought and its parody difficult to discern. In creating it, Ravel, presumably entirely by intuition, becomes the painter of a psychopathological state of fluctuation in which the state of normal awareness and that of illusion merge, then separate.' That seems to me to capture exactly the manner in which the performer should approach 'Alborada', and it underlines the formidably scrupulous balancing act that is required for the recreation of all of Ravel's piano music. The process may have been intuitive on Ravel's part, in the manner of all great art; but we should not underestimate the conscious intellectual act by which he engendered the work, nor his deep understanding of its raw material, drawn from Spanish drama of the Golden Age and the central character of the *gracioso*. Ravel identified with the ambivalence at the centre of seventeenth-century Spanish drama – where, equally, Stuckenschmidt's 'line between serious thought and its parody [is] difficult to discern.'

'La vallée des cloches'

According to the pianist Robert Casadesus, who worked closely with Ravel in the 1920s, Ravel's idea for 'La vallée des cloches' first came to him from hearing the multiple bells of Paris striking at midday. As an image of aural randomness – the characteristic of the opening and close of 'Vallée des cloches', where the counterpoint of bells appears to be achieved without design – this is appropriate, but it is clear Ravel's imagination took flight into a realm far removed from a Parisian cityscape. We cannot know when the title 'The Valley of Bells' came to him, but we might surmise that he hit upon this arresting spatial image as a perfect parallel for the kind of unrestricted, echoing space he imagined for constructing sound layers, sound that would both mingle and remain separate. The piano, with its resonating sound board, iron frame and pedal – and in its ability, at the same time, to articulate complex counterpoint with complete clarity – is the ideal medium for spatial experiments.

Ravel also found a visual symbol – a scaffolding of three staves – to reinforce his concept. Three-stave notation was highly unusual, though not without precedent. The second of Schumann's *Drei Romanzen*, in the nineteenth century one of his most popular piano pieces, is on three staves; and Liszt occasionally adopted this layout (as in parts of 'Les jeux d'eaux à la Villa d'Este', for example, though more for clarity for the reader than to underline a multi-layered structure). Debussy's *D'un cahier d'esquisses*, which had so excited Ravel when he began work on *Miroirs*, is on three staves – intentionally to enhance and clarify its layered sonorities – and this was to become a feature of Debussy's piano writing in *Images*, book 2 (with its two bell-inspired pieces, 'Cloches à travers les feuilles' and 'Et la lune descend sur le temple qui fut'), and the second book of Préludes.

Stuckenschmidt, without elucidating, observes that 'La vallée des cloches' represents 'a new use of the piano.' Bell pieces in fact had been a staple genre of nineteenth-century piano music, notably Liszt's, such as 'Les cloches de Genève' and 'La campanella', and the exquisite late pieces 'Cloches du soir', from *Arbre de Noël* (written partly on three staves), and 'La cloche sonne', based on an old French melody. Liszt's late masterpiece 'Bénédiction de dieu dans la solitude', one of his most far-reaching explorations of piano sonority, is replete with allusions to bells, both earthly and heavenly.

In chapter 2 I also suggested that there might be echoes of the bell-like sonorities of the gamelan in 'La vallée des cloches' – the right hand's opening figuration is far more suggestive of Eastern pentatonicism than it is of Parisian church bells. (Perhaps Debussy was aware of this suggestion when he came to write his Eastern-inspired 'Et la lune descend' two years later.)

Faure tells us that Ravel wanted the final chords to sound like the Savoyarde – the name given to the huge bell that rings out daily across Paris from the Basilica Sacré Cœur on the high *bute* of Montmartre. And he was able to demonstrate this memorably:

Though he was not a virtuoso in the grand sense of the word Ravel was fully able to demonstrate the resources of the instrument and its palette of sonorities. He knew how to create a dazzling crescendo, and a diminuendo vanishing to nothing, all those special characteristics of his music, and he had the perfect knack for capturing with minute precision a fleeting image – for example he had me repeat, tirelessly, the effect of a guttering candle in the last bars of 'Scarbo', through a sort of rapid, vanishing movement, with the hands darting diagonally away from the keyboard. He gave me the means in 'Vallée des cloches' for executing the rapid arpeggio motif in the bass register of the final bars, which represents the sudden, fateful tolling of the bell, the 'Savoyarde', as he called it. He showed me the perfect gesture for achieving it. I didn't get it at first try, and he laughed and said, 'It's quite a knack.' Goodness knows he loved these tricks – just like the little mechanical objects he bought for next to nothing, which would caterwaul when wound up with a key. Dear Ravel! Eternal child!

For all the exotic characteristics of 'Vallée des cloches', Ravel employs in the central section an overtly nineteenth-century cantabile style, and one of the longest and most richly sensual melodic lines he ever wrote. (Again, it is possible that Debussy's melodic outpouring in 'Et la lune descend', though characteristically briefer and fragmented, was a response to this work.) It is one of the many arresting features of this piece that its Zen-like exploration of bells – which the performer is instructed to play 'with great calmness, very softly, without accentuation' – should be able to accommodate the unbuttoned quality of the *largement chanté* section. There are many instances in Ravel's piano music in which he asks for a melody to be brought expressively into the foreground (and occasionally, as in 'Le gibet', brought out 'without expression'), but nowhere else does he use the instruction *largement chanté*, with all the amplitude and 'full-throated ease' that this implies (a translation might be 'broadly sung'). There is no greater outpouring of melody in all Ravel outside 'Lever du jour' from *Daphnis et Chloé* (though 'Le jardin féerique', especially the sublime orchestral version, comes very close.) Not even the slow movement of the G Major Piano Concerto achieves this unbuttoned quality.

The unity of this transfixing piano music is often commented upon. Ravel seems to have captured his intention in one single moment, and as one single spacious entity (Stuckenschmidt offers the bell-casting image 'in one pour'). This is the impression that we get from almost all his music – almost certainly illusory, for the perfection belies the effort. What interests me from a performing angle is the way unity is achieved across the whole of *Miroirs*, with the highly problematic placing of this piece of musical Zen, 'Vallée des cloches', at the end. Each piece will stand alone, and a separate performance of 'Alborada del gracioso' is a popular and effective ending piece on many a programme. But in their correct place the final two pieces make a startling juxtaposition, taxing the performer's concentration, but also the ability to control and characterise musical narrative. And the listener needs to be persuaded of the validity of not cheering at the end of 'Alborada' – one of Ravel's most hair-raising climaxes – and hence of the superior imaginative intentions of what follows, literally anticlimax.

The task Ravel set himself in writing *Miroirs*, his explorations and their outcome, prepared the way for *Gaspard de la nuit*. Ravel's discovery of Bertrand's prose poems, the subject of the next chapter, and his friendship with Viñes, who first put the book in his way, preceded the formation of the Apaches and his friendship with Fargue. Bertrand's own *Gaspard* was for a time forgotten, but the idea remained, half buried in his mind. After *Miroirs* Ravel was fully equipped to tackle what was to become one of the most celebrated masterworks of the piano repertoire.

4

Gothic Fantasies: Aloysius Bertrand – *Gaspard de la nuit*

When I was working on 'Scarbo' with le Maître, he said to me, 'I wanted to produce a caricature of romanticism'. But he added, in a low voice, 'Maybe I got carried away.'

Vlado Perlemuter, *Ravel après Ravel* (1970)

Maybe all of those who play 'Scarbo' – or indeed the whole of *Gaspard de la nuit* – get carried away in the same way as the composer himself, as he confessed to the French pianist Vlado Perlemuter. It is impossible not to be gripped and transported by this masterpiece, and it is perhaps one of the prerequisites for playing it that one should be. But all pianists need to be reminded of the pitfalls of such transport. Eva and Paul Badura-Skoda, many years ago, perfectly captured the pianist's dilemma when they juxtaposed two pithy comments on the art of performance. It is time they were repeated. The first comes from C. P. E. Bach: 'A musician cannot move others unless he too is moved. He must of necessity feel all of the effects that he hopes to arouse in his audience'. This, surely, is indisputable. But here is Busoni, a century and a half later: 'If an artist is to move others, he must not be moved himself – otherwise he will lose control of his technique at the vital moment'. We find ourselves nodding in agreement, remembering those moments when the sheer diabolical intensity of Ravel's art in 'Scarbo' – as well as the cascading passions of 'Ondine' and the gothic horrors of 'Le gibet' – have caused the wrong kind of grief on the keyboard.

Yet how can one perform this wonderful music and not be moved by it? The question takes us to the heart of the art of performance, and indeed to the creative act itself, whether the composer's, poet's, painter's or pianist's. Few artists ever create in a transport of passion; that is simply not how it is done. Yes, there are stories of sudden visions, sudden leaps into creative inspiration – Samuel Taylor Coleridge's short poem 'Kubla Khan' comes to mind, and perhaps one or two of Chopin's Préludes came to him all in a rush on wet and windswept evenings in the wilds of Majorca – but the majority of great artworks are the result of painstaking labour. Oscar Wilde, on being asked how a certain piece of writing was going, declared that he had spent all morning putting in a comma and all afternoon taking it out again. Ravel would have understood perfectly. Of one his most sublime creations, the slow movement of the G Major Piano Concerto, he exclaimed: 'That flowing phrase! How I worked over it bar by bar! It nearly killed me!'

The question remains: how do we reconcile our two propositions? How does a performer achieve the glorious, transcendental scope of *Gaspard*, achieve a full identification with the extraordinary emotive power of this music, and yet remain meticulously in control? Control is both everything and nothing: without it the piece fails, for this is a virtuoso work which depends on the excitement generated by feats of pianistic acrobatics. Scarbo's antics, in particular, are diabolical for the very reason that they should appear impossible – unless enacted by the kind of supernatural being of which he is the archetype. Yet control as an end in itself will not give birth to 'Scarbo': how often one hears a performance of prodigious muscular skill in which the dramatic narrative is missing, that imaginative core without which technique remains just technique, marvellous on one level but imaginatively and artistically void. The performer, and hence the listener, remains unengaged with the end beyond the means.

Perhaps performing should be something like William Wordsworth's famous definition of a poem as 'emotion recollected in tranquillity' – although one would hardly call the experience of performing *Gaspard* onstage as tranquil. But what Wordsworth described was an emotional experience, deeply felt and understood, that informed his poetry at one remove: a controlling detachment is achieved by the poet because the experience is prior to, not simultaneous with, the creation of the work of art. If we accept that this corresponds in some way to the realities of musical performance, then perhaps we can understand how the twin necessities of emotional engagement and technical control can be reconciled. But what precisely is the emotional engagement required for performing *Gaspard*? How should we respond to this music in a way that maintains our vital personal response, but which transcends it to become an authentic 'interpretation'?

The original poems which inspired the music (see Appendix C) provide a way in – and a compellingly necessary one. We have already seen, in the case of *Jeux d'eau*, that the tiny Régnier quotation attached to it was published, at Ravel's insistence, in the programme at the first performance, and that he later admonished his pupil Henriette Faure for not having read it. The poems published alongside each of the three pieces that make up *Gaspard* are far more substantial, and it is clear that Ravel wished the music to be understood – 'interpreted' – in direct relation to them, in the same way that Liszt would have expected the quotations accompanying his own music to be an integral part of the experience.

Most pianists today are aware of the three poems attached to the score of *Gaspard de la nuit*. Less well-known, certainly in the English-speaking world, is the complete collection of poems by Aloysius Bertrand which so captured Ravel's attention as a young man and from which he selected his three (exactly in the same way that Liszt selected his three poems for his 'Petrarch Sonnets' from a much larger body of sonnets written by the early fourteenth-century poet Francesco Petrarca). Bertrand's small volume of fifty-three prose poems, *Gaspard de la nuit*, on which he worked throughout his short life, was first published in 1842, the year after his death. Faure tells us that Ravel expected her to have read the whole collection before embarking on her preparation of his own *Gaspard*.

Bertrand subtitled his book *Fantasies in the Manner of Rembrandt and Callot*, an allusion to the seminal figure of German romanticism, the novelist, critic and composer E. T. A. Hoffmann, whose writings deeply influenced not only Bertrand but also several subsequent generations of European poets, painters and musicians. Hoffmann's works, including his *Fantasiestücke in Callot Manier* (Fantasy Pieces in the Style of Callot) began appearing in French translation between 1829 and 1831, just at the time Bertrand was working on *Gaspard*. One of Hoffmann's many occupations was as a writer of fantasy tales, short stories of the bizarre and ghostly, precursors of and models for the tales of Edgar Allan Poe (another writer of crucial importance for Ravel). Hoffmann also became, through his fictional Kapellmeister Kreisler, the voice of the new romanticism sweeping Europe at the beginning of the nineteenth century, and in his loosely novelistic *Fantasiestücke*, which is dominated by the eccentric Kreisler, he devised an acute, almost Surrealistic commentary on the music and cultural climate of his times. His writings were admired by Wagner, Baudelaire and Debussy; he provided the narrative source for innumerable ballets and operas of the nineteenth century (among them Tchaikovsky's *Nutcracker* and Jacques Offenbach's *Tales of Hoffmann*); and he was the inspiration behind one of the greatest of romanticism's piano works, Schumann's *Kreisleriana*. As a composer Hoffmann devoted a considerable part of his life to writing an opera, *Undine*, based on a story by Friedrich de la Motte Fouqué, the very tale that is the source of Bertrand's poem 'Ondine' and hence of Ravel's piano piece by the same name (as well as Debussy's 'Ondine' from the second book of Préludes). So even before Schumann's twin homages to Hoffmann (*Fantasiestücke* of 1837 and *Kreisleriana* of 1841), Bertrand, with *Gaspard de la nuit*, was devising his own. From its inception he intended his subtitle, *Fantasies in the Manner of Rembrandt and Callot*, to proclaim his indebtedness to Hoffmann. The significance of the seventeenth-century artists Jacques Callot and Rembrandt – which takes the connections of Ravel's *Gaspard* even further back in time – we will discuss shortly. Later in the nineteenth century, Bertrand's only published volume of poetry, *Gaspard de la nuit,* was taken up by Baudelaire and Mallarmé, the father figures of the French avant-garde, who were themselves central influences on the imaginative development of Debussy and Ravel – just as Hoffmann and the novelist Jean Paul had been for Schumann. Baudelaire's remark in the introduction to his own prose poems *Le spleen de Paris* started the trend: 'It was while leafing through, for at least the twentieth time, the famous *Gaspard de la nuit* that the idea came to me to try something analogous.' In fact, Bertrand's *Gaspard* was not famous at all, having largely disappeared after it was published in 1842. It was Baudelaire who made it famous, and even then only among the initiated. Mallarmé related how he had to search second-hand book shops for a copy. It wasn't until 1868 that a new edition was published in a series called *Curiosités romantiques* – curiosities, maybe, but which contained a straw in the wind in the form of a frontispiece by Félicien Rops. Rops was to be a central figure in the Symbolist movement that was just then stirring in France. Symbolism, grounded in the philosophy and practice of romanticism and given new life by Baudelaire and Mallarmé, was to be one of the most influential artistic credos on a long line of writers, poets, painters and composers in the last quarter of the nineteenth century, and reverberant well into the twentieth.In 1895 came a reprint of the original 1842 edition (it was then to have another eight reprints up to 1920), and it might be assumed that this was the volume that Ravel got to know early the following year, lent to him by Viñes. In fact, from a remark of Ravel's, recorded in Viñes's diary, that the small volume which his friend had found in London 'was extremely rare,' it seems that Viñes might have come across the original edition.

In his diary Viñes recorded how in their late teens he and Ravel would share their enthusiasms for the stories of Poe and the poetry of Baudelaire, swap music and books, sketch together – Ravel did gloomy, 'very black' illustrations of themes from Poe – and try out new chords on the piano. Among composers they devoured the music of Wagner, Chabrier, Rimsky-Korsakov and Debussy (Viñes mentions the *Proses lyriques*, songs for which Debussy wrote his own 'absolutely wonderful' texts). In September 1896 Viñes recorded a reading that lasted late into the evening of 'Bertrand's *Gaspard de la nuit*, which I let [Ravel] take with him.' Over a year later Viñes asks for it back: 'He said he would bring it to my flat tomorrow as it was at the bottom of a trunk.'

So it seems Ravel did not keep Bertrand permanently by him, as Schumann did Jean Paul (which he claimed was his bedside reading). But it is clear the small volume had a major influence on him, staying in his imagination, working its way over the years from dormant seed to full-blown creative consciousness. He began his own *Gaspard de la nuit* in early 1908, and it was first performed by Viñes in January of the following year.

To keep Bertrand's *Gaspard* to hand, as bedside reading indeed, is to discover how insistently these small, concentrated prose poems can stay in one's mind. Perhaps we don't today advise our offspring, as Mallarmé did his daughter, to 'take up Bertrand, for here is everything'; time and fashion have moved on. But it is easy to understand how the literary-minded Ravel would have been gripped by Bertrand's miniature narratives, by their startling juxtaposition of the lyrical and the grotesque, their perfection of structure, their boldness of imagery. The fifteen years Bertrand spent putting his poems together resulted in a concentration of material, a paring away, so that each poem comes across with a far greater intensity than its brevity would suggest. This would have had great appeal for the miniaturist side of Ravel, who released this incipient richness in some of the most densely wrought and emotionally charged piano music that he ever wrote. It seems clear that his musical response to *Gaspard de la nuit* grew from the complete work, not only from the three excerpts Ravel chose as his immediate background (and as we have seen, this is confirmed by Faure). Ravel makes this point for us by requisitioning the poet's title.

The poems in their entirety present a narrative, albeit a fragmented, even cinematic one. What is at once striking is Bertrand's control of dramatic incident: the reader becomes an onlooker, as if witness to the multiple productions of a miniature theatre, by turns satirical, farcical, macabre, cruel and lyrical. Colloquial dialogue is juxtaposed with a sharply focused stage setting, which changes from poem to poem, and an exquisite lyrical imagery. Something of the flavour of the whole can be captured from a list of the people, images and objects that Bertrand dwells on throughout: among the characters are a variety of misfits, tramps, poseurs, poor students, soldiers, courtesans, monks, dwarves, witches and sprites; low life is juxtaposed with the peacock preening of the nobility; there are repeated images of blood, deformity and nightmare, allied to storms, moaning wind, graveyards, bell towers, Gothic spires, stained-glass windows, weathercocks and spiders; fragrance is pervasive, the perfume of petals and almonds, flowers of jasmine, a bouquet of violets, a love letter scented with musk; musical instruments abound, often broken and out of tune, as in 'Leaving for the Sabbath': 'And when Maribas [the soldier] laughed or cried, it sounded like the moaning of a bow across three strings of a smashed violin', and from 'The Grand Companies': 'a deflated bagpipe whined like a brat cutting a tooth'. Bertrand's manipulation of language appears effortless, capturing with minimal means a sharply realised sense of place, a startling image or a concentrated sound, as in 'Pity even the glow-worm, which a drop of rain hurls down to the oceans from a mossy branch' (from 'Rain'), and 'The weathercocks cried like sentinel cranes' ('Roundelay Under the Bell').

The whole work also shows us that the figure of Scarbo is ubiquitous, that he appears not only in poems bearing his name. (In fact there are two poems entitled 'Scarbo' – Ravel chooses the one from the end of the volume in the section 'Pièces détachées'.) In many of the poems he is a leering dwarf or gnome, sometimes named, sometimes not. He even appears in the explicatory introduction (the first 'Preface') as a laughing gargoyle. Here we are introduced to the character of Gaspard himself, whom Bertrand establishes as the 'author' of the book – a mysterious old tramp in tattered frock coat and beard whom Bertrand meets one day in a public garden in old Dijon. In Gaspard's rambling conversation with Bertrand – more a rambling monologue about the meaning of art, of God and the devil – he relates how, in the cathedral square one day, he had heard laughter and had turned his head up towards 'one of those monstrous figures that the sculptors of the Middle Ages attached by the shoulders to the eaves of the cathedrals, an atrocious figure of a dammed soul who, a prey to suffering, stuck out his tongue, gnashed his teeth and wrung his hands. It was that figure who laughed.' Bertrand is incredulous:

> 'You had a speck in your eye!' I cried. 'Neither a speck in my eye, nor cotton in my ear. The stone figure had laughed, laughed with a grinning, dreadful, diabolical laugh, but sarcastic, incisive, picturesque'.

Bertrand becomes caught up in Gaspard's monologue in much the same manner as the wedding guest in Coleridge's *The Rime of the Ancient Mariner* is pinned down by the haunted and cursed old sailor who unburdens himself of his story of betrayal. Finally Gaspard thrusts a manuscript into Bertrand's hands:

This manuscript will tell you how many instruments my lips have tried before arriving at the one that is pure and expressive, how many paint brushes I have used on the canvas before seeing born there the shadowy aurora of chiaroscuro. There are deposited many processes, perhaps new, of harmony and colour, the sole result and sole reward that my laborious study may have achieved. Read it; return it to me tomorrow. Six o'clock tolls from the cathedral; the hours chase the sun stealing off among these lilacs. I am going to lock myself in to write my will. Good night.

Even in this short extract we can catch the vividness of Bertrand's writing, and we also notice the natural manner in which poetry, painting and music are evoked as parallel or even unified works of art. Baudelaire would take up this Romantic ideal in his articles on Delacroix and Wagner and in his numerous journalistic pieces on the annual art exhibitions in Paris. Through Baudelaire these ideas became embedded in Symbolist literature at the end of the century, the literature that so entranced the young Ravel and his friend Viñes.

When Bertrand goes in search of Gaspard to return the manuscript, he finds that the old man has vanished. He turns out to have been none other than the devil himself, 'Gaspard of the night' – and as the old man had already insisted that 'the devil doesn't exist', it seems grimly appropriate that he doesn't turn up. This contradiction lies at the heart of Bertrand's poem, a work supposed to have been written by one who had previously asserted that Art comes from God. The contradiction is underscored in the short 'Second Preface', where the contrasting manners of Callot and Rembrandt, to which the subtitle of the book refers, are explained: art is born from a conflict of opposites, from a combination of the grotesqueries of the engraver Callot (whose precise and varied depictions of low life were much admired by artists of the romantic era) and the deep wisdom of such a painter as Rembrandt, 'who communes with the spirits of beauty, science, wisdom and love'. Rembrandt is seen as 'the white bearded philosopher', Callot as 'the braggart soldier who caresses the gypsy girls and who is noisy in the taverns.' This is another version of the celebrated Schumann dichotomy, represented in his journalism and music (exactly contemporaneously with Bertrand) by the opposing figures of Florestan and Eusebius.

Even in the First Preface of *Gaspard de la nuit* Bertrand is writing as a poet. The poetic manner he will display throughout these prose poems is prefigured in Gaspard's exhortation that he had 'neither a speck in his eye nor cotton in his ear.' Sharp visual images allied to concentrated evocations of sound are two of the abiding characteristics of the overall work. Ravel would have savoured these characteristics: at exactly the time he discovered *Gaspard* he was composing a work for two pianos called *Sites auriculaires* (Scenes for the Ear). So it is with Ondine's exhortation to 'Listen, listen!' that Ravel chooses to open his triptych of pieces. In the poem we are asked to listen not only to the water sprite's seductive 'murmured song', but to the droplets of water she brushes across her lover's window panes, 'lit by the dull glow of the moon.' In her castle, in the depths of the lake, we are told her father 'whips up the croaking waters with a branch of green alder'; and Ondine, shedding a tear as she fails to lure her lover to a watery grave, suddenly bursts into laughter, a sound which, as she vanishes, becomes transformed into a shower of spring rain splashing against the windows.

'Le gibet' (The Gallows) and 'Scarbo' work similarly, drawing the reader into an intensity of imagined listening and seeing; sound and sight, hearing and seeing, seem to fuse. 'Le gibet' narrates a series of increasingly macabre suggestions as to the nature of a pervasive sound in the air: it could be the wind, or maybe the sighing of the man dangling on the gibbet; it could be a beetle 'plucking a single bloody hair' from the bald pate of the corpse, or a spider 'embroidering a length of muslin for that strangled neck'. Is it actually a sound, or is it a vision – sound or sight? It is both: 'It is the bell that sounds from the walls of a town beyond the horizon and the carcass of a hanged man reddening in the setting sun.'

The dwarf in 'Scarbo' is evoked by the same means: the poem begins 'Oh, how often have I *heard* him and *seen* him, Scarbo … !' (my italics); the poet recalls the buzz of the dwarf's laughter 'in the shadows of my alcove', and the sound of his fingernail 'scraping … on the silk drapes around my bed.' Like Ondine (and like Gaspard himself), he finally vanishes, but not before his antics threaten to overcome the onlooker with a giddiness and vastness inducing near-panic – 'the dwarf would then rise up between myself and the moon, like the spire of a Gothic cathedral.' We can see here – and in 'Le gibet' too – how the familiar conventions of the twentieth-century horror film were rooted in romantic imagery (and that Mary Shelley's *Frankenstein* had a variety of companions). The minute figure of Scarbo becomes that familiar giant shadow on the wall, magnified by a trick of light, his pointed cap taking on the proportions of a cathedral spire. But in reality he has no substance, being a creature of fantasy and fear, and the poem describes how, like a candle becoming fragile, transparent and ultimately nothing, Scarbo expires into the air. Bertrand's image is not quite the usual one associated with a guttering candle; rather, he compares Scarbo's expiration to the softening of the wax, turning blue as it begins to show light through ('diaphanous as candle wax'), a gradual vanishing process which contrasts strongly with his previous antics. Finally 'he would snuff himself out' – Scarbo, even now, remains in full control, and we realise that this visitation is a repeated occurrence, that we never get the better of our fears which habitually revisit us ('How often have I heard him and seen him …').

Ravel achieves the menacing (and thrilling), protracted magnification of Scarbo in music of stupendous power and equally stupendous difficulty. Yet once this is mastered, what remains difficult for the performer is the structure of the coda – less difficult in technical terms, but highly problematic musically. How is the melting and vanishing to be achieved without a sense of anticlimax? It is possible that the notion of anticlimax is integral to the artistic intent, appropriate to Ravel's stated intention to caricature romanticism. In this sense 'Scarbo' bears the stylistic traits of modernism (compare the ending of 'Scarbo' with its opposite, the tempestuous coda of Liszt's *Mephisto Waltz*, a piece which must have been in Ravel's mind in his own essay in the diabolical). But without the greatest care and thought on the performer's part, Ravel's masterful depiction of Scarbo's disintegration can simply cause puzzlement for the listener. It certainly helps to know what is being depicted – and I maintain that as wonderful as the musical experience is throughout all three parts of Gaspard, it is greatly enhanced by knowing the poems, for performer and listener alike. How could it not be, considering how unerringly Ravel has found musical equivalents for Ondine's laughter, her watery element, the macabre *mise-en-scène* of the gallows with its blood-red sky, the shiver-inducing laughter of Scarbo, his grinning somersaults and manic spinning? One wants to know about these things as much as one wants to know what is going on in an opera: without knowing, the imaginative experience is incomplete. In *Gaspard de la nuit* Ravel's piano, in the Lisztian manner, is transformed into a theatrical stage, upon which the pianist 'plays'. For Charles Rosen *Gaspard* 'starts not from the poems of Bertrand, but from the piano's capacity to represent the images of those poems' – a remark that is luminous with implications for performers and their ability to meet both the technical and the imaginative challenges of this work.

It remains to consider a few details of performance of a general enough nature not to be confined to Appendix A. Viñes tells us that Ravel wanted the song of Ondine submerged in the accompanying figurations at the opening, which seems exactly appropriate considering how, as a sprite (a creature of the elements), she is born of the water, is made of it and will return to it when she dies. In surrounding her with her own element, conjured from a figuration combining a trill with a Lisztian tremolando – and in which she 'murmurs her song' – Ravel creates a perfect aural symbolism.

And for those pianists who haven't picked up the correct reading from the Peters edition of the right-hand figuration: this figuration does not change in bar 5, continuing exactly as it began. Ravel's manuscript is very clear on this point, though the misprint in the original French edition has been long disseminated, causing unnecessary strain for several generations of pianists.

Ondine is not a witch, as I have sometimes heard suggested; she is a water sprite, associated with the mermaid, and her element, apart from water, is the art of seduction. She is not evil, and the opening figuration should not evoke the chattering of teeth. (In all cases of extramusical context it is well to get the images right: the musicologist Vladimir Jankélévitch, for example, in his book on Ravel, says that Scarbo 'bursts like a soap bubble', which not only replaces Bertrand's highly original metaphor with a cliché, but gets the idea wrong too. Ravel's Scarbo does not burst like a bubble – he vanishes in the manner Bertrand so carefully depicts.)

Ondine originated in Homerian mythology as a siren, one of those beautiful female creatures whose songs lured Odysseus's sailors into the water with mindless desire. Ravel certainly related to the sexual allure of his Ondine. The climax of 'Ondine' – as well as the build-up to it and the subsiding afterwards – is built on impeccable musical procedures, but the implications of sexual climax are clear, or at least should be. For Ravel there were several recent precedents for the expression of overt sexual arousal, including Wagner's *Tristan und Isolde* and Debussy's *Prélude à l'après-midi d'un faune*, two works that had a deep influence on him. And there was also the palpable sexual undertone of Debussy's own *Tristan*-derived opera, *Pelléas et Mélisande*, another work that Ravel revered. But in terms of piano music Ravel takes the voice and style of sexually charged musical symbolism directly from the nineteenth century: he interprets Bertrand through the virtuoso pianism of Liszt, and thereby briefly dons the mantle of sexual charisma worn by Liszt himself. It is this aspect of romanticism which, surely, 'carried [him] away'.

The differences between Debussy and Ravel are perfectly illustrated by their respective 'Ondine' pieces. Debussy's, some five years after *Gaspard*, is one of the most enigmatic and challenging of the second book of Préludes (challenging, that is, in terms of sonority, character, structure – it has none of the Lisztian challenges of Ravel's 'Ondine'). Harmonically it has the experience of Stravinsky behind it, but this does not explain the characteristically Debussyan manner. Its mercurial whimsy is unlike anything Ravel could have attempted, as is its method of blending fantasy and sensuality to achieve a flickering eroticism, at once disembodied and voluptuous.

Ravel's effects are achieved in a quite different way, by a complex variation of decoration – again, this is Liszt's practice – which adorns a repeated melodic line with circular patterns. The opening tremolando, against which we hear Ondine's murmured song, takes us into a unified sound world which remains the musical landscape throughout, even when the murmur grows to a passionate cry. Only once does the enveloping and swathing figuration cease, leaving the sprite's voice as quiet, unadorned melody. In terms of the narrative, Ravel creates at this moment the sense of loneliness after climax, and the effect is to make us all the more aware of what has gone before, what is missing. It is a simple enough dramatic device, common to music, narrative, or theatre – multiplicity followed by singularity, sound by silence – but Ravel's handling is so masterly that we experience the effect as if for the first time.

Debussy, on the other hand, never allows us to settle long into a fixed sonority or swoon to the curves of endless melody. His tale is one of constant interruptions and multiple scenes. His Ondine barely sings but rather dances, frisks and seduces with her changing shapes, moods and personas. The art of composition, of structure and musical intention, is radically different – and altogether more modern, more difficult. Ravel didn't essay anything of a similar vein until his *Valses nobles et sentimentales*, in which finely wrought harmonic textures and the most minutely judged subtleties of rhythm are at the service of refined sensation – this is Ravel at his peak of his genius as a miniaturist. Nothing could be further from the audacious virtuoso style of *Gaspard*.

Ravel insisted on a very slow, unwavering tempo for 'Le gibet'. He had an argument with Viñes over it, who claimed it failed to grip audiences at Ravel's tempo and so bored them. This is indeed the problem, but it is usually dull pianists, not tempi, that bore audiences. To sustain a musical structure at a slow tempo is one of the supreme skills of pianism (it is the slow movements of Beethoven's sonatas, for example, which are among the greatest tests). This has little to do with tempo memory, that necessity for tempo recall which enables the performer, at all times, to know how to relate different sections of a long piece. It has more to do with rhythmic awareness, an ability to judge relative emphases within a phrase so that a phrase *sounds* like a phrase, sounds like a sentence or paragraph of a thought, something unfolding in time in the same way as discourse or narrative unfolds – with a certain inevitability, but also with a sense that what is being said has an air of spontaneity, an existence for that moment only. Such unfolding in time is not the same thing as playing in time, or at least not in the way in which that term is usually understood. Playing in time is taught as playing with a strict pulse. I would contend that *really* playing in time involves flexibility, an ability to play *off* the pulse while maintaining the illusion of regularity. (It follows, however, that a complete understanding and constant awareness of the underlying pulse is essential.) Playing 'Le gibet' metronomically is not the answer; this, as Viñes perhaps recognised, leads to boredom. Ravel's concern for an unwavering tempo is the viewpoint of a composer, not a performer. A performer knows that the effect of regularity is achieved by irregularity. I am not saying that 'Le gibet' should never be metronomic – indeed, in places it can be strictly so – only that the metronome will not provide the final answer to the problem of tempo. Phrasing is a process of forward momentum (even at the slowest of tempi) articulated through a balance of weak and strong accents; the regularity of the pulse has nothing to do with it. This is easily demonstrated by playing a phrase of 6/8 as six in a bar – hence six equal stresses, hence stolidity and monotony – and then in two (two groups of 3 eighth notes), which creates a sense of flexibility through the alternation of different stresses. Yet in both cases the metronomic pulse will be the same. In addition, the performer will create emphasis by delay, and direction by the minutest forward propulsion – what I call playing off the pulse. The larger-scale pulse structure, however – that which is governed by the principal emphases in the whole duration of a phrase, which will be few – will seem completely regular.

And the key to 'Scarbo' too, once the keyboard choreography is mastered, is the character, as well as the execution, of the rhythm. This rhythm is intimately associated with the antics of Scarbo himself. He springs and somersaults, hops and spins. The technique is Lisztian, the Liszt of 'Gnomenreigen' and *Mephisto*, and requires immense agility and flexible wrist movement rather than power. Power comes in bursts, especially at the extended climax just before the end, but what is required most of the time is a light touch and lightning movement across the keys. Above all the performer must identify with the romantic thrill, the frisson of fear, the projection of the kind of narrative that would delight children and adults alike. This is not of the same character as Liszt's *Dante* Sonata, which is altogether more serious, and where the souls of the dead do seem truly to be wailing in hell. Ravel's 'Scarbo' suggests fear, but it is not the fear of hell. Scarbo the devil is actually harmless. The fear we feel is one we want to experience again, like the thrill of the circus or the tremor of fright in fairy stories. 'Scarbo' is magical.

5

The Perfection of Style – *Valses nobles et sentimentales*

It is at the piano that a poet of sound often finds his most
beautiful rhymes, testing with his own ear multiple audacities
of acoustical reaction, so as to calculate the finest effect for
future listeners. It is where he measures, with exquisite delight,
differing degrees of seductiveness or astringency, where he
develops his alchemy of sound in which is distilled his most
intoxicating perfumes or his most fatal poisons.

Émile Vuillermoz, 'L'œuvre de Maurice Ravel' (1939)

The twin poles of Ravel's aesthetic in his solo piano music are *Valses nobles et sentimentales* to the north and *Gaspard de la nuit* to the south. My polar choices are not especially significant, unless we care to see the cool, exquisitely clean precision of the *Valses nobles* as an example of northern intellect and rationality, and the hectic, sexually charged drama of *Gaspard* as befitting a conception of the alien, unbridled south. (In a revealing remark comparing Beethoven and Mozart, Ravel suggested the former was more the Roman kind, while Mozart was Hellenic. 'I myself feel closer to the open sunny Hellenes,' said Ravel.) Such neat categorisations do neither work full justice, but they do serve to underline how different these two great works are – poles apart, indeed. What remains startling, and endlessly exciting for the pianist who performs them, is the realisation that they come from the same pen.

The consequence of this realisation, for interpretation and performance, is that the pianist can very usefully experiment (in the privacy of the practice studio) with playing the *Valses nobles* like *Gaspard* and *Gaspard* like the *Valses nobles*. What this will reveal is that each of these major works inevitably contains elements of the other, and that together they allow the pianist a deeper understanding of an artist who fiercely protected and concealed the impulses behind the creative process. Put another way, the pianist will reach a greater understanding of *Gaspard*, and how to communicate this in performance, through an intimate knowledge of *Valses nobles*, and vice versa. Precision and refinement, allied to an exquisite control of texture and small-scale structure, are the hallmarks of the *Valses nobles*; they also display, less obviously but keenly apparent to the pianist who lives long with them, an emotional charge, a 'feeling', that is the equal in impact to the more sustained emotional narrative of *Gaspard*. It is notable how many *expressif* and *très expressif* markings there are in *Valses nobles* – fourteen in all; *Gaspard*, at twice the length, has six, as well as the stern instruction *sans expression* in 'Le gibet'. The expressive power of *Gaspard* is overt, and Ravel wished it to be curbed, refined; that of *Valses nobles* is subtler, quieter, and needed highlighting. Equally, for all the theatrical and virtuosic demands of 'Ondine' and 'Scarbo' and the self-consciously contrived grotesqueries of 'Le gibet', *Gaspard* at every moment is a work so precisely constructed, so perceptive in its understanding of the possibilities of pianism, so strictly controlled at the points of maximum audacity, that it demands as refined an understanding of colour, texture and rhythmic flexibility as anything in *Valses nobles*.

We can see the poles defined by these two great works as inherent in two opposing genres. *Gaspard* defines the virtuosic side of pianism, the audacity of the professional soloist daring all in a public display; *Valses nobles* defines the intimacies of private music making, the domain of the amateur (though the opening waltz appears to promise otherwise). The dialectic of public and private was imbedded in nineteenth-century music making, with the virtuoso in command of the concert hall and the amateur in command (to varying degrees) of the drawing room. The demand for music playable by amateurs was huge and accompanied the inexorable rise of the professional performer and the mounting complexity of the music performed publicly. This accounts for the existence of Chopin's nocturnes, Schumann's *Kinderszenen* and Liszt's *Consolations*. These great composer-pianists wrote music for themselves to play as virtuosos, but they also needed to write music that would sell to, and be playable by, amateurs at home.

The composer was a different animal by Ravel's time, and Ravel had no need to earn his living as a performer, though he performed in public (and conducted), rather badly. But the old forms remained, the public and the private, the virtuoso and the amateur, and it is certain that the presence of the formidable virtuoso Ricardo Viñes, literally by Ravel's side, had a profound effect on the genesis of *Gaspard de la nuit*. While we cannot say, on the other hand, that *Valses nobles* was aimed at amateurs – Ravel would have preferred that they leave his music alone – the eponymous waltzes of Schubert, which were his starting point, most certainly were. Behind Ravel's *Valses nobles* lies the presence of amateur music making, the small-scale, self-contained piece devised to amuse and console. Ravel's previous piano work, *Ma mère l'oye*, for four hands, had already shown his taste for such composition, with the first performance given by children.

Valses nobles et sentimentales was given its first performance by the composer Louis Aubert, its dedicatee, in May 1911, in a curious experiment mounted by the Société Musicale Indépendante (a group for the propagation of new music, founded a year earlier by Ravel and other former pupils of Fauré, with Fauré himself as president).

The committee decided to give a *concert sans noms d'auteur*: all the music in the concert was to be anonymous, and the listeners would be asked to guess the composer and write in the name next to each title in the programme. Ravel's friend the critic Calvocoressi was at the concert and recalled:

> Many people who would have applauded the *Valses* with the utmost vigour had they known Ravel had written them remained indifferent; and unfavourable comments arose freely, during the interval, from lips usually ready to sing Ravel's praises. . . . I cannot remember whether the majority found for Ravel, but I doubt it. What I remember quite well is that I did not.

Almost nothing is recorded of Ravel's reaction at the time, apart from his stoicism in quietly withstanding the many sarcastic remarks. Calvocoressi believed that his friend's attitude to criticism, 'favourable, or unfavourable, was and . . . remained one of absolute, often contemptuous indifference.' This may have been the attitude Ravel wished to convey, but the real picture was more nuanced. It is not a sign of indifference that, after the inaugural concert of the Société Musicale Indépendante the year before (at which *Ma mère l'oye* had been premiered), he had asked to be sent the reviews – 'as many as possible,' as he wrote to Vuillermoz. The fact that this particular concert was, in Ravel's words, 'in everyone's opinion a great success' clearly made it easier for him to read his critics. His own comment on *Valses nobles*, in his characteristically matter-of-fact Autobiographical Sketch, simply recalled 'the protestations and boos' that greeted the performance, and revealingly, in contrast to Calvocoressi's assessment, he mentioned 'the slight majority' that found in his favour. This had been of more importance to him, perhaps, than he had liked to confess. (Vuillermoz, who had also been at the concert, remarked that 'though stoic, he was in all likelihood a little bitter.')

What was so difficult for the first audience of *Valses nobles*, an audience that for a concert of new music would have been musically literate and sophisticated? It seems they were too sophisticated for the obvious Straussian (Johann) flavour of the work, while the notable dissonances of harmony came across either as either naive inexpertise or a joke (it is significant that some considered the work to be by Erik Satie). Even Ravel's discerning friend the critic Jean Marnold (to whom Ravel had dedicated 'Le gibet'), writing in the *Mercure de France* the following year, found that 'the complicated harmonies ... were disproportionate to the essence of the exercise.'

But it is not entirely surprising that many failed to spot the composer. After *Gaspard* and *Ma mère l'oye* Ravel changed his style to what he called 'a distinctly clearer writing, which sharpened the harmony and emphasised the contours of the music.' He uses the word *durcir* – to harden. Even today this hardening of dissonance, this sharpened profile – signalled in the magnificent audacity of the opening bars – is one of the most notable characteristics of the work. It is just as apparent in the bittersweet harmonies of the softer, intimate Waltzes, such as no. 2, which opens with alternating major sevenths over minor triads, and no. 5, with its constantly clashing chromaticisms and cluster chords that so influenced the jazz harmony of Bill Evans half a century later. At its most extreme the dissonance approaches bitonality in the middle section of the seventh Waltz, though Ravel pointed out later that he had simply employed a chord found at the opening of Beethoven's E-flat Sonata, op. 31 no. 1. The difference of course was that by separating out the ingredients of this chord, so that each hand appears to be on a different key centre (when in fact Ravel is exploiting the nature of appoggiaturas and withholding their resolution), he not only 'emphasise[s] the contours' of the music but creates contours where none had before existed. By so doing he certainly 'hardens' the harmony. (With his composition students Ravel delighted in proving the formal accuracy of his harmonic procedures, as Roland-Manuel recalled: 'I learnt that there was not a single procedure [*aggregation*] in my beloved *Valses nobles et sentimentales* that could not be justified by Reber and Dubois.')

And what would the first audience have made of no. 8, the Épilogue? The surface languor of this music is deceptive, for not only do we have here, in clear delineation, the characteristically astringent dissonances, but also a disintegration of structure, where echoes of previous waltzes, dislocated memories, intrude and break up the surface pulse. Ravel would certainly have been struck by the similar process in several of Debussy's Préludes, book 1, published only the year before, such as 'Les sons et les parfums tournent dans l'air du soir' (a waltz), 'La sérénade interrompue' and 'Minstrels'. In a letter of May 1910 Ravel writes of 'playing Debussy's Préludes again. They are wonderful masterpieces.' He had only just received the new publication from Durand. Three days later his excitement remained when he wrote to another friend: 'I have received Debussy's Préludes. There's a certain 'Cathédrale engloutie' and a 'Sons and parfums' etc. and all the rest too, which are splendid.'

In other respects *Valses nobles* bears little relation to Debussy, though the riveting final bars of the Épilogue, marked *ppp en se perdant*, perhaps echo the process of attenuation at the end of such Préludes as 'Voiles' and 'Des pas sur la neige'. But those of Ravel's first listeners who had failed to relate to the previous seven Waltzes would have found this Épilogue, and its final bars, inexplicable.

And what of his loyal colleague and pianist for the occasion, Aubert, one of the few members of the Society who were in the know? Perhaps he failed to capture the panache and the magic, the subtle ironies, the suggestive curtsies of the imagined dancers, the flicker of decadence. Possibly he failed to surmount the technical difficulties – of touch, texture and pedalling – of a kind so different from the acrobatics of *Gaspard* but equally challenging.

Above all, for the performer, it is the characterisation of the waltz, the way in which the dance rhythm is identified and projected, which defines the ineffable mood and atmosphere of the work. It seems that Ravel was at his most demanding and dogmatic when teaching this piece, its rhythm especially, making the twenty-three-year-old Perlemuter repeat the cross-rhythms in the opening Waltz 'ten times, hands separately,' as he recalled, adding, 'He was so insistent on precision.' Henriette Faure's similar recollections capture, amusingly, her petrified state of mind when she played the Waltzes to him at her first lesson:

> He was seated. He got up, stood close to the piano and subjected me to a torture that fifty years later I have not forgotten, stopping me continually, going back over the tiniest details, for a breath, a silence, a single pedal, an inflection – and along with all this, like a clock in the background, his endless 1.2.3., 1.2.3. It was exhausting. I had to integrate fantasy with rigour, to find the dream world, the ideal elegance, within the greatest possible rhythmic precision. This martyrdom lasted near on two and a half hours.

It is also clear that Ravel was proud of, indeed possessed by, the unique quality of what he had achieved, that he viewed the work with the fierce and uncompromising pride of ownership. (Such an attitude would be the source of Calvocoressi's belief that he viewed criticism with contempt. But the fact that he was convinced of the quality of his creative achievements does not mean he was unaffected by criticism of them.) Perlemuter, over twenty years later, recalled:

> Despite the years that have passed, I cannot recall without a certain emotion Ravel making me work on these *Valses*, there in his study, next to the piano, the score in his hands. I had never seen such a keen look in his eyes. He had about him such a desire to be understood, of leaving not a single detail to chance, not only in the text but in

the interpretation of it. The desire for perfection of the letter led
one involuntarily to the spirit.

We know that 'perfection of the letter' rarely leads quite so simply
to 'the spirit,' but as an aphorism it holds an essential truth and
reminds us again of Ravel's oft-quoted remark about wanting his
music simply to be played rather than interpreted. But the distinction between interpretation and playing the letter of the score is far
from simple, as Ravel himself must have known. This is confirmed
by Perlemuter's observation that Ravel was concerned not only
with the letter of the text 'but in the interpretation of it.' Details
of the text, instructions regarding tempo, articulation and dynamics, are never as clear-cut as they seem. Details need a context, a
musical *raison d'être*, a function, just as do the words in a sentence.
The word 'interpretation' itself, in different contexts, means subtly
different things. Ravel often used it as a pejorative term, meaning
a loose, unthinking, self-indulgent performance as opposed to one
that demonstrated an objective understanding of the composer's
intentions. To a great concert artist, interpretation means what
is achieved, uniquely and artistically, on the concert platform, an
identification with the spirit of the music that includes both a
subjective response and objective understanding. Perlemuter knew
this, as he made clear when he referred to the 'spirit' of a work. But
his own use of the word 'interpretation', in the passage above, also
included the meaning 'to understand', as in 'How do I interpret
your instructions?' Ravel, it seems, in the painstaking lessons he
gave to Perlemuter and Faure, undertook to make these instructions
absolutely clear.

It is not surprising that both pianists emphasised Ravel's insistence on rhythm in *Valses nobles et sentimentales* – they are dances,
after all – nor that they found his instructions as a teacher so
daunting. Ravel's waltz rhythm – elegance allied to the clock-like
precision that so occupied Henriette Faure – is not at all easy to

master, especially as it is overlaid with the most refined variations of texture and stress that can easily throw the rhythm, and hence the style, out altogether. But the pianist will finally discover that what cannot be escaped – 'his endless 1.2.3., 1.2.3.' – can actually be embraced, and that difficulties of emphasis, agogic accentuation and subtle elasticities of pulse (often indicated) then begin to melt away.

Towards the end of 1913 Ravel made a piano-roll recording of *Valses nobles* for the German company Welte-Mignon, whose player piano was far in advance of its competitors in its much-publicised ability to capture accurate tempi, expressive nuance, dynamics and pedalling (even half pedalling). Edwin Welte, the director, had sent his machine and his technicians to Paris to record '"lions" like Debussy and Ravel.' Debussy too was recorded at this period, short pieces including a selection of his preludes and *Children's Corner*, the result eliciting from him the flattering comment that 'it is impossible to attain greater perfection of reproduction than that of the Welte system.' Ravel also recorded the first two movements of his Sonatine (no doubt fearing the third movement was beyond him technically).

There would be later piano-roll recordings by Ravel, in the 1920s, some of which, though released under his name, were actually performed by his close friend Robert Casadesus; by this time a considerable amount of his piano music certainly was beyond him. *Valses nobles*, however, seems authentic Ravel, complete with awkward corners, characteristic old-fashioned arpeggiation of chords and desynchronised left and right hands. (It seems reasonable to assume, as can be assessed from later transfers onto disc, that these characteristics are authentic and not merely the result of poor reproduction techniques; one of the transfers, made in 1992 by Dal Segno, is onto a modern concert grand.) Welte's technicians were able to correct wrong notes, but they seem to have left some of Ravel's errors alone, perhaps to give the impression of authenticity. While considerable allowance has to be made for the inaccuracies of reproduction – setting up the rolls on comparable instruments to the ones Ravel played on is not an exact science, and the rolls themselves have degraded over the years – enough remains to assess Ravel's performance in terms of stylistic intentions. The most remarkable performance is of the seventh Waltz, the most difficult technically – unless the technicians and the vagaries of the technology really have enhanced or distorted the picture. The climax is electrifying, building up to an impassioned denouement by way of a sudden and marked increase in tempo at bar 39 and its later repeat, an instruction absent from the published score. It is highly likely that Ravel would have forbidden this tempo change in others and that he was unaware of it in his own performance, but he allows himself to be carried along by the natural sweep of the music and remains perfectly in control of the line, wrong note notwithstanding. (At bar 58 Ravel, in his excitement, clearly strikes an E-flat in the bass instead of an E, though the second time around he gets it right. The rest comes across as remarkably accurate.) I am assured by Roy Howat that this accelerando would most probably not have been the result of fluctuations of playback speed, as the Welte system adequately guarded against this within a single piece; however the overall tempi, set by the speed at which the roll turns, cannot be taken as immutable evidence of Ravel's actual tempo. To my mind his performance is superior in every way to that of Casadesus, whose microphone recording of the *Valses nobles* from the early 1950s is at this point not only messy, but also lacking in the essential lift and swirl of Ravel's waltz idiom. (Perlemuter's recordings, however, capture this aspect of the music perfectly.) Casadesus's tempo is much the same as Ravel's, providing some corroboration of the accuracy of the Welte roll. What is remarkable in Ravel's performance is that his pianistic weaknesses never come at the expense of style and mood; his projection of his beloved waltz rhythm is palpable, even when, as in the first Waltz, control wavers. Amusingly, in the opening bars he takes some time to get going, and then when he does he has to rein himself back. But the overall panache of the up-tempo Waltzes and the gentle irony he brings to the others are an invaluable lesson in music making.

To my mind, as bewitching as is the orchestration Ravel devised for the ballet version, *Adélaïde, ou La langage des fleurs*, it is over-perfumed for these terse, exquisitely wrought statements of waltz rhythms. Angela Hewitt, in the comments she wrote for her complete Ravel recordings, calls the orchestration 'incredibly schmaltzy', and one can see what she means. This is very much a pianist's comment. The pianist has to imagine and suggest sonorities and textures that are almost unrealisable, and it is this very tension between illusion and reality that makes the piano, and piano music, so challenging and fascinating (and it is why it makes it such an ideal instrument for descriptive and programmatic music, offering suggestions which remain undefined). The orchestration also blurs the contours and diminishes the dissonances of the piano version (as, for example, in the 'bitonal' middle section of no. 7), as well as seeming to fulfil all possibilities of sonority, inevitably foregrounded by Ravel's orchestral wizardry. Pianists, on the other hand, have to find a myriad of nuances through a myriad of fleeting suggestions, just with fingers and pedals.

However, from the ballet version, for which Ravel wrote his own scenario, the pianist can learn an essential insight: that the characterisation of *Valses nobles et sentimentales* need not be overly serious. If there is an intensity of expression – and this is Ravel's own instruction for the second Waltz (*avec une expression intense*) – it is not a tragic or earnest expression. 'But what could this intense expression be other than that of an impassioned heart?' asked Jankélévitch. 'This is why, despite his wish to remain unaffected, he sometimes gave way like a simple romantic to the languor of the ritardando.' We can add that in the second Waltz, and elsewhere, he gives way to rubato too. But these moments are also tinged with irony – in the *languissant* of the sixth Waltz, for example, and in the subtle placing of the syncopation in the main theme of the seventh. But it is Ravel's 'wish to remain unaffected' that is the key, the ironic presence which gives to the music its unique ability to touch our sensibilities in a way that the conventional romanticising of this music would not even begin to do (indeed, conventional romanticising kills all great music). It is a myth that Ravel's music must be played straight and that he intended it to be played this way. What he intended was that it be played on his own terms, and he believed passionately that what he had indicated in the score was sufficient for the pianist to achieve this. (His efforts to teach his own music reveal, clearly, that his intentions were not as clear as he had thought.) His recording of *Valses nobles* is far from straight, not because of imperfection but because of Ravel's complete identification with the idea of a waltz, one that dominates our perception of his performance and shines through his weaknesses as a pianist.

The ballet scenario is a rather flimsy affair, and I have never felt that in terms of narrative or mood it has much to offer the pianist – apart, that is, from the shade of irony that hovers in the background. The setting is Paris in 1820, and the story is about a courtesan, Adélaïde, who when we first encounter her in her salon is inhaling the scent of a rose, symbol of voluptuousness. She is wooed by the lovesick Lorédan and the more dashing Duke, an eternal triangle that, as in so many nineteenth-century opera and ballet scenarios, is set to end in melodramatic tragedy. But Ravel's scenario is emphatically not to go the way of the death and despair of Verdi's *La traviata*, and the young lovers, minus the Duke, eventually fall happily into each other's arms. Ravel's orchestration is perfectly suited to such a tale.

For pianists, however, Régnier's epigraph – 'The delicious and ever novel pleasure of a useless occupation' (from the preface to his novel, *Les rencontres de M. Bréot*, first published in 1904) – is perfect for placing the overall intention of the work, though I am repeatedly struck by the extent to which it is ignored. It does take some pondering however, as it is considerably subtler in meaning than the quotation Ravel used from Régnier for *Jeux d'eau*.

Régnier's novel is a homage to the libidinous manners of the eighteenth century, encapsulated in the figure of Monsieur Bréot, who delights in music but even more in sexual licentiousness. So the useless occupation, which is nevertheless immensely pleasurable, is life itself (and, by implication, making love and making music). Ravel in turn symbolises this 'delicious pleasure' by the decadent frivolity of the waltz, and all that is implied by what was originally a highly risqué dance. The whole enterprise of *Valses nobles* is one of masterfully disguised irony (the ironic seriousness – or the seriousness of the irony – is superbly poised and very difficult to pull off in performance). Ravel would also have intended a double meaning with his epigraph, as a reference to the act of creating art in the first place. It is his own art, the music itself and the act of writing it, that is the 'useless occupation.' The words have behind them the laconic drawl of the dilettante – the very last thing that Ravel was – for whom art requires little effort and affords an endless stream of novelties. Régnier also intends a comment on 'art for art's sake', whose roots lie in the early nineteenth century (and which was much vaunted by one of Ravel's literary heroes, Edgar Allan Poe) – so his phrase is an ironic critique of this much-prized slogan and its implications.

Ravel's imaginative achievement in *Valses nobles et sentimentales* is to identify the essence of pleasure associated with the waltz (and captured so effortlessly by Régnier) and turn it into great art. *Valses nobles* embodies the irony at the centre of Régnier's words and dramatises the conflict between high art and entertainment. This was the reason why many in Ravel's first audience were so wrong-footed, signally failing to catch the irony – though the title itself should have been enough of a clue, a borrowing from Schubert that in 1911 could only have been ironic.

The orchestral score does have benefits for the pianist, opening the ear to possibilities of voicing and texture – and it might be

Example 9. Ravel, Waltz no. 7, *Valses nobles et sentimentales*, bars 19–20. The tie marks over the barline indicate a pedalled resonance.

tempting to take some of the tempi, dynamics and nuances into the piano score. In fact, however, Ravel left an instruction concerning orchestral transcriptions that suggests otherwise: 'Nuances, accents and slur marks can and often must be distinguished in an orchestral transcription. - [tenuto] doesn't mean > [accent]'. The pianist should know this anyway, an understanding that comes in part from the obvious fact that the orchestra does not have a pedal. This is relevant to such a moment as the delightful 'lift' in bar 19 of Waltz no. 7 (see example 9 and Appendix A, p. 166), marked as a pedalled resonance which is, of course, absent from the orchestral version.

What is accepted today as a legitimate addition to the piano score is an inner voice, bars 31–4 of Waltz no. 4, played by horns and cellos in Ravel's orchestration (see example 10). Ravel's wish for this to be included in the piano version is documented by Perlemuter in *Ravel d'après Ravel*, and it is now printed as the authentic reading in the Peters *Urtext*.

In his comments on the fourth Waltz Perlemuter said: 'I see on my music, in his [Ravel's] hand, the addition of an ascending phrase, which added to the printed text enriches it in a remarkable way.' Unaccountably, his book fails to notate this new reading, despite printing many other musical examples. So a generation of pianists – other than those familiar with, and probably puzzled

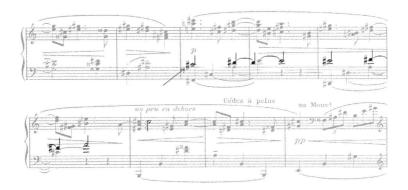

Example 10. Ravel, Waltz no. 4, *Valses nobles et sentimentales*, bars 29–37, showing the additional line which Ravel gave to Vlado Perlemuter.

by, Perlemuter's two recordings (1961 and 1977) – has been largely unaware of this highly effective addition to the piano score. Even today many are surprised when hearing it.

The performer, of course, is at liberty to play the fourth Waltz as originally written. Ravel plays it this way, in his 1913 recording, even though he had written the orchestration in March of the previous year. Neither does Henriette Faure mention the reading, which seems a strange oversight if Ravel had given it to her (she worked with Ravel in 1923, and Perlemuter worked with him in 1927), so it seems almost certain he had not. Recordings by two other pianists who knew Ravel very well, Casadesus and Jacques Février, also use the original piano score. It seems clear that Ravel, loath to alter his works once they had arrived at publication, was content to let the issue remain unresolved. The master of artistic discipline did not, in this rare instance, make up his mind.

The Épilogue takes us beyond the waltz into a kind of cinematic hallucination. One thinks of the manic swirling towards oblivion in *La valse*, but here in reverse, in an aural haze where motifs of the earlier Waltzes fleetingly come into focus and then fade. As Henriette Faure eloquently observed:

The paradox is that within this hazy texture [*ce flou*] each motif presents its particular character, now spirited, now finely sculpted, now elegant. The difficulty comes in presenting each shape without compromising the tempo, in creating absolute precision within this atmosphere of dreams. Gradually, in Ravel's world as in Liszt's and Schubert's, the music fades into a silence in which all that remains is suggestion.

The contrast with the intense life of the preceding waltzes is startling, and the listener becomes separated from reality.

Ravel's art here presents the greatest irony of all: the profound seriousness – the acoustical miracle that is the Épilogue – reminds us that everything was intended, that every note was placed with the most meticulous intention; the Épilogue suggests that the waltz is, after all, as serious a business as life itself. We had suspected as much, and our final realisation is that Régnier's 'useless occupation' is emphatically not the last word, and that 'pleasure' is manifestly inadequate as the sole reason for pursuing art.

6

The Great War – *Le tombeau de Couperin*

> *I hear that Saint-Saëns has proclaimed to the admiring crowd*
> *that during the war he has composed music for the theatre,*
> *songs, an elegy and a piece for trumpet. If instead he had spent*
> *his time turning out mortar shells then perhaps his music*
> *would have benefitted.*
>
> Ravel, letter to Jean Marnold, 7 October 1916

Of all reactions to the experience of war, Ravel's is among the most fascinating. During the First World War he was not in the trenches, but neither was he very far behind them: he served as a truck and ambulance driver, tending the wounded and constantly within sound, and often within range, of the guns. His bravery, which he denied, was simply and profoundly extraordinary. *Le petit* Ravel supped on horrors, but his reaction was to protect himself with their antithesis. Not for him the explicit extroversion of expression-ism – the harrowing imagery of the war poets or the bitter irony of Debussy's *En blanc et noir* – but rather the calming, civilising elegance of eighteenth-century French dance forms. His piano suite *Le tombeau de Couperin*, though conceived just before war was declared in 1914, was brought up as a child of war. Ravel hung on to his original conception and completed the suite in 1917. Each of its six movements is dedicated to close friends who were killed in the war.

On 8 August 1914, just after war was declared, Ravel wrote to his brother Édouard: 'As I felt I was going mad I have taken the wisest course: I am going to volunteer.' This would not have been the wisest course for his safety, but it was clearly the wisest for his conscience and hence his peace of mind. 'I will go (if they want me) because I want to go,' he wrote to his friend Cipa Godebski. Though characteristically single-minded, this decision was all the more astonishing in that it meant he would be leaving his ailing and aging mother, to whom he was devoted. His alarmed friends cajoled and argued, but (to Godebski again) their pleas 'would not have the slightest influence on [his] resolution.' And to Roland-Manuel he wrote:

> But Good God, Good God [which he wrote as *N. de D. de N. de D.* – Nom de Dieu], I know full well, my dear friend, that I'm work-ing for the fatherland by writing music! At least I have been told this often enough in the past 2 months to convince me of it, firstly to prevent me from volunteering, and then to console me when I'm rejected. But nothing has prevented me, and I am not consoled.

Ravel usually spent the summer months in St. Jean de Luz, in the Basque region of southwestern France, near his birthplace in Ciboure, a short distance down the coast. He was there in the summer of 1914, full of plans for compositions, among them what he called at that time a 'symphonic poem' he entitled 'Wien', which later became the ballet *La valse*; a 'French suite' for piano, which became *Le tombeau de Couperin*; and his Trio for Violin, Cello and Piano. 'In five weeks I have done the work of five months,' he wrote to Lucien Garban in September. 'I wanted to finish my Trio before joining up.'

The diminutive Ravel was rejected for being four pounds under-weight. But in March 1915 he finally secured a post as a truck driver for an artillery regiment, and by 1916 he found himself behind the lines at the Battle of Verdun, the longest and most brutal battle in the history of warfare. Even now it is hardly possible to arrive at an accurate casualty figure for Verdun, though it is believed that over half a million perished from February to December in a confrontation of armour, high explosives and young men that was of no strategic importance whatsoever. The front line was in the same place at the end as it was in the beginning. One hundred and fifty miles to the east, Parisian life went on largely untouched, the city's theatres, nightclubs and restaurants thronged with civilians and off-duty soldiers.

Ravel came to little physical harm at the front, though he was operated on for dysentery, but the experience of the war, as it did all of those who survived it, scarred his psyche for the remainder of his life. In January 1917 he was also stricken by the death of his mother. From this point on, the pace of his composition would slow considerably, and he would find it increasingly difficult to complete his works. In June he finished what would turn out to be his last solo-piano composition, his 'French suite' – a Prelude, a Fugue, three dances and a Toccata. One of the deceased dedicatees was the half brother of his dear pupil Roland-Manuel, and another the husband of the pianist Marguerite Long. Long gave the first performance of *Le tombeau* in 1919.

While Ravel needed to be totally honest with himself and others about his motives, his modesty would have prevented him from fully articulating his altruism, which he concealed with irony. 'After all, the fatherland is hardly waiting for me to save it,' he observed. Roland-Manuel records that his friend wanted above all to 'know': 'And yet I am a peace-loving person. I have never been brave, but there it is, I have a fascination for adventure, so strong that it becomes a necessity. What will I do, what will we all do after the war?'

Ravel foresees here, with quiet acuteness, the emptiness awaiting him and all those who would manage to survive.

His letters from the front dwell on his physical remoteness from the conflict, almost as if he feels guilty that he is relatively protected. For most of the time, he points out, he sees and hears much, but experiences little. One of the few times he articulates the horror of Verdun is in a postcard to a friend from April 1916, in which the scene that he paints after a battle has the intensity of cinema:

> I saw something unimaginable, a nightmare town, horribly deserted and silent. It wasn't the din from above, nor the little puffs of white smoke all in a line in the clear sky; it wasn't the tremendous, invisible struggle that was so harrowing; it was the feeling of loneliness at the centre of this town which lay in sinister sleep under the brilliant light of a beautiful summer's day. Undoubtedly I will see more terrible and more repugnant things, but I don't think I will ever experience anything more profound or strange than this kind of mute terror.

Silence after battle, or away from the battle, is one of the tropes of war imagery, disseminated through memoirs, poetry and cinema. In his poem 'A Night Attack', Siegfried Sassoon (who witnessed the war as an infantry officer at the Battle of the Somme, launched by the British in an attempt to take the pressure off the French at Verdun) recalls the tranquillity far behind the lines:

> For now we've marched to a green, trenchless land
> Twelve miles from battering guns . . .
> Wide, radiant water sways the floating sky
> Below dark, shivering trees.

Ravel wrote of a similar experience, describing a Sunday spent 'in the most lovely countryside: a torrential stream between steep banks, a waterfall on the left, and on the right a little tunnel covered with foliage and white roses, into which the stream vanishes. But still away over there the hell goes on.'

Another trope of war is the presence of birdsong in the silence. 'Beyond the German line a blackbird sang,' writes Sassoon in his poem 'The Distant Song'; and Sebastian Faulks's 1993 novel *Birdsong* – which draws on the harrowing imagery of Sassoon's memoirs as well his poetry – describes 'a moment completely quiet as the bombardment ended and the German guns also stopped. Skylarks wheeled and sang high in the cloudless sky.' This trope too is recounted by Ravel, as recalled by Hélène Jourdan-Morhange:

> As a truck driver at Verdun [Ravel] witnessed the most indescribable chaos and the most deafening noise of war. The silence following the battle seemed supernatural, the peace returning to the countryside, a limpid sky and then suddenly, at daybreak, the song of a warbler [*fauvette*]. He was so captivated by this unexpected song that he vowed to write a piece, 'La fauvette indifférente'. But war and illness prevented him from realising this project.

This must be the same piece 'about which he spoke many times' to his friend and pupil Manuel Rosenthal, 'a piece from *Le tombeau de Couperin* which was to be called *Le rossignol indifférent*.' So Rosenthal remembers the warbler as a nightingale. But the association with *Le tombeau*, not made by Jourdan-Morhange, is especially intriguing. It seems certain that, whatever the bird, Ravel was thinking of the titles of Couperin's bird pieces from the third book of his harpsichord Suites (ordre 13 livre 3), especially 'Les fauvètes plaintifs' and the celebrated 'Le rossignol en amour'. Roy Howat, noting an additional echo of Rameau's title 'L'indifférente' (from the Suite in G in *Nouvelles suites de pièces de clavecin*) and following up Rosenthal, suggests that we might hear Ravel's experience of the birdsong 'quietly encapsulated in the Menuet of *Le tombeau*' at the point where the minuet returns in bar 73, 'piping as a quiet descant

over the last echoes of the desolate *musette*.' This is a fitting idea –
impossible to verify other than in imaginative terms, but it *feels* right.

Whatever the case, our attitude towards *Le tombeau* is inescapably
affected by our knowledge of the war. Either we are shocked that
such an elegant, formal and apparently untroubled work should
have been brought to fruition at a time of such cataclysm – and
hence accuse Ravel of the same insouciance as the fun-loving Pa-
risians just 150 miles to the east – or we embrace the work in the
full knowledge of its contemporary as well as archaic context, and
deepen our understanding of its imaginative impulses by noting the
dedicatees who had lost their lives, the possible echo of birdsong
(and what that would have meant to Ravel at that moment, and
to the thousands of others who experienced it) and even the word
tombeau. The usual translation of this word is 'tomb'; but in terms
of the suite, *tombeau* should be taken to mean 'homage' – a homage
to Couperin – just as it would have in the eighteenth century, when
it was accepted, as Howat says, that a 'posthumous tribute had no
need to be sombre'. But the dark irony of the word, for Ravel, is
also plain to see.

There is a third attitude we might take towards *Le tombeau de
Couperin*. We can regard it as an autonomous art object having no
relation whatsoever to anything outside itself – its *self* being the set
forms of an eighteenth-century harpsichord suite, a sealed system,
as it were. Ravel himself, or an important part of him – the part
he was happy to show – would have encouraged such an attitude.
But it has been the argument of this book that there are ways of
understanding artworks that go beyond the object, an attitude we
also find validated by Ravel. Roland-Manuel recalls a comment
Ravel made towards the end of his life that suggested an awareness of 'mysterious influences [*puissances mysterieuses*]' at work
on the products of the imagination, beyond skill and technique.
Comparing his early String Quartet to the much later Piano Trio,
he declared that 'with little regret he would exchange the *know*

how of the works of his maturity for the artless *power* displayed by the String Quartet of his youth.' Roland-Manuel continues:

> Coming from him this is something of a surprising statement. It shows, nevertheless, that this little man of steel, so sure of himself and usually so mistrustful of anything to do with 'inspiration', could not escape an awareness, common to us all, of the mysterious influences that bypass our understanding and without which we could do nothing. The power of these hidden forces, with which his work normally had little communication, decreased [he felt] the more assured and authoritative his work became.

If it is accepted that such 'mysterious influences' are at work in the creation of art, then it is also clear that they lie so deep below the surface as to be barely analysable. In *Le tombeau* the war shades the work, for us, purely by the fact of its contiguous existence, while the music itself expunges all traces of the conflict. (This does not prevent the extraordinary reaction of Glenn Watkins to the Toccata, in which he hears 'the steep ascent of aircraft, followed by the plummeting dive,' and 'a rain of meticulously coordinated and deadly machine gun fire at high and low altitude.' These are claims he feels entitled to make by adducing Ravel's desire to join the air force.) This expunging was not so much a deliberate act but, because Ravel was the kind of artist he was, an inevitability. All he could do was indicate his profound sincerity by adding the particular dedications – a moral necessity – while knowing that the only art he could make had to be depersonalised, and in this case independent of the horrifying facts of warfare. In this he was showing his affinity with the Mallarméan ideal of impersonality, later taken up by T. S. Eliot (as we saw in chapter 1). At this point in Ravel's life, the refuge of impersonality – now not so much a denial of the self as a removal of the self from the creative process – was his only way of surviving his war experiences psychologically intact.

Such a position was not only grounded on bitter experience but also buttressed by Symbolist theory. 'What can possibly make us understand the identity of the true craftsman of a beautiful work?' asked Paul Valéry. 'For he is positively *no one*.'

This all feeds into, and helps to clarify, Ravel's remarks to Roland-Manuel at the end of his life concerning an artist's *conscience* and the nature of sincerity. He adduces with approval Mozart's 'simple pronouncement [that] music can undertake anything, it can do or depict anything it dares, *providing it charms and remains finally, and always, music*' (my italics). And then comes this proclamation:

> The fact is that I refuse simply and absolutely to confound the artist's *conscience*, which is one thing, with his *sincerity*, which is quite another. Sincerity goes for nothing if the artist's conscience isn't engaged in the process. Our conscience requires that we develop our craft. So my objective is the perfection of technique. I aim constantly towards this, knowing I will never achieve it. The important thing is to get closer all the time. Art, without doubt, has other *effects*, but the artist, to my mind, should have no the other aim.

'Perfection of technique' takes the ideal of impersonality to its most extreme point, and his remark here sits rather uneasily with his other remark to Roland-Manuel concerning 'mysterious influences'. It was exactly this striving for technical perfection, as we have seen, that he feared would dim such influences. In the case of *Le tombeau* we might see Ravel's terms *conscience* and *sincerité*, which he places in opposition to one another, as exemplifying the split between his experience of the war and his identity as an artist. His 'sincerity' is the manner in which he reacts to the war, his feelings about it, his compassion, his fierce sense of duty as a human being. In another context he might have identified this as his 'conscience', but in fact he reserves that word, in his musings to Roland-Manuel, exclusively for his identity as an artist, and he uses it to include the meanings 'integrity' and 'being' (in French the word *conscience* means both conscience in our sense and consciousness): what enables his artistic being to manifest itself is his tireless concern with developing his craft. He does not deny the sincerity of his feelings, but he mistrusts the place such sincerity has in the process of artistic creation. (Elsewhere he associates sincerity with spontaneity, which as the *raison d'être* for artistic creation would, for him, simply lead to 'babble'.)

Again, this is highly apposite to *Le tombeau de Couperin*. Ravel did not hide his feelings with regard to the war, nor his sense of patriotism. But pursuing his plan for a civilised and elegant French suite was not a simple assertion of patriotism any more than it was a sign of indifference. (In fact, his conscience as an artist compelled him to a dignified protest against the League for the Defence of French Music, whose aim was to ban performances of Austro-German works. He was adamant in his opposition and refused to join.) For Ravel, the compelling need was to be faithful to his original vision of his suite, and to insist that his spontaneous feelings and insights about the war, his sincerity and compassion, had nothing to do with it. His task was to be faithful to his art as he conceived it, not to make 'sincere' statements about the state of the world. He was fully aware of the dichotomy this set up between experience and the creative act, of the potential split between the sentient artist and the technical processes of his art. But he knew and trusted – and this is where the 'mysterious influences' come into play – that somehow the concentration on process would release the imagination, acknowledged in the acuity of his concluding observation: 'Art, without doubt, has other *effects*, but the artist, to my mind, should have no other aim.' And in such a manner *Le tombeau* was born.

Two further influences on *Le tombeau* remain to be examined, and they are curiously intertwined. One is a novel that Ravel read while convalescing from his illness in 1916: one of the great novels of the French language, *Le grand Meaulnes* by Alain-Fournier. Ravel was so drawn to it that for a number of years he had plans to turn it into some form of music, either for piano and orchestra (according to Orenstein) or cello and orchestra (according to Chalupt). Roland-Manuel tells us, tantalisingly, that even as late as 1922, while Ravel was staying with him in Normandy, his friend 'pursued in the forests of Rambouillet and Lyon–la Forêt the fleeting shade of *Le grand Meaulnes*; but this beautiful prey slipped away.' We will see shortly how apt is Roland-Manuel's language here in relation to the imagery of the novel, to its fragile magic and discreetly erotic charm.

The other influence emerges from the eighteenth-century context of *Le tombeau*. Debussy once referred to Couperin as 'the most poetic of our harpsichordists, whose tender melancholy is like the enchanting echo that emanates from the depths of a Watteau landscape, filled with plaintive figures.' Debussy's use of an aural image to describe a visual reaction is especially appropriate. He was referring to the *fête galante* paintings of Couperin's exact contemporary, Jean-Antoine Watteau, paintings full of young people dancing elegant minuets and making music. (The art historian Michael Levey has written of the effect of music in Watteau, where 'the entwined harmony of voice and instrument . . . becomes a symbol of love.') I would suggest that there is also an echo or, to reverse the metaphor, a faint gleam of Watteau emanating from the depths of Ravel's *Le tombeau*. The way in which Watteau's themes are interlinked with Alain-Fournier's will become clear if we first examine the novel.

Most biographies of Ravel glance at his discovery of *Le grand Meaulnes*. One of Ravel's letters talks of the novel's 'charm', how it had 'nothing to do with the war,' and that he hadn't 'enjoyed a novel so much in a long time.' He would have learned that its author, having published his only novel in 1913, was killed in action the following year at the age of twenty-seven. (Life expectancy for the young men of Europe between 1914 and 1918 regressed to the levels of the Middle Ages.) If nothing else, Ravel would have keenly felt the precariousness of existence represented by Alain-Fournier, and perhaps reflected that artworks confer a kind of immortality on their creator. Stuckenschmidt, one of the only commentators to suggest a connection between the novel and Ravel's interior imagination, observed that, although his specific plan for music came to nothing, 'something of the inspired, serene power of Fournier's prose did pass over into Ravel's next composition [*Le tombeau de Couperin*]'.

I would say that it was not only the prose that inspired Ravel, but Alain-Fournier's own preoccupations: his acute and moving analysis of the processes of the imagination; his evocation of a bygone era, a lost world (some English translations have entitled the novel *The Lost Domain*); and his understanding of the necessity for the human psyche of the concept of 'play', of fantasy; of the vital presence within the novel of what Baudelaire called 'that queen of the faculties', imagination itself. The ever-vigilant and controlled Ravel would also have been struck by the novel's warning, for Alain-Fournier's achievement lies in his creation of an imaginative world that also contains its own trenchant critique: the power of the imagination is potentially destructive.

The story turns on the devastating personal consequences for its hero of the imagination unbridled. The world of innocent delight that he discovers and then loses while still an adolescent becomes the object of his obsession. The 'lost domain' is the ancient chateau he stumbles upon, where children and adults in fancy dress are awaiting a wedding which never takes place, and where he falls in love. His desire to recover this idealised world (and the beautiful Yvonne de Galais), where dreams and reality are interfused, is repeatedly thwarted. The real world drags against the world of his imagination as adolescence gives way to adulthood.

It is a novel of many layers: the lost domain is suffused with the symbols of the *commedia dell'arte*, of Harlequin and Pierrot, and with overtones of Watteau's *fête-galante* paintings, in which young people in *commedia* costume saunter in idealised landscapes amidst crumbling statues. But in the novel love affairs, at first suffused with charm and magic, become matters of life and death, of honour and self-sacrifice. When the *commedia*, in the form of a circus, invades the real world of village and schoolroom, the seemingly harmless disruption sets off a chain of events that eventually leads to the novel's tragic denouement. The novel's principal theme is concentrated in its hero's cry, towards the end, addressed to the girl who had broken off her engagement on the day of the wedding party. 'Ah, what harm you've done us all! You who have never wanted to believe in anything.' But Meaulnes's own obsessive willingness to believe in the imaginative power of the lost domain means that the harm is of his own creation.

The novel is also about time, about the inexorable movement from childhood, when time seems suspended, to adulthood, when time presses and has consequences. The story begins with a date which isn't quite a date – 'He arrived at our house one Sunday in November 189—' – so the time is both fixed and free, once upon a time and always. In the lost domain time stands still, captured like an enchanted moment in a Watteau painting. In terms of the space the domain takes up in the narrative, and Meaulnes's single night there, it is actually quite brief, but it dominates his being and hence the whole novel. The lost domain existed once upon a time, and it exists always.

Time is also one of Watteau's themes, heightened by the presence of those ancient statues that are part of the landscape and that signal to the young revellers (and to us) that everything has its end, that their living beauty will fade and turn to dust. This is why, for Debussy, the enchanting figures in the parks and gardens are 'plaintive'. Paradoxically, the very moment of love, or ecstasy, or quiet happiness, that Watteau paints with such easeful insight is captured through a vital play of colour and movement across the canvas. The paintings express the reality of transience. The enchanted moment is but a moment, partly discerned by the revellers themselves, who, in Verlaine's defining image from his own *Fêtes galantes*, are 'sad beneath their fanciful disguises.'

There is no comment on Watteau from Ravel, but neither is there much on Couperin. Even *Le tombeau*, Ravel said, was 'not so much a tribute to Couperin himself as to French music of the 18th century.' But if it is a tribute to eighteenth-century music, then it is also a tribute to an eighteenth-century artistic ethos, and at the opening of the eighteenth century Couperin and Watteau were France's two greatest living artists. As for their influence on subsequent periods of French culture, during Debussy and Ravel's formative years – during the second half of the nineteenth century – it was immense. Howat has admirably detailed the popularity of harpsichord music in France during this period and what almost amounts to a cult of Couperin, Rameau and Louis-Claude Daquin. (According to Ivry, the harpsichordist Wanda Landowska claimed that 'L'Arlequine' by Couperin 'was one of Ravel's favourite pieces, and she often played it for him.') But there was equally a cult of Watteau, for which the brothers Edmond and Jules de Goncourt were largely responsible through their highly influential essays on art (eventually collected under the title *French Eighteenth-Century Painters*), and for whom Watteau is 'the great poet of the eighteenth century.' The Goncourts defined for a generation the mood of Watteau's paintings: 'In the recesses of Watteau's art, beneath the laughter of its utterance, there murmurs an indefinable harmony, slow and ambiguous; throughout his *fêtes galantes* there penetrates an indefinable sadness.' Verlaine expressed the spirit of Watteau in poems he entitled *Fêtes galantes*, and Debussy set six of them as songs.

The Goncourts set the tone and the standards. 'The world of Watteau,' they proclaimed, is 'the deification of the ideals of the eighteenth century, the spirit of the period.' In such a climate, which survived into the twentieth century and became all the more acute during France's struggle for survival between 1914 and 1918, Ravel's eighteenth-century French suite could hardly have failed at some level to reflect the world of Watteau and what the Goncourts called his 'robed allegories.' In a broad sense we might view Ravel's suite as a kind of allegory – at the very least the term *tombeau* sets up an arresting symbol of both past and present. We have already seen that a *tombeau* was an accepted form of eighteenth-century homage to the dead, and that Ravel's own homage was not only to Couperin and the music of his period, but also to dead comrades. *Le tombeau*, in the way it echoes eighteenth-century musical styles, creates a narrative of manners, sensibility, taste, decorum, refinement – all associated with an historical moment long past – as a comment on what the twentieth century could no longer sustain. The fact that *Le tombeau* is part of a respectable musical tradition of classical allusion (including Edvard Grieg's *Holberg Suite*, which contains a Rigaudon and a Musette; and Debussy's *Suite bergamasque*, with its Minuet and Passepied, and his *Pour le piano*, with its Toccata) does not at all diminish the importance of its historical moment, 1914 to 1917; nor does the fact that Ravel conceived the work just before the war started. The enhanced symbolic strength of *Le tombeau* would have become clear to him as events which he could not possibly have consciously foreseen (those 'mysterious influences' again) unfolded.

One of the seminal books of the twentieth century devoted to Couperin and the culture of the early eighteenth century is Wilfrid Mellers's *François Couperin and the French Classical Tradition* (1951). Working outwards from a specific passage in Couperin's 'L'Arlequine', he had this to say in connection with the ideas I have been discussing:

> The passage is a fine example of Couperin's ability to attain to great sonorous richness with the minimum of means; it is this kind of effect which made so deep an appeal to Debussy, and still more to Ravel, since they found in its emotional quality something that was not irrelevant to their position in the modern world [i.e., their position as outside convention]. This quality is extremely subtle. . . . As a whole, the piece is balanced between a bumpkin simplicity and a sophisticated hyper-sensitivity, in a manner that almost justifies a

comparison with Watteau's wonderful painting of Gilles. Both Watteau and Couperin seem, in works such as these, to be attempting to transmute a personal loneliness or distress into the world of the *commedia*, precisely because the theatre can idealise the crudities and indignities of everyday life into 'something rich and strange'. It is the tenderness of the feeling – the sympathy with the outcast – that is so remarkable in Watteau's pictorial, and Couperin's musical, representation of the Fool.

Alain-Fournier's *Le grand Meaulnes* is occupied with the same theme. While Ravel would have fully understood this aspect of the novel, whether he associated it with Couperin can only be a subject for conjecture. In *Le tombeau* the representation of the Fool was not his concern (although the Rigaudon might be interpreted in this way). What is certain, exactly at the period of his work on his suite in 1917, was his own extreme loneliness and distress. He was ill, friends had been killed, his mother had just died, and composition was his only route back to health and stability. There seems to be little doubt that his belief in the values of another epoch and in the associated imaginative values of fiction – his necessary immersion in worlds removed from the brutal realities of 1917 – were at multiple levels brought to bear on the creation of *Le tombeau de Couperin*.

Ravel's exhaustion after the completion of *Le tombeau* was not alleviated by the end of the war the following year. That year, 1918, also saw the death of Debussy. Stuckenschmidt observed that although Debussy's death 'left no documentary traces behind in Ravel's papers . . . we can be certain that the news moved him deeply and that it contributed to his growing feeling of solitude.' The fact that he wrote no more solo piano music after this point would have been for a number of reasons, but the absence of Debussy may have been one of them. Apart from a curious experiment (lasting one and a half minutes) for five hands at two keyboards, entitled *Frontispice*, it would be another ten years before Ravel again turned to piano writing with the two great concertos. Manuel Rosenthal affirms that, 'like Debussy, to whom he often referred, Ravel proclaimed that "the piano is the composer's harmonic treatise. It's there one finds everything."' No doubt the piano would have remained Ravel's principal tool for composition, but after *Le tombeau* his desire, or ability, to create solo piano music seems to have evaporated. His creative engagement with Debussy of course also took place in arenas other than piano composition (so, while criticizing Debussy's *L'isle joyeuse* as poorly written for the piano, Ravel also viewed *La mer* as badly orchestrated, and 'the larger forms [as lacking] architectonic power'; in *L'après-midi d'un faune*, however, Debussy 'achieved perfection'). And it seems that Ravel had little interest in Debussy's piano *Études* of 1915, that he missed, or at least was not prepared to engage with, their extraordinary originality of design and sonority. But he ceased writing solo piano works in 1918. Certainly he would have recognized that his duel with the composer whom he had called 'our incomparable Debussy, the most phenomenal genius in the history of French music,' had finally come to an end.

7

The Intimate Ravel: Ricardo Viñes and Henriette Faure – Sonatine, *Pavane pour une infante défunte, Ma mère l'oye* and Other Works

With Debussy music was in evolution; with Ravel it was in crystallization, and a quite exceptional spiritual stillness was needed for the process to be accomplished flawlessly.

G. W. Hopkins, '(Joseph) Maurice Ravel' (1980)

It remains in this final chapter to discuss the early pieces, as well as two of Ravel's most popular piano works, the Sonatine and *Ma mère l'oye*. The early works were closely associated with Ravel's friendship with the Catelonian pianist Ricardo Viñes, so it seems appropriate here to look a little more closely at Viñes's influence and his pianism. Also in this chapter I draw again on Faure's *Mon maître Maurice Ravel*, which, along with comments on details of the scores, provides nuggets of insight into the nature of the man himself. It is an oversight of Ravelian scholarship that while the account by Vlado Perlemuter (admittedly a far more famous pianist than Faure) of his lessons with Ravel is well-known in English translation (as *Ravel According to Ravel*), Faure's richly informative memoir remains available only in French (and is now out of print).

Sonatine

Ravel's memory was certainly at fault when he recorded in his Autobiographical Sketch that 'after the *Miroirs* I composed a Sonatine for piano.' This would take it into the last months of 1905, but Durand had published the Sonatine in September; and we know that Ravel played the first movement, or at least a version of it, in January 1904 at one of the famous soirées of Madame de Saint-Marceaux (*née* Marguerite Bagnies). Calvocoressi tells us that Ravel entered this movement into a competition run by a Parisian journal for 'a first movement of a piano sonatina, length not to exceed 75 bars.' In the event, the competition was cancelled, as Ravel's was the only entry. Ravel seems to have added two further movements just before he began work on *Miroirs* (he played 'Oiseaux tristes', the first of the set to be written, to his fellow Apaches in October 1904).

Jankélévitch catches the characteristic Ravelian mode of the Sonatine when he compares it to the 'chaste artlessness [*chaste ingénuité*]' of the String Quartet. He also divines that special quality of ambiguity in the first movement that is fundamental to our understanding of Ravel and so essential, and difficult, to communicate in performance. For the performer it is the ingredient that prevents sentimentality. Writes Jankélévitch: 'The quiverings of melancholy are touched by hints of light-heartedness and an imperceptible smile.'

Henriette Faure, as usual, is revealing about Ravel's attitude to the Sonatine, putting into perspective questions regarding the nature of interpretation:

It is the inner spirit of the opening melody that governs the movement, a movement whose elan, breaks [*brisés*], contrasts [*oppositions*] and alternations of tempo overcome the constraints of classical form like a flower arrangement overflowing the contours of a vase. The interpretation of these pages can be quite free in those places where there is a quiver of heartfelt expression, of spontaneous feeling. 'You play this movement a little too rigidly', Ravel said to me. 'But just because I ask for a certain flexibility doesn't mean you should play like those pianists who wilfully distort the second theme, which is more classical. They elongate the dotted quarter note, so making three eighth notes out of two. They all do it, it's an epidemic.' 'But why?' I asked. 'Well obviously they prefer their own imaginations to my reality.'

In that last remark we can hear Ravel's inimitably ironic tone of voice, described by Vuillermoz as dropping abruptly at the end of a phrase to underline his point. It would be accompanied by a particular gesture, in which he would 'rapidly slide the back of his right hand behind him, execute a kind of ironic pirouette while averting his eyes, which gleamed with mischief.' His voice would drop 'by a fourth or fifth,' recalled Vuillermoz, 'and one can find these exact inflections in *Histoires naturelles* or in *L'heure espagnole* ... the *quasi parlato* melody born from the characteristic Ravelian voice.' We can find this falling fourth at the very opening of the Sonatine.

Ravel's own recording of the first movement, made on a piano roll in 1913, is faster than he seems to have instructed Perlemuter. ('It's almost always played too fast,' relates Perlemuter. 'Ravel insisted the tempo should not be rushed.') Ravel rushes, though his performance is highly revealing. As always in his recordings, once the urge to perform is upon him, he goes for the spirit of the music. The final result lacks control, but it closely resembles the characteristics of Faure's account: *les oppositions* are brought out, and the first theme is full of spirit, while the second has a more classical precision. Above all the music flows, maintaining a unity even within the indicated changing tempi. It is tough rather than effete. There is not a hint of sentiment anywhere, but it manages to be deeply expressive – though Ravel's characteristic nervous energy when performing is at the expense of the 'imperceptible smile' that Jankélévitch diagnoses. (Faure's *brisés* might be a reference to the *brisés* of classical ballet, the rapid foot movements – a kind of fluttering – that parallels the figurations accompanying the Sonatine's opening theme.)

Ravel's performance of the second-movement minuet is quite fast too, and somewhat clumsy. (And the performance style that leads him to arpeggiate chords creates almost no distinction between these and the chords where it is specifically asked for – in bars 16–17, for example.) But what comes across is a strong focus on pulse, which dominates the music without restricting the flow. Ravel's playing is always fully committed and expressive even when his execution is faulty. Dynamic contours are strongly and effectively marked, and as usual changes of tempo are perfectly judged.

Faure's comments draw attention to the different accentuations and stresses he wanted, but which 'in a clumsy interpretation can give to the movement the character of a waltz.' Ravel certainly avoids this in his recording. 'Ravel asked me particularly not to exaggerate the inflexions, which would make it sound like what he termed a "*bal de barrière*".' (Théophile-Alexandre Steinlen, one of the most successful illustrators of the period, whose pictures appeared in a host of magazines and journals during Ravel's lifetime, illustrated exactly the kind of dance and tawdry milieu Ravel would have had in mind with this remark. Steinlen's coloured illustration 'Bal de barrière' (1898), rather in the manner of a Toulouse-Lautrec poster, shows two couples waltzing under the lights of a large dance hall, with loungers looking on.)

'Ravel loved playing the ending [of the Menuet],' Faure recalled. 'I will never forget the expression of grandeur he gave to the ascending melodic line, or the sudden radiance and authority of the final chord, which he played with that special springy action he had. Then he would immediately get up from the piano, and his face would be expressionless, impenetrable.' Marguerite Long recalled that Ravel wanted it to be played 'in the tempo of the minuet in Beethoven's E flat Sonata, Opus 31, No. 3.' The circularity of this advice – what, after all, *is* the tempo of Beethoven's own minuet? – suggests that this was another of Ravel's ironic remarks, made in response to a query about the 'correct' tempo.

Ravel did not record the final movement, whose dashing display was clearly beyond him. He did, however, attempt to play it: in an amusing conversation with Roger Nichols, Perlemuter recalled turning pages for Ravel during the last movement (this would have been in the late 1920s) 'and not knowing where it might be tactful to do so.'

Early commentators complained about the difficulty of the Sonatine. In a letter of April 1906 to Léon Vallas, whose wife had given the premiere the previous month, Ravel commented that he was 'startled by their objections with regard to its difficulty. What will they say about *Miroirs*, which I myself cannot manage to play correctly!' Ravel exhorted Faure to play the last movement with complete abandon throughout, 'without prudence and without mercy.' She diagnoses it as 'youthful, dauntless, constantly on the move, like myself, so I was at ease with it.' Perlemuter partly contradicts this, though he hedges his bets and claims Ravel 'wanted it very fast but not rushed [*précipité*].' The piece is so perfectly written for the instrument that the exquisite moments of lyricism (*tranquille* and *très expressif*) take their place naturally, without strain, within the very fast tempo. Although technically it is not the most challenging Ravel, it remains one of his most glorious and exciting essays in colourful virtuosity, requiring considerable finesse, and I do not subscribe to Marguerite Long's lofty view that it 'presents no particular difficulties.'

Pavane pour une infante défunte

The *Pavane*, an unashamedly gorgeous piece of music, was to Ravel what 'Clair de lune' was to Debussy: they were both early works, fulsomely lyrical and sensual, that became immensely popular but which later they would have preferred to disown. The *Pavane* was composed in 1899 and given its first performance by Viñes in Paris in 1902. By that time Ravel had written the landmark *Jeux d'eau*, which was premiered by Viñes in the same concert.

The dedication to Princess Edmond de Polignac (*née* Winnaretta Singer, heiress to the Singer sewing machine fortune), who commissioned the work, tells us something of the rarefied milieu Ravel occasionally frequented, principally by invitation to the salons of Madame de Saint-Marceaux, who was devoted to music, and where the young Ravel rubbed shoulders with the lions of the cultural scene. Composers needed patrons as much then as did their predecessors in the previous century. Five years earlier Debussy was in a similar position: 'Mme de Saint-Marceaux has discovered in me a talent of the highest order! It makes me die laughing,' he wrote to Chausson. But unfortunately Debussy disgraced himself over a broken engagement to a singer to whom he had been introduced by Madame de Saint-Marceaux. His career did not suffer long. Viñes, in his diary entry for February 1902, tells us he was invited for the first time to Madame de Saint-Marceaux's home so that she could hear him play the music of Debussy. (He dined there, and afterwards Ravel arrived, along with others, including the composer and conductor Reynaldo Hahn and André Messager, musical director of the Paris Opéra – Debussy's *Pelléas et Mélisande* was about to be given its premiere, conducted by Messager.)

Ravel did not quite disown his *Pavane*, for he orchestrated it in 1910; this version was first performed under Henry Wood in England the following year. He also recorded it on piano roll. Perlemuter failed to discuss it in his radio programmes with Jourdan-Morhange, apart from saying that Ravel was not interested when he brought it to him, 'and made a face.' With Faure, Ravel seems to have given the piece more attention – perhaps his gallant courtesy prevented him from dismissing his young pupil's interest in it, though he listened to her playing it, she recalled, 'with that somewhat testy air that I had got to know so well.' Faure's memory of details is useful: the arpeggiated chords should be played 'very rapidly, as usual, and the overall tempo not too slow so as not to weigh the piece down. The orchestration handles a slow tempo more successfully.' Then comes this insight:

> Ravel seemed only to recover his good humour when we reached the final page, where the half-note pulse of the accompaniment takes on a mechanical aspect. Already we can see emerging here the mechanical trait that was so dear to him all his life. He told me: 'God knows, we have heard the melody enough, so although the accompaniment needs to be subservient to it you should highlight its slightly mechanical character.'

We should note this, then, despite the instruction in the score on the last page, *marquez le chant* (bring out the melody). And we should note too the advice on the tempo, though as usual Ravel's own tempo, in his recording, seems too fast. His piano-roll performance is not an ideal model. It seems that the technical aspects of the reproduction are faulty, resulting in uneven phrasing and voicing, though we cannot be sure to what extent Ravel's own skill at these points let him down. However, the general idea of the momentum of this piece is clear, as is the articulation of the first page. Ravel clearly uses pedal, though he manages at the same time to suggest an articulated, but never dry, eighth-note accompaniment. But the instruction at the head of the score for *une sonorité large* (a full sonority) is a very clear indication of what the piece requires, and performers should not inhibit this sonority through a fear of over-pedalling. (There is no logical reason for the absence of pedal markings in the opening bars, given that Ravel indicates it at bars 28 and 60.)

Early Works and Ricardo Viñes

Ravel's earliest piano work, *Sérénade grotesque*, was written when he was about seventeen, though it was not performed until 1901 – by Viñes, to whom it was dedicated. It then vanished from the public eye. 'My first compositions, which remain unpublished, date from around 1893,' Ravel recorded in his Autobiographical Sketch in 1928. 'Emmanuel Chabrier's influence was apparent in the *Sérénade grotesque*, and that of Satie in the *Ballade de la reine morte d'aimer* [for voice and piano].' Neither of these works was published until 1975.

Ravel had met Viñes in 1888 when they were both thirteen, just a year after the boy from Catalonia and his mother had arrived in Paris. The Spanish mothers struck up an acquaintance while Maurice and Ricardo were attending the junior classes at the Paris Conservatoire. In the diary Viñes kept over several decades, Ravel first appears, without a name, in the entry for 22 November 1888: 'In the afternoon the boy with long hair called ". . ." came over with his mother.' It seems he had intended to fill in the name once he had learnt it, but it appears in the next day's entry: 'We went for the first time to the house of the boy with long hair called Mauricio.' And then in December he finally and carefully records the full name: 'In the evening to *le chevelure* [the one with the hair], by which I mean Mauricio Ravel.' From here on the entries record innumerable sessions at the piano, concerts, avid shared reading and drawing and, later, just as enthusiastic visits to art galleries. (In 1898 they go to an exhibition of Odilon Redon pastels; Ravel 'is dead with admiration.') From August 1892 comes a diary entry describing how the boys spent 'almost all the time at the piano, trying out new chords and playing over our ideas.' The *Sérénade* seems to have been written around this time.

Viñes spoke almost no French when he arrived in Paris and he had had no formal schooling, yet he rapidly taught himself several languages and developed a deep passion for literature and painting as well as music. An entry in his diary for 26 March 1895 reads: 'I went and browsed a bit in the second-hand book shops, without finding anything interesting. I returned home to work and at 5 Ravel came over and made me listen to his new and strange compositions, and showed me the works of Arthur Rimbaud that had just been published. What a genius this Rimbaud.' This was when they discovered *Gaspard de la nuit*.

Viñes must also have developed Ravel's interest in Spanish literature and music, and it seems certain that he helped Ravel define his own Spanish identity, that he was the catalyst for what Henriette Faure described as 'le Ravel Français d'origine Espagnole'. The Spanish mothers were of course in the background. Ravel once said: 'The Spanish folk songs sung by my mother in the evenings to rock me to sleep . . . formed my first musical education'; and on another occasion, 'My mother used to lull me to sleep singing *guajiras*.' Ravel's mother was actually a Basque, but despite Ravel's pride in his Basque origins, it does seem it was her Spanish ancestry that drew him the most. Manuel de Falla identifies

> the subtly genuine Spanishness of Ravel . . . a Spain he had felt in an idealised way through his mother. She was a lady of exquisite conversation. She spoke fluent Spanish [which] evoked the years of her youth, spent in Madrid. . . . When Ravel wanted to characterise

Spain musically, he showed a predilection for the *habanera*, the song most in vogue when his mother lived in Madrid.

All of this explains the Spanish tinge to many of Ravel's early works throughout the 1890s (not least the allusion to a Spanish princess in the *Pavane pour une infante défunte*, a title which takes a dandyish delight in the sound of words rather than their meaning, a title of appearance over substance). *Sérénade grotesque* has strong Spanish elements, with early echoes of the keyboard idiom of 'Alborada', and an intriguing hint of the title too: *grotesque* has echoes of *gracioso*, while a *sérénade* is an evening song as opposed to an *aubade* or *alborada,* which is a morning song. In 1895 came the 'Habanera', which along with 'Entre cloches' formed the two-piano work *Sites auriculaires*. ('Habanera' was later orchestrated to become the third movement of *Rapsodie espagnole*.) The 'Habanera', said Ravel, 'contains the germ of several elements which were to predominate in my later compositions.' At its first performance in 1898, *Sites auriculaires* caused mirth and some offence – partly because of its facetious title (Scenes, or Sites, for the Ear, with overtones of Sites for the Little Fingers), and partly because its inherent dissonances were exacerbated by a lack of performance preparation, with Viñes and his partner, Marthe Drone, playing from a barely legible manuscript ('I play . . . Ravel's *Sites auriculaires*, pretty badly both pieces. I was ahead by a beat in "Entres cloches", producing an inexpressible effect'). The manuscript also has an epigraph from Baudelaire's *Les fleurs du mal*, the first line of 'À une dame créole': 'Au pays parfumé que le soleil' (In a fragrant land caressed by the sun). This fits the exotic evocations of the 'Habanera' (though Howat has pointed out that 'Entre cloches' also has exotic elements: the manuscript, but not the printed score, groups the eighth notes of the opening bars as 3 + 3 + 4, 'suggesting a Latin American flavour perhaps blended with elements of Basque *zortzico*').

The rarely played *Menuet antique*, again dedicated to Viñes, also comes from 1895; Viñes premiered it in 1898. (Like the *Pavane*, it was later orchestrated by the composer.) The work has echoes of Chabrier's *Menuet pompeux* and maintains a certain ironic archaism, with Ravel's beloved clashing seconds and sevenths articulated by strongly marked syncopations. The middle section, in piano style close to the more famous *Pavane*, achieves a delightfully sensual elegance, with a glance at Chopin's Barcarolle in F-sharp Major in bars 65–6.

Viñes had a tremendous impact on the music scene in Paris at the beginning of the twentieth century. It is not easy to assess the range of his playing from his few recordings of the 1930s (including some Debussy and Albéniz, but sadly no Ravel), and his diary makes it clear that he regarded the new technology of recording with great suspicion. 'He disliked the whole concept,' the musicologist Elaine Brody has written. 'Without a public to listen to him, inspiration was lacking. He played a piece slightly differently each time, never in exactly the same way.' Nevertheless, his recording of Debussy's 'Soirée dans Grenade' is essential listening for anyone who plays Debussy. It has an unmistakable Spanish idiom, rhythm is foregrounded and the tempo is surprisingly but compellingly fast. He brings to it the character of Albéniz. As we saw in chapter 3, Debussy and Viñes had an immediate rapport when they first met. It was Ravel who introduced them, and Viñes noted in his dairy, 'Ravel told me that Debussy likes my playing enormously, especially my sonority.' Later Debussy dedicated 'Poissons d'or' to him.

Debussy was extremely exacting when coaching 'Poissons d'or' (as demanding a teacher, it seems, as Ravel). The pianist Maurice Dumesnil, who played it to him, came to the conclusion that it was only Viñes's performance of this piece that satisfied him. Viñes's recording, however, though brilliantly articulated, is brittle and curiously inflexible, and does not bear out Debussy's comments (to Dumesnil) concerning the freedom of rhythm he wanted, and the lightness of the figurations. In fact, despite his early enthusiasm, Debussy once observed that Viñes's playing was 'too dry', and he had other criticisms too: 'À propos my new *Images* [book 2]. We must gently persuade Viñes there is work to do! He still doesn't sense the architecture clearly enough, and despite his incontestable virtuosity he distorts the expression. Naturally I wouldn't dare tell him.'

On the other hand, many of Viñes's contemporaries remembered playing of immense colour and subtlety, and it seems clear that the recordings, which date from late in his career, are not fully representative of the Viñes of the early Apaches days. 'At one time or another, Ricardo Viñes would put all the poetry of his touch into a piece of Claude Debussy,' recalled Tristan Klingsor. 'We listened, ravished, to the *Sarabande*.' Brody mentions rave reviews of Viñes's playing from the 1890s, 'his irreproachable style, his warmth and his extraordinary use of the pedal.' Viñes received a big prize at the Conservatoire in 1894 – ahead of Alfred Cortot ('who played and sight-read to perfection,' wrote Viñes, 'but without charm, like the good student he is'; and we might recall that Ravel had also beaten Cortot in a competition three years earlier) – and he mentions the crucially important piece of information in his diary for 16 January 1895 that he had received, as the prize, a Pleyel grand with a third pedal, the middle-pedal sostenuto – which is of considerable significance for all pianists wondering how to sustain long bass notes in Ravel's and Debussy's piano music. (See 'The Sostenuto Pedal', Appendix B.)

Léon-Paul Fargue was very close to Viñes and an admirer of his friend's artistry in the early days – 'for all of us his playing was simply dazzling', he recalled – and on Viñes's death in 1943 he wrote a vivid obituary portrait. 'Who could resist the image of Ricardo in full spate, literally leaping on his friends, grabbing them by a shirt button, eagerly sharing his passions, his enthusiasms, his infatuations, with such strength and conviction?' And in 1933 Calvocoressi wrote: 'Viñes, alert and cheerful, ever on the track of new music and new ideas, as keen on literature and painting as on his own art, whenever he turned up, the life and soul of our meetings. We loved his childlike ingenuity as much as we admired his playing and appreciated the colossal amount and rare quality of his disinterested work as a pioneer'.

Ravel made other close friends in the early years of the twentieth century – particularly Ida and Cipa Godebski, to whom he dedicated the Sonatine, and through whom he became acquainted with the literary group of *La revue blanche* – and though his friendship with Viñes cooled, they were not estranged after the premiere of *Gaspard de la nuit*, as has often been maintained. However, Viñes did not premier any of Ravel's piano music after *Gaspard* (which is to say, he premiered all the early works, plus *Jeux d'eau*, *Miroirs*, and *Gaspard*, but not *Valses nobles* or *Le tombeau de Couperin*). In a letter to Calvocoressi from 1922 Ravel is still referring to Viñes affectionately as 'Ricardo', though he is stern in his disapproval of his performance of *Gaspard*:

> I will not ask Ricardo [to record it] for 2 reasons: first, I believe he's in Spain around that time; second . . . Viñes never wanted to play these pieces, and especially *Le gibet*, in the manner the composer desired they should be played. I did say *wanted*: I don't know whether you were present at one of those discussions when he assured me that if he observed the nuances and tempos I wanted, then *Le gibet* would bore the public. He would never budge an inch.

It is revealing that the first reason Ravel gives is merely the practical one that Viñes would be in Spain – suggesting that he is relieved not to have to explain his real reason. And it is interesting that he refers to himself as 'the composer', thus distancing himself from any personal interest in the argument. Ricardo is still Ricardo. In the 1920s Viñes was frequently away from

Paris, promoting a host of new compositions by Latin American composers, and during the 1930s he settled in South America. He returned to Paris in 1935, but his career had evaporated. He attended Ravel's funeral in 1937 and died in Barcelona six years later. His final years, dislocated by war and poverty, were 'very painful to him,' according to his niece Elvira Viñes. In his obituary Fargue wrote: 'I first got to know him at one of his concerts I went to with Maurice Ravel, and from that time began our musical understanding and our deep friendship.' And he ended: 'Everything he took up in Arts and Letters became part of him. He was a great musician, a genuine human being who always lived happily and ardently among real things.'

Menuet sur le nom d'Haydn

In the summer of 1909, to commemorate the centenary of Haydn's death, the magazine of the Société Internationale de Musique (S.I.M.) commissioned several composers to write a short piece making use of the five letters of Haydn's name. If the musical sequence A to G is repeated against the template of the alphabet, the letter *A* will fall on *H*, *O*, and *V*, so the letters *Y* and *N* in *HAYDN* will become the notes D and G. The letter *H* is already the German designation for B-natural, so the note B is chosen instead of A for the beginning of the name. Hence the composers were to use the motif B–A–D–D–G.

Debussy, Reynaldo Hahn, Paul Dukas, Vincent d'Indy, and Charles-Marie Widor all made contributions. The task especially appealed to the artisan in Ravel, who contrived a remarkable construction in which he delighted in indicating every appearance of the sequence with the appropriate letters, including a backward version (bars 19–20 and 29–30) and one where he turned the name (and the stave) upside down to reveal D–G–G–C(♯)–B (bars 25–26). The intellectual effort is concealed within the form of a delicate minuet enriched with extraordinarily bold chromatic harmony, in which nearly every chord employs a combination of sevenths, ninths, elevenths, and thirteenths.

Ma mère l'oye

Ravel's suite of piano duets was written for and dedicated to Mimi and Jean Godebski, the children of his close friends Cipa and Ida. It proved too difficult for them to play, however, and the first performance, in 1910, was given by a student of Marguerite Long's, the eleven-year-old Jeanne Leleu, and her partner, the fourteen-year-old Geneviève Durony. (Ravel dedicated to Leleu, three years later, the Prélude he had written for a sight-reading competition.) The children's stories that are quoted at the head of the three middle pieces were printed in the programme. In the same programme Ravel played the premiere of Debussy's *D'un cahier d'esquisses*. The following year Ravel orchestrated *Ma mère l'oye* and turned it into a ballet for which he wrote a new scenario.

Ma mère l'oye is a masterful combination of precision and simplicity, humour and tenderness, sublime skill allied to an extraordinarily loving and deeply insightful representation of a child's fairy-tale world. In its refined clarity it is the single work of Ravel's that most clearly defines and manifests two aspects of his genius found everywhere in his work, but in a more diffuse form. The first is what Manuel de Falla called 'the absence of vanity': Ravel's refusal to yield to the expectation that music should 'affect a certain haughty aspiration to what was thought to be transcendental.' The second is the characteristic that Manuel Rosenthal identified: 'His essential gift was to always know how to express an immense tenderness. . . . No one else knew how to find this tone with such purity. In this Ravel was like a child. He knew how to guard within himself the richness and mystery of childhood, which the adult world overshadows.' The result is that *Ma mère l'oye* achieves a profundity of expression that is itself transcendental.

'Pavane de la Belle au bois dormant' (Pavane of the Sleeping Beauty)

In the first two pieces, Ravel told Faure, the music should 'evoke the naive, the unreal, the unknown.' She played badly, she recalled, 'and he didn't play much better, but I was under a spell and I rediscovered in him the soul of a child that has returned to a fairy kingdom.'

'Petit Poucet' (Tom Thumb)

The epigraph relates the well-known tale by Charles Perrault of Tom Thumb leaving a trail of breadcrumbs so he can find his way home. But on the way back he discovers the birds have eaten all of them. 'The difficulty of this piece confounded us and we became somewhat paralysed. Then Ravel laughed and lightly tapping the score he said "we are as lost as he is."'

'Laideronnette, impératrice des pagodes' (Laideronette, Empress of the Pagodas)

> She undressed and stepped into the bath. At once all the little pagodas sing and play their tiny instruments, some have theorbos made from nutshells, others have viols made from almond shells, for it was right they should play instruments suitable to their size.

Ravel told Faure that, after the mechanical little dance of the first section, the middle section is where Laideronnette proclaims her authority – 'after all, she is the empress.'

'Les entretiens de la Belle et de la Bête' (Conversations between Beauty and the Beast)

'When I think of your kind heart you do not seem so ugly.'

'Oh yes good lady, I have a kind heart but I am a monster.'

'There are many more monstrous than you.'

'If I had the wit I would pay you a great compliment in order to thank you. But I am only a beast. . . . Beauty, will you be my wife?'

'No, Beast!'

'I will die happy for having the pleasure of seeing you one more time.'

'No my dear beast, you will not die, you will live to be my husband!'

The Beast had vanished and she saw kneeling before her a prince more beautiful than love itself, who thanked her for lifting the spell.

Faure relates that while playing this piece with her, Ravel was in a very good mood. 'You are the pretty one and I am the monster. It's a graceful waltz. Not too slow, not heavy, take care over the big crescendo, as if they are having an argument.'

'Le jardin féerique' (The Magic Garden)

When Ravel came to the end of the play-through with Faure, he said to her, 'This needs more reverence than we gave it. It's a garden in which the flowers are so tall they're taller than a man.' This was a bold statement from one who was so sensitive about his own diminutive stature. With Faure, Ravel had learned to be fully at ease.

Henriette Faure

Henriette Faure (1904–1985) was nineteen when she first played to Ravel (not seventeen, as she states in her memoir, written some fifty years after the event). In her first lesson she played *Valses nobles et sentimentales*, and as we saw in chapter 5, Ravel subjected her to 'a torture that fifty years later I have not forgotten.' So began a series of lessons, several times a week from September 1922 to January 1923, culminating in a two-and-a-half-hour recital of Ravel's complete piano music at the Champs-Élysées theatre in Paris, attended by many of the most influential musicians of the time: Roussel, Schmitt, Aubert, Jacques Durand, Vuillermoz, Roland-Manuel, 'artistic directors, conductors, a number of virtuosos with their scores and of course the unknown and suspicious crowd.' Ravel came with his brother Édouard and Hélène Jourdan-Morhange, refusing a box because 'he had a horror of making an exhibition of himself.' In the interval Ravel did not appear, and someone suggested he had 'hidden himself away.' Clearly Ravel was as nervous as Faure. But afterwards her 'demi-god' was the first to see her, and he congratulated her for such a long time that several of her friends, apparently not knowing who he was, grumbled about 'the little Monsieur who never seemed to be done.' Faure subsequently had a successful career promoting Ravel's music, and she recorded most of his major works.

When she arrived for her lessons at Le Belvédère, Ravel's home, at Montfort l'Aumary, not far from Paris, he would always greet her somewhat shyly but with great courtesy. 'Each time the ritual unfolded in the same way – a walk in Montfort, the cemetery, the cloisters and then the long and scrupulous observation of his garden, which he adored.'

> Ravel was a charming companion, scrupulously polite and kind, and very talkative on non-musical subjects, such as the 1914 war, his cushions, his sofas, his eye for carpeting, his striped seating and curtains and the multitude of knick-knacks he had collected, which for the most part were of questionable taste.
>
> Our conversation was always on the level of small talk, and I found it impossible to draw him out on more important subjects, so stubbornly was he set on staying on the surface of things. I believe this provided a strong protection of his inner self.
>
> Only once did I risk breaking through his defences. We were about to work on *Gaspard de la nuit* and I exclaimed how seductive were these three poems of Bertrand's. He responded, with a scarcely concealed excitement, that I should read the whole book, that it was marvellous, that all the romanticism of the 19th century was contained in that little volume. And exactly as if I was forcing my way in to Bluebeard's castle I cried out, 'Ah, so you are sometimes a romantic then?'
>
> What happened next was astonishing and rather sad. Ravel looked at me without seeing me, and his manner became distracted, distant, troubled. I would say he was at a loss for words. This lasted quite a time, and as we were at table I saw him repeatedly turning his spoon in the jam, and his awkwardness persisted.

Faure offers considerable insight into Ravel's own playing as well as his teaching method. After the small talk, the garden visit, the delighted tour round his collection of knick-knacks and little me-chanical toys, came the work, and at that point his face would take on a completely different expression, alert and tense. The man who until then had been easy-going, unconcerned, all at once became a musician and an exacting taskmaster. In the lessons

> he wanted the immediate realisation of his ideas, even down to the smallest details, and nothing could be left to chance. And he was as quick and nervous in his movements as in his playing. He rarely wrote anything on the score, but he played and demonstrated his music very persuasively. From the first two or three chords he played one could tell the special stamp of Ravel. He caught at once those abrupt strokes of harmony, their inner force, the crisp arpeggiation, the sudden tight crescendos. And he also had a way of floating the sound (he called this 'the glide'), of striking the chords so they emerged as if from the shadows, with a kind of echoing resonance. But if he was required to articulate, say, a sudden flurry of notes after a limpid melodic line, no one could command the unity of expression as well as he, the strict control of tempo, phrasing, proportion, so as to give the impression, from beginning to end, of one continuous thread.

Many pieces among Ravel's piano works come to mind as Fauré's reference point here, but none perhaps provides a more suitable illustration than the first two pieces of *Miroirs*, 'Noctuelles' and 'Oiseaux tristes'. It is almost as if she is recalling the structure and progress of the music as she writes. Her own recording of *Jeux d'eau* (now extremely difficult to find) manifests similar traits, especially in terms of unity and crispness of articulation. A fast tempo is strictly maintained and there is not a vestige of rubato, yet the phrases are constantly moulded through precisely realised dynamic gradations. It is a wonderfully refreshing performance and bears out perfectly the lesson she learnt concerning the laughing river god of the epigraph (see chapter 2).

Her playing clearly delighted Ravel, and it is equally clear that he took enormous pleasure in imparting his ideas to her. (He gave her a photo, from 1913, of himself playing the piano and inscribed it, 'À ma charmante et parfaite interprète Henriette Faure, Maurice Ravel 10/11/22'.) His gallantry is touching and her lively recollections of her fears and his foibles often very amusing. She relates, for example, that she was as scared of breaking his precious objects on the shelves next to the piano as she was of not being able to execute his minute instructions. (Another visitor to his house recalled that it was 'crowded with bibelots, one more out-of-date and unusual than the next . . . which bear witness to a vivacity of spirit and a humor which were his alone.')

Conclusion

In my attempt to reconstruct the feel and presence of Faure's lessons with Ravel, I have relied, of course, on Faure's own attempt, her recollections some fifty years after the actual event. I am struck by the vividness of Faure's memoir and its air of authenticity, which is corroborated by the recollections of others. But one tiny detail is at odds with Perlemuter's account – the kind of detail that a biographer will wonder about and no doubt give far too much attention too, but which is all part of a concern with the minutiae without which the mosaic cannot be assembled. Faure says that Ravel rarely wrote anything on her score. Perlemuter implies the opposite, and is constantly drawing attention to places where Ravel has written instructions, such as this for 'Ondine': 'All over my score he wrote "faster, more melting [*plus vite, plus fondu*]." What does this tell us? Perhaps simply that by the time Perlemuter arrived Ravel had changed his methods, that he had become even more determined to stamp his authority on the score. But I think it tells us something more. It tells us about the fluid nature of objective truth, the random nature of memory and reconstruction, and of the randomness that is a sign of authentic human inconsistency. It tells us that the whole picture can only include untidy ends, blurred details, contradictory statements – that the whole forever remains open to conflicting interpretations.

I am struck, for example, by Faure's extraordinary comment, rarely quoted, that 'Maurice Ravel demanded of his performers the complete abandonment of their personal feelings [*annihilation complète de leur participation sentimentales*].' This must have been what it felt like for her, but I cannot believe that this was Ravel's intention, or even that Faure herself complied. In context the remark has immense validity; out of context it is nonsense.

The apparent extremity of Ravel's position is a sign of his intense concentration on detail and process, on the elimination of the extraneous so as to reveal the essence, on his fear of indulgence leading to sentimentality. He worried that the pure lucidity of his music could be so easily marred, but he also knew the extent to which his music revealed his inner being, and this he had fiercely to protect. ('Whenever I reached those places which he marks *expressif*,' Faure recalled, 'he would say, in a worried and slightly testy manner, "Get on, get on, and don't weep over it."')

Without question Ravel was ambivalent on the issue of interpretation. (His remark about abandoning personal feelings comes in the context of his more celebrated utterance 'I don't ask for my music to be interpreted, only to be played.'). Of the many stories about his inconsistency on this point, I will give two examples. The first concerns a recording of the orchestral version of *Pavane pour une infante défunte* for Columbia, made in 1932, at which Ravel was present. He insisted on such a slow tempo that it was clear the performance would overrun the twelve-inch disc by two and a half minutes. The Columbia director suggested a break for refreshment and took Ravel to a nearby bistro. When they returned the conductor had completed the recording, having reduced the timing to four minutes, thirty-two seconds. The performance was played back to Ravel, who commented that it was perfect.

And René Chalupt recounts an amusing story in which Ravel was listening to Ricardo Viñes playing one of his works, having initially told him to 'play it as you want.' He then 'made him begin his performance all over again, instructing him almost note by note until this great pianist ended up conforming precisely to the composer's instructions.' (As we have seen, however, Ravel did not manage to get Viñes's compliance over the tempo of 'Le gibet'.)

Within Ravel's exhortation 'Play it as you want' lies the understanding that a score, by itself, is incapable of indicating every detail of the composer's intentions; otherwise, the implied question 'How should I play this work?' would never need to be asked. This was why Ravel had to expend all his energy, when teaching his music, to make his intentions clear. So Ravel too knew that a score could not simply be 'played'. But it seems that once the instructive mode had seized hold of him, an extreme didacticism came to the fore.

The 'interpretations' that he had every right to loathe were those which went against the composer's unambiguously expressed instructions. When he told Paul Wittgenstein that 'performers *are* slaves', he was reacting with indignation to a performance of his Concerto for the Left Hand in which Wittgenstein had actually changed the score, radically altering textures and sonorities, and hence the notes as well. As Orenstein says, in Wittgenstein's recording of the concerto he takes such liberties as to give 'the impression of playing his own arrangement.'

So at the end of this book we have come back to the score, what it can tell us and what it can't. At one level, for the performer, the score is all we have, and without question we have to accord it profound respect, just as we respect the tiniest details of biography from which larger questions can be drawn and addressed. But on another level, the music can only be brought off the page by a performer's imaginative engagement with the sounds as heard, and this engagement will require a considerable degree of (necessarily judicious and informed) personal response, a refined decision-making process that can only be the performer's.

In my epigraphs I quoted a remark by Ernst Krenek, and at risk of being didactic myself I will repeat it here, in my own words, as a plea for the essential autonomy of the performer's art. Any problems that might arise from interpreting Ravel's piano music stem mainly from the fact that interpreters try too hard to suppress their own imaginations. The quotation from Harold Bloom that I placed beside it might suggest, however, that I believe that all interpretation is essentially misinterpretation (as Ravel would certainly have thought). Bloom concluded: 'and so all criticism is prose poetry.' He was talking about the act of critical commentary, the necessity of engaging with art works in the quest for understanding. That has been the process of this book, and I have to confess that in this regard I have reduced poetry to prose. The necessary redress is to cease talking about Ravel's music and return to performing it and listening to it – to reassemble the poetry of his ineffable *miroirs*.

Appendix A: Details for Performance

Some of the comments below are highly detailed and will make sense only with a score, with bar numbers, to hand.

Jeux d'eau

After Henriette Faure's first play-through to Ravel of *Jeux d'eau* and his admonishment that her fountains were 'sad', she began again, she recalled,

> at a livelier tempo, and I played those rapid sixty-fourth notes, lead-
> ing up to some of the themes, even faster, in the Ravelian manner,
> and I gave a little more air to the curves and the breathing points,
> and marked the phrase endings even more, with a kind of rapid
> movement of the hand; and above all, by thinking joyfully, I turned
> what I had thought to be a musical contemplation into a brilliant
> divertissement.

The 'sixty-fourth notes . . . leading up to some of the themes' can only refer to three places (bars 18, 37 and 77), though her advice would also be appropriate for the thirty-seconds in the first bar (and this is how she plays them in her own recording of *Jeux d'eau*; see chapter 7). Her decision to give 'a little more air to the curves and the breathing points [*respirations*]' perfectly captures the nature of the melodic decoration, which is done partly through dynamic shaping and partly through a slight squeezing or hurrying of the figurations, without compromising the pulse. The curves (*courbes*) of the phrasing, and the breath at the end of each unit, can be seen in bars 19–26 and the new theme beginning at bar 38. These need to be carefully shaped – at bar 21, for example, Ravel has indicated a precise dynamic contour – and giving them 'air' is a helpful way of imagining the choreographic elegance and freedom required.

Along with sound and texture, and associated questions of touch and pedal, the performer also needs to engage with the rhythmic structure. What I have called the mechanical rigour of the eighth-note pulse can impede the overlying grace and shimmer of the figuration unless the performer responds to the way in which Ravel subtly breaks up the rhythmic line. The figurations in the right hand are in constant variation, principally alternating sixteenths and thirty-seconds and later introducing sextuplets. All this is obvious enough. But what the performer should also notice is how this alternation often articulates an underlying dotted rhythm (implied in the opening bar and made explicit by the part writing in the left hand at bar 5) and hence a suppleness within the rhythmic structure. Furthermore, the grouping of the larger half-note units constantly changes, as signalled by the changing time signatures, thus creating an ambiguity at the heart of the structure: the first two bars actually articulate a single bar of 3/2 (three half notes), mirrored by another 3/2 bar immediately following (so the second half of bar 4 can be isolated as a bar of 2/4). This kind of structural fluidity is always present, even where the piece appears to settle into a regular 4/4 bar structure: notice, for example, how the principal stresses in bars 34–7 come at the beginning of each downward arpeggio, and none of them are on bar lines. When the 'correction' comes in bar 38, where the projected melody begins firmly on the downbeat, it is preceded by that momentary Ravelian hiatus in the pulse, an ascending figuration (marked *rapide*) that has the effect of adding an extra, but unspecified, moment of time to the end of the previous paragraph (or perhaps to the beginning of the next).

All this the performer needs to articulate without overemphasis – so as not to impede the momentum – but with a constant awareness of the differing stresses and accents, which are themselves a product of the harmonic rhythm as well as the melodic shape. By these means suppleness is created at the heart of the regular pulse. So on the first page, for example, the sense of 3/2 at the opening is implied by the harmonic rhythm (a thrice-iterated tonic pedal) as well as the repeated motifs; likewise, the (concealed) dotted rhythm in each half of bars 1 and 3 is suggested by the subsidiary harmony on the 4th eighth note of each group, articulated each time by the rapid upward arabesque in the right hand.

Such procedures are the basic elements of Ravel's compositional process, and performers do not have to search very hard to find them. But their projection is vital for bringing the music off the page and creating maximum intelligibility for listeners. Ravel's fountains are the result of the most meticulously crafted fusion of colour and line, of harmonic and rhythmic inventiveness melded with melodic decoration. A sense of the music's gracefulness and freedom can only be communicated when the larger-scale phrase structures are articulated, while keeping the discreet eighth-note pulse perfectly in control.

The ending is masterful, and the instruction *sans ralentir* – without slowing up – is of course crucial to the effect. After the improvisatory material, marked *très rapide*, beginning at bar 72, the pulse reasserts itself, though it is now slower. From bar 78 there is again a strong sense of two beats to the bar, as well as a regular two-bar phrase structure. The listener is led through a series of repeated melodic phrases signalling a winding down, a movement towards closure, which means that the actual moment when the fountains vanish comes upon us suddenly: the final chord is heard, as if halfway through a phrase, on the weakest beat (Ravel again employs the time-signature alternation of the opening, reversing it). He was to produce a similar effect some years later at the end of 'Scarbo'. The end of *Jeux d'eau* creates a dreamlike vanishing, where momentum is not so much halted as dissipated. The effect also depends on the pedal, and the last sounds we hear are pianissimo sixths and sevenths over the tonic chord, which create an echoing, barely audible continuation of the preceding figuration.

Miroirs

'Noctuelles'

The pictorial dimension of 'Noctuelles', discussed in chapter 3, is achieved through the strictest procedures of structural and harmonic logic in Ravel's inimitable manner, which manages to combine the orthodox with the audacious. Overall the piece employs an ABA structure, fast–slow–fast, with the recapitulated material in the second A section a fifth lower than in the first. All this is straight-forward and fully audible. But it is the manner of the unfolding of each section that appears so complex, the way in which the structure, so often in one-bar repeated units, seems to grow from the image, constantly referring to it or nourished by it. (Of *Miroirs* Viñes said: 'This music is very specifically descriptive. It would be a mistake to interpret it otherwise.')

However, the overall structure is not quite as simple as I have implied, for the simple formal description 'ABA' does not take into account what happens between the B section and the return of A, a substantial twenty-two bars in which elements of the two sections are juxtaposed. The moment of return is actually blurred – the first two bars are missing – and we are in the recapitulation before we are fully aware of it. This is a masterful transition, allowing us to experience once more the exquisite realisation of the 'Noctuelles' image of the opening from a different perspective.

Harmonically, there is orthodoxy in the firm cadence into D-flat in the third bar, with the first two bars acting as a dominant; the audacity lies in the way this dominant is disguised, in the way Ravel uses all twelve tones in the very first bar except for the key note D-flat, which is withheld until the cadence. (This whole process, over three bars, has a strongly pictorial role, evoking hovering followed by swooping flight, an effect that also relies on the rhythmic change in the third bar.) As so often with Ravel, the most dissonant harmony can be reduced to orthodox chord progressions: in the passage we looked at above, bars 6–9, when extended into bars 10–12, create a ii–V–I cadence. There is audacity too in the chains of sevenths in the middle section – a beloved Ravelian harmonic trait – and the way these dissonances are put to the service of a haunting expressivity.

One of the characteristics of impressionist piano music is the way it requires the pianist to create an intensity of colour by means of the pedal – but not by the pedal alone. Pedalling is allied to a precision of finger articulation, so that clarity and resonant colouring can be attained at the same time. 'Noctuelles' would be unthinkable without the sustaining pedal (in a way, perhaps, that the Prélude from *Le tombeau* would not). Yet it needs precise finger articulation to project the full effect of its textures and sonorities – and, at the same time, an essential lightness of touch for the weightless moths' wings.

'Oiseaux tristes'

Henriette Faure recalled that Ravel

> was essentially concerned to bring two levels into relief. The cry of the birds on the upper level, a little strident, in rapid arabesques – and then the stifling darkness of the forest on the lower level, sultry and muffled, veiled in pedal, motionless. . . . And I must mention how crucial is the role of the bass for capturing the impression of oppressive heat, not percussive, but penetrating.

It is not clear whether the descriptive instruction she relates here came directly from Ravel. It is more likely that Faure, when she finally wrote her memoir, conflated her own experience of the piece with Ravel's frequently quoted remarks about the birds of Fontainebleau (which she would have known from Vuillermoz's original memoir, and which she too quotes in her account). My instinct is that Ravel would have been unlikely to have coached her by way of such images; he would more likely have concentrated on voicing, rhythm and tempo (so the 'two levels' remark seems like authentic Ravel, as do the remarks on pedalling and the sonority of the bass). All the evidence from his known observations on the performance of his music points this way.

Faure also notes that the piece displays

> the character of an improvisation. . . . I will perhaps surprise the reader by saying that this is, in fact, one of those rare pieces of Ravel that comes alive through rubato, a disciplined rubato in the manner of Chopin. . . . It is interesting to note, in passing, those places where Ravel, who was fiercely insistent on unity of tempo, loved to indulge in his poetic pieces in all kinds of improvisations.

And she then cites the extraordinary *presque ad lib* section at the end of 'Oiseaux tristes'. There is a similar instance towards the end of 'Noctuelles'.

Ravel usually writes such passages in half-size notation, the sign found in Chopin and Liszt for decoration and improvisation. Such notation also indicates a lightness of touch (in Ravel, often marked *léger* or *très léger*). But a delicate flexibility of pulse is often implied too, and sometimes specifically indicated: in 'Noctuelles', the passage at bar 36 and its more extended version at bar 120 are preceded by the instruction *poco rubato*. *Jeux d'eau* has a similar cadenza-like passage (bar 72) in half-size notation, although here the touch required can be steely, with the dynamic reaching a brilliant fortissimo.

As regards the improvisatory feel of 'Oiseaux tristes', Faure could have mentioned the opening birdsong, as Perlemuter does. Ravel, he said, told him that the arabesques 'must not be played strictly in time, but quicker [*plus bref*]. Ravel wrote this himself on my score. If you play strictly what's written, it loses character. You mustn't be afraid of elongating its final note. Once you sharpen the contour of this arabesque it stands out.' He might have added that it also sounds more like birdsong. And Perlemuter does not mention what occurs when this improvised rhythm is placed against the ostinato triplets in bars 8 and 9: clearly the parts cannot be aligned as the score states. The pianist needs to keep the accompaniment strict and the birdsong as free as before, just the kind of rubato Chopin was supposed to have executed in his own playing.

In her own account Faure refers to Liszt's famous description of Chopin's rubato: 'Look at those trees,' he said to a pupil. 'The wind plays in the leaves, stirs up life among them, the tree remains the same. That is a *Chopinesque rubato*.' Viñes, on the other hand, described it slightly differently: 'Even though Ravel loved exact interpretation, he was also the creator of a rubato – a rubato *en place*, measured, which is the opposite of Chopin's, which leaves the interpreter greater freedom.' Viñes implies here that Ravel's rubatos are written into the notation, but this is not exclusively the case. There are numerous instances of a highly subtle rubato in *Valses nobles et sentimentales*, indicated by such instructions as *très expressif* and *languissant* (languidly), as well as various specific instructions for slowing up.

'UNE BARQUE SUR L'OCÉAN'

During her lessons on this piece Ravel told Faure that it mustn't be 'weighed down by uniformity, by the formulaic approach with which he had heard pianists treat it, which bored their listeners.' He said that she had 'to diversify'. (This hardly squares with his remark about wanting his music to be played, not interpreted.) So with 'Une barque' Ravel must have worried that he had not made his intentions clear enough. Diversification can be achieved only by means of varying the pulse, dynamics, sonority, texture – the common elements of a performance, not all of which are possible to indicate precisely. Only tempo can be strictly ordained (though see Ravel's comments on metronome marks in the note '*The first concerns a recording*', p. 218), but in fact at the head of 'Une barque sur l'océan' Ravel gives no metronome indication, asking merely for 'a flexible rhythm.' (The difficulties involved in assessing the right tempo for a piece of music are unintentionally revealed by Perlemuter, when he advises that a certain passage should be 'not too fast, without dragging', that another should be 'slow but moving', and another 'very fast but not rushed'.) Dynamics and accentuation can be marked only relatively, and we are given no help regarding the dynamic *extent* of the numerous hairpin inflections. (Viñes said that Ravel wanted crescendos 'en général très marqué' – in general very marked, exaggerated – which would certainly apply to 'Une barque' and to 'Ondine' too.)

Ravel instructs that the piece should be 'très enveloppé de pé-dales' (swathed in pedal) – crucially important, but hardly more than a blanket instruction. Colour (or sonority) might be indicated with such words as 'brilliant' or 'luminous', but Ravel gives no such instructions, which is certainly not to say he doesn't expect a huge variation of colour. (He does, however, in bar 83, indicate 'without colour' for a rapid ostinato passage for the right hand, marked *pp*, in which he clearly intends a dynamically uninflected monotone.) 'Feeling' is indicated four times by the markings *expressif* and *très expressif*. But what is done, pianistically, to create such expression? Do we linger over the pulse, stress the melody, enrich the harmonic texture? Each case will be different, and each pianist will find a different solution.

The half-size notation towards the end of 'Une barque sur l'océan' (beginning in bar 117) is not a sign of rubato: the calming of the sea is captured within the rhythmic pulse by the notation, the light-touched arabesques taking their place in the larger pulse as the piece drifts towards its close. This is a good example of Viñes's rubato *en place*: to the listener the pulse appears to slow, to hesitate – instead of continuous arpeggios there are now spaces in the rhythmic fabric – but in reality the pulse remains precise.

One further word on Ravel's plea for the performer to 'diversify' in 'Une barque': Ravel, as we have seen, refused to allow Viñes to record *Gaspard de la nuit* because the pianist would not take 'Le gibet' at the very slow tempo asked for – not such a sin, perhaps, as altering the notes (as Wittgenstein had in his performance of the Concerto for the Left Hand), but in Ravel's view a sin nevertheless. The slow tempo, said Viñes, 'would bore the public.' It is a nice irony that it was on the very account of boredom that Ravel urged Henriette Faure to 'diversify' in 'Une barque sur l'océan'.

'Alborada del gracioso'

Regarding 'Alborada del gracioso', Faure recalled:

> Whenever I opened my music at the title of certain pieces, those pieces where he was especially keen I should understand his aesthetic, he would say, very quickly and quietly, 'Ah! Attention'. From that moment I was under his command. . . . In the case of 'Alborada' his concern was always with the unity of the tempo, which he termed 'inexorable.' He told me: 'The incisive, acrobatic character of Alborada cannot be achieved at too fast a tempo, but at the same time the tempo needs to be lively and must never slacken. Apart from the freedom allowed (oh, so slight!) in the nostalgic vocal line of the middle section you must make sure, with an iron discipline, that you never speed up or slow down the initial tempo. . . .' So herein lie the strength and character of this *pièce de métal*. Ravel

knew exactly the tempo he wanted – lively and poised at the same time – and he ordered me to do it.

And the performer might ponder, with a certain relief, Faure's remarks on the famous repeated-note passages (and she also mentions the repeated notes at the opening of 'Scarbo'). 'In those places,' Ravel told her,

> it's not necessary to get obsessed by the precision and clarity of the repeated notes. That would only result in a slackening of tempo. I use this figuration in my pieces as a sort of pretext: it stands for a kind of vibration, but articulated within the initial tempo, and in 'Alborada' it must not be allowed to compromise the rhythm of the leaping left-hand chords. When the alternating glissandos cut in, the repeated notes are reduced to a secondary role.

This is all very well, but the repeated-note passage at the opening of 'Scarbo' is noticeably different from the triplet figurations of 'Alborada' and is marked as such, 'très fondu, en trémolo' – very blurred (or melted), like a tremolo. Perlemuter recalls Ravel's intentions for 'Alborada' somewhat differently: 'Ravel wanted me to play this passage [at bar 43] lightly like a flute [*légèrement fluté*], recalling the orchestra.' This is not quite the same as Ravel's suggestion of 'a kind of vibration' and is certainly not a tremolo. There is a further irony in that Ravel's own orchestration of 'Alborada' gives this moment to a far-from-melting muted trumpet, and at the parallel passage after the middle section the trumpet is paired with a side drum.

The fact remains that any sensitive and alert attention to the music at this point will reveal that it is the rhythm that should take precedence, not the clarity of the repeated notes. The repeated notes, especially in the passage beginning at bar 52 (the point where in his orchestration Ravel does finally introduce the flute), have a melodic contour, and if the performer articulates this, rather than a mechanical sequence of triplet-grouped sixteenth notes – and discerns that the rhythm of the passage is 6/8 alternating with 3/4 – then everything falls into place and the *gracioso* will dance his seductive jig.

The monody of the middle section offers another of those instances of rhythmic freedom ('oh, so slight!' as the terrified Faure amusingly affirms) – this time associated with melody, not decoration, as it is elsewhere in *Miroirs*. The melody suggests a *copla*, the wailing recitative found in flamenco, and Ravel marks it *expressif en récit*, indicative of the kind of vocalized freedom and richness of tone he had in mind. Each phrase is notated with significant rhythmic variation, a sign of improvised song, but held taut by the framing accompaniment, which is strictly on the pulse, alluding to the distant stamping of feet and metal percussion, the suggestion of a dance echoing from afar. The performer should already have been alert to this by the pianissimo marking on the score, though Perlemuter offers some additional advice: Ravel wanted here, he recalled, 'une rumeur lointaine' which is not 'a distant murmuring', as *Ravel According to Ravel* translates it, but something more menacing and in keeping with flamenco, 'a distant rumbling'. And once again, for all the strictures, we learn from Perlemuter that the instruction 'Tempo 1' at this point should not be taken too literally, as Ravel's marking 'eighth note = eighth note needs to be interpreted . . . and not too fast.'

'La vallée des cloches'

Earlier I spoke of the way in which this piece needs to accommodate, without strain, the Zen-like outer sections and the fulsomely lyrical middle section. The performer must sense that the music achieves this accommodation through multiple means – harmonic, rhythmic, dynamic, structural, spatial – all working towards the same end. From the *très calme* at bar 12, the pulse structure is fluid, with the time signature constantly in flux, which allows an inter-play of repetition and variation, of stasis and movement, like the tolling of bells beginning and lapsing. The lapsing is underlined by the terracing of the dynamics, in bars 16–18, from *mf* to *pp* and by the subtle change of pulse – the syncopation ceases – at the point where the *pp* is reached. But cessation here is also simultaneous with expectancy, because the long diminuendo is on a dominant seventh chord. At first the stability of the C tonality seems secure, as the bell on B-flat appears to be separated from it, tolling in a different spatial plane and somehow unconnected to its harmonic function as a seventh needing resolution. (This effect has been set up from the beginning, where the pitch of the bells appears to be separated from the harmonic function, and especially by the introduction of the thrice-repeated E-sharp in bar 6.) The glory of the sudden surge forward into melody which follows is created by a perfect cadence (and a crescendo): the listener, in a retrospective realisation of a functioning dominant seventh, then perceives this as a release and a liberation from stasis, a resolution fully maintained by the soaring strength of the melody, despite the dissonant B-flat sounding deep in the bass. (The consonant root, F, is actually withheld for six bars, creating a further sense of catharsis when it finally comes at bar 26.) B-flat also tolls in the accompaniment, maintaining the continuity and syncopated rhythm of the bells. So the central section is a new departure, but one born of the earlier material, and achieves an organic unity by means of the thrice-struck bell motif and the continuous organisa-tion of the harmonic and spatial planes.

The performer needs to hold taut this central section – the ex-tended apex of the whole arch structure (A–B–C–B–A) – through scrupulous rhythmic and dynamic control, while sensing the in-exorable movement back to the home key (which at the opening of the piece had only been implied, never stated). At the *très calme* in bar 42 the harmonic structure settles for the first time on a C-sharp, which underpins the return of sections B (a fourth lower) and A (same pitch). The magnificent Savoyarde, struck four times at decreasing dynamic levels, is built from interlocking perfect fourths (G-sharp, C-sharp and F-sharp); harmonic resolution, within the long silence of the final bar, is imagined rather than heard.

Gaspard de la nuit

The most important detail for 'Ondine' is the unchanging grouping for the right-hand figuration at the opening (see p. 87). Ravel told Henriette Faure that she should 'correct the heaviness of her thumbs' in 'Ondine' by practising Liszt's 'Feux-follets', and he insisted on the 'style' of the piece, 'no rhythmic weakness [*amollissement rhythmique*], but wedded closely to the framework of the poem.' (To Perlemuter he said that the triplet rhythm across the bar lines from bar 76 to bar 78 should be done flexibly, *souplement* but most pianists would do this anyway, especially when the accompanying dynamic inflexion swells towards the centre of the triplet, as here.) Ravel talked of the 'suggestive magic' of the glissandi and how the melody at one point (as he spoke, he 'leafed through the pages,' so it is not clear exactly where this point is) was 'naked in diaphanous whiteness' ('la mélodie nue dans une sonorité blanche, diaphane'). All these remarks suggest a rare lack of inhibition on Ravel's part, a consequence of his imaginative engagement with the nature of his own creations.

As Perlemuter points out, Ravel insisted that the rests at bar 83, just before the recitative, not be extended, so that what followed would not become 'a piece within a piece' – and above all that the performer not slow down in this bar. He wanted the arpeggio at bar 88 to start in one single motion so as to incorporate the initial bass grace notes into the upward swoop, without any holding back.

In 'Le gibet' he insisted, of course, on the correct articulation of the accents, and on the slowness of the tempo and the instruction 'sans expression'. (Faure, he remarked, played the piece 'like Ricardo Viñes; an admirable artist but he understood nothing of this piece.' Clearly her first play-through was too fast.)

One of the clues to mastering the character of the bell motif lies in the exact observance of the tenuto mark on the third iteration. It is the falling away of the dynamic at this point which is so important, and which needs to be articulated in precisely the same way each time, against the cross-rhythm of the melodic line. A sense of the poem's desolation is contained in this rhythm, as much as in the surrounding textures. (Debussy, a few years later, created a similar effect by purely rhythmic means at the opening of 'Des pas sur la neige'.) As in 'La vallée des cloches', the effect depends on the pianist's awareness of separate planes of pulse. Rhythmic control is as crucial to the effect of 'Le gibet' as control of sound.

Above all Ravel was concerned that Faure should not play 'Scarbo' too loudly, warning her it was a piece of extreme contrasts, a piece not only of terror but of mystery too. As I observed at the end of chapter 4, 'Scarbo' is magical. (One might add to the warning on dynamics that neither is the character of 'Scarbo' dependent on a headlong tempo.)

Faure recounts an amusing episode prior to her all-Ravel recital in Paris in 1923, when the director of the Maison Gaveau, on being introduced to her, remarked that she was too small to be seen on stage. 'You might not see me, but you will hear me,' Faure replied. Ravel at once looked worried, and asked her, 'You are not going to play "Scarbo" like one of Liszt's rhapsodies, are you?' 'Ah,' she returned, 'I have too much love for you to betray you like that for a single instant'. No doubt this remark made Ravel even jumpier.

To Perlemuter Ravel said he wanted the hairpin markings of 'Scarbo' 'très éclatants' – very explosive (with overtones of 'dazzling' and 'resonant') – 'not only where they are needed for expression.' Clearly Ravel is indicating the interface between dynamics and rhythm, that point at which articulation serves not only colour and sonority, but the structural integrity and character of the whole. A precise understanding of how all these elements are interfused is the central requirement for performing *Gaspard de la nuit.*

The opening D-sharp tremolando, he told Perlemuter, should be 'comme un tambour' – like a drum. However this remark needs some interpretation, as the instruction on the score is 'très fondu, en trémolo', with the addition of 'Ped.' This is a purring, menacing side drum if it is one at all, a distant vibration following the initial fright of the first accent. (See also p. 156 for Ravel's comments on the tremolandos in 'Alborada'.) Orchestral effects are apparently everywhere in 'Scarbo', but in that inimitable Ravelian manner which conjures sounds that don't actually exist outside the piano (see chapter 4, p. 86, and the note '*in* Gaspard de la nuit *Ravel's piano*', p. 205). Reversing the usual idea of piano transcriptions of orchestral music (a staple of the music room and concert hall throughout the nineteenth century and well into the twentieth), Ravel remarked that, rather than a piano transcription, what he wanted to write was 'an orchestral transcription for piano.'

Most commentators (but not Perlemuter or Faure) point out that the tempo equivalences Ravel marks at bar 430 do not in fact add up. In the real world, however – the world of sound and performance – they do. The tempo of bar 430 depends on a sense of accelerando preceding it, which is unmarked but almost impossible to resist. (If it is resisted, the tension of the musical narrative fails; in his recordings Perlemuter, like many other performers, creates an accelerando.)

Beginning in bar 448, Ravel asked for 'an enormous amount of pedal' for the rising chromatic figuration and, again, an unusually exaggerated crescendo, but delayed 'so as to prepare for the brilliant crescendo leading to the final episode.' Jourdan-Morhange (rather sniffily, one feels) remarks on how Ravel shows his 'weakness for Liszt' in his instruction that the final hairpins (from bar 586 onwards) should be 'stormy'. And finally, yet again, the ever-vigilant Ravel writes on Perlemuter's score at the very end of 'Scarbo', 'Sans ralentir'. We might be forgiven for hearing this as if in capital letters: DON'T SLOW DOWN.

Valses nobles et sentimentales

WALTZ NO. 1

The physical characteristics of Ravel's piano music, the way it is choreographed on the keyboard, the way it belongs to the keyboard, are superbly displayed in this opening Waltz. Ravel clearly found those opening chords with his hands, and his long thumbs. What he created was not simply a startling sound redolent of the excitement of the dance floor, but a pianistic equivalent to the act of dancing. The first Waltz embodies the physical act of dance within its musical framework. (This happens again, especially in the fourth and seventh Waltzes.) Ravel instructs that it be played 'très franc', meaning very decisive, straightforward – but it can mean uninhibited too, and this is central to the spirit of this opening. That Ravel delighted in this quality is confirmed by a letter he wrote when occupied in the early stages of composing his orchestral piece *La valse*: 'You know of my deep sympathy for these wonderful rhythms and that I value the joie de vivre expressed by the dance far more deeply than the Franckist puritanism.'

The cross-rhythms are one of the most difficult aspects of the first Waltz, requiring a complete independence from the 'endless 1.2.3.' – there are four on the first page alone. In bars 5–6 the accented Ds, bizarrely offbeat, suggest to me the steam organs accompanying fairground carousels; in bars 7–10 the pianist has to take great care to articulate the hemiola only in the left hand and avoid a parasitic accent on the second beat of the right hand (bars 8 and 10). This is a trap for the unwary, as is the cross-rhythm produced by Ravel's phrase groupings in the right hand at bars 13–14, which is often ignored. The final cross-rhythm on the opening page comes at bars 17–20, where the exultant *ff* chords leading to the D major cadence are actually in 2/4. This effect is dependent on the correction offered in the final bar of this section, where the all-conquering 3/4 asserts itself and demands that the next section follow without the pianist even taking a breath – hence the stern warning 'Sans ralentir'. At the equivalent moment in the last bar of the Waltz this instruction is replaced by 'un peu pesant' – slightly weighted. There is an implication here of a very slight holding back, which is now possible because there is no continuation, no unstoppable 3/4; the end has come. It serves nothing at all to try and create continuity between this Waltz and the next. Indeed, the attempt merely spoils what follows.

WALTZ NO. 2

In many ways the second Waltz is the rarest gem of the set, the simplest pianistically and with that ineffable quality of expression that Paul Crossley has called Ravel's 'infinitely lonely lyricism'. But it is not only the lyricism that touches us: the melodic outline has a harmonic underpinning of extraordinary poignancy, yet it is achieved through procedures of the most refined and precise rationality. For the performer it is essential to realise that the *expression intense* comes from within the procedures of the music – as always the waltz rhythm leads the way. Although the tempo instruction reads 'quite slow', this should be gauged only by comparison to the previous Waltz; the metronome marking of 104 does not feel at all slow. Henriette Faure writes of 'shades of rubato, very slight, very slight, and quickly suppressed by Ravelian vigilance.'

Waltz no. 3

This is the daintiest of the set, almost doll-like in its *petite* grace-fulness, inhabiting a world similar to Debussy's 'Serenade for a Doll' from *Children's Corner* but even more demanding in terms of articulation and nuance of phrasing. Ravel told Perlemuter that the comma at bar 20 should be understood to mean 'comme une révérence' (like a curtsey). The swell in the bar preceding the comma is the clue to this gesture – indeed, it is the whole bar, plus the comma, that contains the curtsey. Ravel, Perlemuter commented wryly, was 'so insistent on such details of punctuation' (although, alas, in many editions this particular one is missing).

Waltz no. 4

Another kind of waltz gesture is captured perfectly in the fourth Waltz, in which the three beats are articulated across two bars. Again the dynamic swell (repeated every two bars and later expanded over four- and three-bar phrases) is crucial to its realisation and will bear some exaggeration so as to make it unmistakable. The result is an aural image of the smooth circular motion of waltzing partners on a dance floor, the graceful whirls and twists of dancers in supple motion. The whole effect is reliant on precise dynamic and rhythmic control, the pulse inexorably regular until the single moment (bar 36) it relaxes by a hair's breadth, an enticement to seduction that is at once withdrawn. Ravel gave Faure the title 'Venetian Waltz' for this piece, which delicately points up its seductive pleasures. We saw in chapter 5 that he gave Perlemuter an alternative reading at bars 31–34.

Stuckenschmidt points out that 'Ravel's fourth waltz is so close in mood and key to the third of Schubert's *Valses Nobles* that one can play the two pieces one after another without doing violence to them stylistically.'

WALTZ NO. 5

For this Waltz, Ravel gave Faure the image of a little doll, in velvet, silk and curls and the title 'Waltz 1830'. To Perlemuter he said, 'In the spirit of a Schubert Waltz', which Ravel also wrote on his copy, along with the word 'simple'. Herein lies the heart of Ravel's irony. Both these (somewhat contrary) pieces of advice are valid, and immensely helpful, though neither is entirely true of the complex character of this fifth Waltz. The simplicity resides in the conventional waltz accompaniment – the only time in the whole work Ravel resorts to it (it is certainly in the manner of Schubert) – and in the melodic repetition. But little else about this work is simple. Ravel's advice is designed to reveal the music as he wants it played, not to state its character: play it simply and this character will be revealed. The image of the doll reminds us not to be too serious, and the image of Schubert tells us that this dance is gracefully and traditionally 'in time.' The doll is dancing to the most ubiquitous of all dance rhythms – simplicity itself, and here articulated as such – but also to music in which an assumed naivety will reveal an exquisitely balanced sophistication and the essence of the *sentiment intime*. In this Ravel is close to both Mozart and Schumann, two composers whom he revered.

WALTZ NO. 6

The cross-rhythms here are as difficult as anything in the opening Waltz. This is the one that Perlemuter said daunted him the most, even after he had mastered it. It is fast, one beat to a bar, which makes the speed of the quarter note too fast to be understood as a waltz rhythm. In fact, the waltz is in the left hand's hemiola (as it is in the right hand of no. 4), so it needs to be highlighted, though without detracting from the right hand's melody. This Waltz put Faure in mind of Schumann's *Papillons*.

Waltz no. 7

This is the most difficult of the set: it shares with the first Waltz a daringly acrobatic choreography at the climax, and the middle section requires a deftness of touch and nimbleness of movement that will bring clarity to the tinge of bitonality without compromising the lyricism. This middle section had to sound like a 'broken musical box,' Ravel told Faure. The 'lift' and 'drop' in the main theme (bars 19–20) need considerable finesse and stylistic awareness, and Ravel does his best to indicate his intentions: the staccato third beat, allied to those tie marks which have no supporting pillar on the other side, can be understood only in terms of pedal, an indication of resonance. The tenuto marking on the drop, the chord after the lift, can be understood as a kind of squeezing and withholding of the sound (Ravel instructed Perlemuter to delay the drop very slightly); the dynamic indications are also crucial to realising the effect. This is the musical representation of a dance gesture – essentially balletic, a rise and fall, a leap and a landing.

This was the Waltz that Ravel considered to be 'the most characteristic' of the set, though he fails to expand on this statement. Both Perlemuter and Faure stress its Viennese characteristics, which are obvious enough – for example the swoop, either down (bar 40) or up (bar 56) to the third beat, which is snatched off (a distinctly different gesture from the 'lift' of bar 19). Certainly the more extensive proportions of Waltz no. 7 sum up the spirit and the technique of the whole work, and perhaps Ravel considered that its harmonic and melodic outlines represented the range of what he had achieved in the others.

Le tombeau de Couperin

Prelude

The Prélude has an extraordinary harmonic richness which, because of the style of the piano writing – a drier, crisper sound than 'Une barque' or 'Noctuelles', less obviously pedalled, more cleanly articulated, as suits its baroque allusions – is partly concealed. Line is the first impression, rather than colour – though the harmony does its work on our imagination and is responsible for why this music touches us almost without our being aware of why. It is pure Ravel dressed up in the harpsichord style of Couperin.

The pedalling needs to be very discreet (and fingers can create colour too): too little pedal risks robbing the piece of its essence, too much creates harmonic nonsense ('little touches of pedal' was how Ravel advised Perlemuter). The articulation mark on the repeated left-hand E in the opening bars is a clue to Ravel's intention: not a dry staccato, but a note with an afterglow of resonance – and therefore pedalled. On the other hand, placing both notes of the mordent at the beginning of the melodic phrase into one pedal creates the wrong kind of colour, a dissonance which sounds for too long and thus spoils the lyrical purity of the top line. These are imitative of baroque 'snaps' and should be treated as such: they are the main device Ravel employs to convey his imitation, along with those many moments when the left-hand figurations echo the dramatic richness of harpsichord arpeggiation.

It is a mistake to treat this piece in the same manner as Bach is sometimes treated on the keyboard – with an apology, as it were, and doing our best to convey a baroque keyboard style. The full resources of Ravel's piano are at our disposal: this is a homage to Couperin, not a pastiche, and is as characteristic of Ravel as Debussy's 'Hommage à Rameau' is a characteristic piece of Debussy.

The two pieces make an interesting comparison: Debussy makes no attempt at all to conjure up Rameau's harpsichord, merely (but magnificently) using the rhythm of the sarabande to symbolise his desired baroque style. He captures a bygone era, but it is an illusion. Ravel's Prélude is also an illusion, but the harpsichord sound is embedded within its keyboard style. Still, the composer is no less Ravel. (Even in his tiny pastiches of Borodin and Chabrier, *À la manière de . . .* , he fails to conceal himself). The ending of the Prélude is a characteristic Ravelian climax, employing nearly the whole range of the keyboard, while the harmony as the piece develops is audaciously enriched in a manner that sends jazz musicians into swoons of delight. No two pieces better represent the difference between Ravel and Debussy.

Fugue

The Fugue, as we would expect, is perfectly wrought and meticulously skilled in its fugal procedures. It is also exquisitely lyrical, despite the accents. It has a reputation for being difficult to memorise – Marguerite Long used to perform *Le tombeau* without the Fugue for this reason. My advice would be, for those in need, to use the score. Music is all; memorisation has nothing to do with artistry. The final bars are like a musical box winding down ('very much like a musical box' is also Perlemuter's image for the ending of the Forlane), and the performer might take this as the context for the whole piece, so as to capture the precise sound and the precisely articulated rhythm. In this way the accents can sound with a delicate, bell-like bloom, never clipped or angular, though the use of the sustaining pedal should rarely be noticeable. Soft pedal can be used freely. Fauré suggests using only using finger weight, which gives a good idea of the kind of sound required, although touch control through arm weight will do just as well. Perlemuter stresses the Fugue's intensely expressive nature and warns against treating it as an academic exercise.

FORLANE

The tempo is not easy to judge in the Forlane, and for me Ravel's metronome marking – 96 for a dotted quarter note – is too fast. It needs to dance, yet remain flexible enough for the dotted rhythm not to sound mechanical. It should not clip along, but rather lilt. Ravel modelled his dance on the fourth *Concert Royal* of François Couperin, in which the final movement is a forlane. The pianist might judge the character of the dance from Couperin's, though as ever Ravel remains so much Ravel that his Forlane becomes virtually a new invention. The astringent chromatic harmony of the Forlane will sound all the more effective if the chords are lightly textured, not full, so the softer dynamic markings need careful attention: these markings are not for atmosphere but for sonority, and they suggest translucence rather than romantic richness. The groupings of the phrases are a signal of the lilt and swing of this dance, though observation of the phrase marks should not create any abruptness at the end of the phrase; rather, the whole melody needs to be blended in one seamless line, with the phrase groupings created by dynamic inflection. Observe too the accented points – not percussively, but as moments of arrival and departure. This is best achieved by scrupulously avoiding all accent at those points where none is indicated (and therefore especially not at bar lines). The tenuto marks, on the other hand, almost take care of themselves – not accents so much as 'squeezings', like a bowed note on a violin whose dynamic level increases minutely just after it has sounded. And it should go without saying that if any of this is overdone, the result will be an over-mannered performance and not Ravel's Forlane. Mannerism, however, is part of Ravel's intention – the tasteful mannerisms of eighteenth-century style in which the correct manner is all. It is a perilously fine line the performer has to tread.

The melodic voicing needs great refinement throughout, in parallel with the light texture required for the chords. An example comes on the second page in the first episode (beginning in bar 29): highlighting the lower note to show the melodic line does not compromise the colour of the clashing second but rather makes the sonority even more telling; the effect of the second remains, but another dimension is brought into relief.

The second episode needs to be felt with the accent on the second beat (in fact, the characteristic phrase emphasis of the whole piece is towards the second beat, giving it its characteristic lift and mobility) until Ravel delightfully 'corrects' it at the cadence by creating an accented pause on the downbeat, momentarily halting momentum, which then tips forward to resolution on the (now) weak second beat. This moment, as Ravel said of a similar gesture in *Valses nobles*, is 'like a curtsey.' The whole effect, apparently natural and artless, is created through an alignment of rhythmic and harmonic structure, and the pianist needs to be constantly alert to such procedures throughout. This way lies mastery.

RIGAUDON

The audacity of the Rigaudon is proclaimed in the first two bars: the opening statement is an ending statement, so the music appears to end immediately it has begun. This produces an added sense of satisfaction at the end when precisely the same statement completes the work, allowing us to savour the joke. The cross-hand accompaniment alludes to eighteenth-century style, and the A section conveys an unhindered, unbuttoned exuberance that requires total rhythmic accuracy. As ever, the texture of the chords requires the utmost finesse: the sound should have a certain and thrilling 'smack' about it, a harpsichord-like clatter, brilliant and never solid. The haunting middle section has the instruction *Ped*, and this can be courageously obeyed (with light half pedalling, and occasionally longer, on each eighth note) without any loss of face regarding the staccato markings in the accompaniment. In this way the lower fifth will evoke the drone of folk instruments or a small guitar or lute, and the pedal will nurture the resonance of the melody, rounding it and giving it sweetness. We might see this central part of the Rigaudon as the sad clown, perhaps even pairing it with Watteau's painting *Le Mezzetin*, in which the *commedia*-costumed guitarist is depicted in a lonely, tragic pose. We saw in chapter 7 how *Le tombeau* can be related to the iconography of Watteau.

Menuet

One of the essential performing requirements for the Menuet is a feel for the stresses, where they fall and, crucially, where they don't, and how the phrasing is in irregular groupings which are themselves a reflection of the harmonic structure. Ravel has been meticulous in his marking here, and there is a considerable amount of information in the score to help us characterise the dance rhythm (as there is in the Forlane). It achieves its flexibility through articulation and dynamic contour. The movement across the bar line at bars 2–3, unstressed, is picked up in the long sixteen-bar phrase that follows, creating the delightful flexibility of two- and three-bar units which combine to create a seamless forward momentum. The momentum only rests at the dotted-half-note cadence points, and even then the underlying quarter-note pulse continues the forward direction. So the pulse is inexorable throughout, though its regularity is disguised by the irregular placing of the main stresses. There can be just the slightest hint of expansion over the dynamic climax at bars 22–3 (and if not done to the smallest degree is best not done at all), and the performer should notice the careful placing of the peak of the crescendo, which extends to the third beat; the musette, especially, must follow on seamlessly without any loosening of the thread of the pulse, as should the visionary return of the Menuet at bar 73.

The three *expressif* markings (bars 25, 97 and 104) are indications of sound quality and in no sense can be taken as signs of rubato. The first two may have a gently penetrating cantabile, while the third is enhanced by the sonority and momentum of the new accompaniment figuration. The emotional climax at bars 57–61 is given no instruction apart from fortissimo, but it can be felt as *molto espressivo*.

Ravel told Perlemuter that the rapid arpeggio which precedes the return of the main theme at the end (bar 121) should be unprepared, 'like a surprise', a characteristic Ravelian effect – 'like the spring of a cat,' added Jourdan-Morhange.

Toccata

We can be reasonably certain Ravel would not have been able to demonstrate his Toccata to Henriette Faure in the virtuosic manner he envisaged. His advice was of a general nature, as far as any can be discerned (and Perlemuter too recalled little that was specific). Orenstein has unearthed a comment Ravel made to the pianist Jeanne-Marie Darré, 'Play it as rapidly as possible, on condition that every note is heard distinctly,' and Perlemuter confirms it. This, however, is hardly revealing.

What the performer should be concerned with above all, along with rhythmic control, is the quality of the sound, which means a concern with dynamics and, crucially for a piece that seems to require precise definition, pedal. In fact, a considerable amount of pedal is needed, sometimes in dabs and at other times in sustained swathes, and for the dynamic climax of the last pages so as to capture bass notes and achieve a rich orchestral sonority. Ravel's pedal indications on the first page, the only ones in the whole piece, are a clue to what can be used elsewhere. (There are also two *una corda* instructions, which are certainly not the only places soft pedal can be used.) The passage beginning at bar 94, for example, obviously requires long pedals to sustain the melody. At all times the performer should be controlling two simultaneous planes of sound: the articulated, toccata sound, which requires definition and precise touch control, and the background resonance, the orchestral sound, which is done with pedal. The one should never weaken the other. Without pedal the whole piece becomes percussive, dry, and all we hear are the hammers. With careful and often bold pedalling, the articulated sixteenths are enhanced, projected, but never at the expense of their definition; the harmony is enriched, and the inherent lyricism of the piece comes to the fore.

A careful observation of the indications for dynamics, accentuation and note lengths, as well as an awareness of the harmonic rhythm, will make all this very clear. So, for example, there will no pedal at the opening, perhaps a dab on the first-beat accents beginning at bar 5 (depending on the instrument and the acoustic) and then Ravel's first pedal mark underlines the harmonic rhythm, a single beat lasting two bars. No pedal is necessary for the passage beginning at bar 23, nor for its sequential development; but with the arrival of the more extended melodic line, D minor at bar 35, dabs of pedal can be introduced on the accented beats to help this melody resonate – and we can note too that this highlights the melodic shape by emphasising the implied quarter note.

Ravel gave a fine lesson in the art of orchestration and by implication the art of piano playing when he told a composition pupil: 'Instrumentation is when you take the music you or someone else has written and you find the right kind of instruments. . . . But orchestration is when you give a feeling of the two pedals at the piano: that means that you are building an atmosphere of sound *around* the music, around the notes – that's orchestration.' This is precisely what is needed in the Toccata, as much as in such pieces as *Jeux d'eau*, 'Une barque sur l'océan' and 'Ondine'. This is not to say that long, enveloping pedalling is the predominant manner for the Toccata – far from it. But confident orchestral pedalling is crucial for the climax and its build-up from bar 191: this is the point where Ravel underpins the sixteenths with reiterated pedal points – C-sharp, B, and arriving at E in bar 221 – which can be sustained with a mixture of whole and half pedals. The bass fifths at bars 234 and 236 can be given full pedals sustained for two bars, while the magnificent flattened dominant, B-flat, beginning at bar 238 can be treated in the same way. None of this gets in the way of the audibility of the 'staccato' sixteenth notes. The resolution onto E, a foreshadowing of the climax of *Boléro*, can be done, if the pianist so chooses, with a pedal lasting to the penultimate bar.

Finally, the melodic character at the fortissimo beginning at bar 221 should not be overlooked. This passage should not be hacked, but richly orchestrated and carefully phrased. It is, after all, a reorchestration of the tender melody at bar 57, but now tenderness has given way to the climax of passion.

Appendix B: The Sostenuto Pedal

On 16 January 1895 Ricardo Viñes recorded in his diary that he had received, as the prize for a competition he had won at the Conservatoire, a Pleyel grand with a third pedal – the sostenuto middle pedal. Much confusion surrounds this subject, not least because Ravel and Debussy never indicated the sostenuto pedal or mentioned it to anyone. Roy Howat, however, confirms that Viñes's new instrument was not an oddity, and he makes it clear that three-pedal instruments were known in Paris in the 1890s and that Ravel and Debussy (and of course Viñes) would certainly have played on them. We do not know the exact model of the new Steinway Madame de Saint-Marceaux bought in 1896, on which many great pianists and composers were invited to play, but considering the prestige as well as the size of her salon, it is unlikely this would have been smaller than a model A (six feet three inches). Three pedals were standard at that time on New York and Hamburg Steinways on all pianos from the model A upwards. The French piano makers Boisselot, Debain and Montal had invented the system – not Pleyel (as Viñes assumed), who had copied it. Steinway had perfected its own system in 1874.

The actual practice and expectations of composers regarding this pedal are far from clear, however. If it was so important a device, if it was regarded as an exciting and versatile new technology, why was it not indicated on the score? Why do we get so exercised by the instructions regarding tempi, articulation and dynamics and not ask ourselves why the ever-meticulous Ravel failed to insist on sostenuto pedal in, say, the Épilogue of *Valses nobles et sentimentales*, or the last bar of the Menuet from the Sonatine? But then Ravel gave very few indications for any kind of pedalling anyway, apart from some markings for held chords, often in final bars, and a few for *una corda*. (Debussy gave even fewer.) We have already noted the illogicality of Ravel's pedal instructions for the *Pavane*. The only unambiguous instruction would be for a composer to indicate *pas de pédale*, and Ravel never does that.

The answer can only be that it didn't much matter. I don't mean that the composers didn't care – far from it; rather, they understood a tradition of pedal technique stretching back to Chopin in which continual use of the pedal – swathes, minute alternations, half pedals, flutter pedals – was integral to the pianist's art and almost impossible to indicate. Debussy described the pedalling of the aged Liszt, whom he heard as a student in Rome, as 'a kind of *breathing*' – and he even suggested that it ought to be possible to indicate it on the score. But he never did. Viñes mentions that Ravel wanted the upper register of *Jeux d'eau* to have long pedals, but the composer does not indicate it. The well-known instruction at the head of 'Une barque sur l'océan', 'très enveloppé de pédales', is an exception, but it is not the only place in Ravel's piano music where such an instruction would be appropriate, and it is certainly not an instruction for the performer to hold the pedal down continually. It is sometimes suggested that Poulenc loved bathing his own playing in pedal because he had been a pupil of Viñes, who to some (but not to Debussy) was the master of bold pedal techniques. But my instinct is that this had as much to do with the nature of Poulenc – the character of his harmonies, his ear for rich colours – as it had to do with Viñes. (Poulenc would surely have agreed with his contemporary, the pianist Walter Gieseking, who said his own performances evolved 'from the self-evident necessity . . . to play the piano so that it sounds beautiful.')

The final bar of the Sonatine's Menuet, that moment that Ravel loved playing to Henriette Faure, provides an interesting case for examining sostenuto pedal. It is easier to execute with sostenuto, but when Hélène Jourdan-Morhange asked Perlemuter, 'How do you manage not to blur the harmonies while holding the pedal?' he replied:

> You have drawn attention here to something that's as essential for Ravel's music as it is for Debussy's. This is the light fluttering of the foot, which, when it works, enables you to hold the bass and glide the dissonant harmonies across it. They gently fade, leaving the bass note sounding to the end.

So why no mention from Perlemuter, 'one of the keepers of the Ravel doctrine,' of the sostenuto middle pedal? The technique he describes is actually a fundamental pedal technique, and hardly more important for Debussy and Ravel than it is for Schumann, Chopin or Liszt. (Schumann's own piano playing was characterised by a markedly free pedal technique. 'The phrases swam into each other,' recalled a contemporary; 'not really piano playing, but more a ghostly gliding and weaving.')

So the conclusion has to be that Ravel, who would certainly have known Viñes's three-pedal instrument, recognised that the sostenuto pedal could be put to use in various places, but also that the effect could be achieved in other ways. (The majority of pianos would not have had such a pedal.) It is odd, then, to read the recollection of Abram Chasins, another pianist who played for Ravel:

> Ravel, in response to certain pedal effects I had devised for his exquisite Sonatine, exclaimed, 'Why didn't someone show me that such effects were possible with a sustaining pedal? How many more possibilities it would have suggested to me.' . . . Ravel had never before encountered a sostenuto pedal. The effects I showed him

might have been my own inventions, for they did indeed use all three pedals, but primarily the simultaneous depression of both the sostenuto and soft pedal with the foot angled to accomplish that.

But we know Ravel *had* encountered a sostenuto pedal. It is certainly possible, with practice (and 'with the foot angled'), to operate *una corda* and the middle pedal simultaneously, but what are we to make of the rest of the memoir? If we remove the comment about Ravel's not having encountered this pedal, then perhaps it makes more sense: what he had not realised was that *the soft pedal and the middle pedal could be depressed simultaneously.* In *Valses nobles*, as Howat has pointed out, Ravel appears to have conveniently marked the places where the middle pedal is needed as '3 cordes', thus liberating the left foot in order to operate it. (However, it is important to note that this is not an actual instruction for middle pedal, simply an instruction not to use the *una corda*.) Chasins mistook Ravel's remark and assumed he knew nothing of the middle pedal – which has remained a common misconception ever since.

Again we are in the presence of one of those familiar inconsistencies of memory and historical reconstruction. The explanation must be that, because Ravel had no way of demonstrating the *sostenuto* mechanism to Faure and Perlemuter on his own piano, he simply left it alone and reverted to traditional pedal practice as Perlemuter has described it. He accepted that the effects he wanted could be achieved (possibly better achieved, in terms of subtle overlapping colouration) without it. Who would otherwise dare suggest that this master of scrupulous, painstaking techniques had, in the 1920s, forgotten about it altogether?

Appendix C: Ravel's Literary Sources: Fargue, Bertrand and Régnier

Translations by Paul Roberts and Jenny Gilbert

Léon-Paul Fargue: From *Poèmes* (1912)

'THE LITTLE STATION OF FLEETING SHADOWS'

The little station of fleeting shadows, weary at five o'clock. Like a reflection of the sky glancing off tall grasses, the rails, where blue eyes are fleeing, go in search of travellers' red-eye: the brief, muffled tremble of a train emerges from the depths of the heavens.

A ray gilds the exit gate, on the path that turns left, and this large bloom like the hand of a sleeping child. The bus for the Hotel of Little Hell awaits. The stagecoach waits further off, on the blue pathway, under the lime trees.

Marie is dead, but Myrtis's eyes are dreaming in the trees.

An engine, worn out with black, hollow coughing, stands silent. Everything stops and dreams. As before.

Old things yawn, recognize the hour, and go back to sleep. In the sheds the night moths take off, in awkward flight, and circle around other beams. A bird sings, in a questioning tone, from beside the track where night comes, near the water tank, over the tinkling flowerbeds, over the listening flowers, in the tree swollen with shadow, which already contains the whole of the evening.

Friend, you are sad. A lamp browns in a window opposite. A voice cools on the road. A bridle ring clinks, the sound of horses' boredom. Particular memories strike up, uncertainly, like a chorus of shy children.

Oh do not dream. Keep watch over these distant scenes, soft as sobbing, until the curve of dawn, towards the Délivrandes,* where we will suffer again.

'La petite gare aux ombres courtes'

La petite gare aux ombres courtes, lasse de cinq heures. – Comme un reflet du ciel au fil de hautes herbes, les rails, où fuient des yeux bleus, vont chercher les yeux roux des voyages: Le tremblement bref et sourd d'un train qui sort du bas du ciel . . .

Un rayon dore la barrière de sortie, sur le sentier qui tourne, et cette grosse fleur, à gauche, comme une main d'enfant qui dort. La voiture de l'Hôtel du Petit-Enfer attend. – La diligence attendra plus loin, dans l'allée bleue, sous les tilleuls.

Translators' note: Our Lady of Délivrande is the prominent saint of the lower Normandy region, a region of France famous for its statues of black madonnas. Douvre-la-Délivrande is a town on the Normandy coast, and may have been the ultimate destination of the railway. Fargue's reference, in the plural, refers to the statues.

Marie est morte, mais les yeux de Myrtis rêvent dans les arbres . . .

Une machine qui s'exténue d'une toux cave et noire – de se taire. Tout s'arrête et songe. Comme naguère.

Les vieilles choses qui sont là bâillent, reconnaissent l'heure et se rendorment. Les noctuelles des hangars partent, d'un vol gauche, cravater d'autres poutres. Un oiseau chante, sur un ton de question, du côté de la voie où la nuit vient, près du réservoir, au-dessus du parterre aux sonneries légères, au-dessus des fleurs qui prêtent l'oreille, dans l'arbre gonfle d'ombre et qui contient déjà tout le soir . . .

Ami, tu es triste. Une lampe brunit quelque vitre, en face . . . Une voix fraîchit sur la route. Un anneau tinte. – Un bruit de chevaux s'ennuie. – Certains souvenirs se prennent à chanter, d'une voix mal assurée, comme un chœur d'enfants timides . . .

Oh ne songe pas. Veille – et rejoins sur la courbe – enfin – ces lointains, doux comme un sanglot, vers les Délivrandes ou nous souffrirons encore . . .

Aloysius Bertrand: Three Poems from *Gaspard de la nuit* (1842)

'ONDINE'

> *. . . I thought I heard*
> *a vague harmony that cast a spell over my sleep,*
> *and near me a murmuring*
> *like fragments of song from a sad and tender voice.*
>
> Charles Brugnot, *The Two Genies*

'Listen! Listen! It is I, Ondine, who brushes with these water drop-lets the resonant diamond panes of your window, lit by the dull glow of the moon; and here, in a robe of shimmering silk, is the lady of the castle who, from her balcony, gazes out at the beautiful starry night and the beautiful sleeping lake.

'Each eddy is a water-sprite swimming in the current, each current is a path that meanders toward my palace, and my palace is a fluid structure, in the depths of the lake, in the place where fire, earth and water meet.

'Listen! – Listen! – My father whips up the croaking waters with a branch of green alder, and my sisters caress with arms of spray the cool islands of grass, water lily and iris, or mock the bearded willow as he trails his fishing line.'

Ceasing her murmured song, she begged me to put her ring on my finger, to become the husband of a mermaid, and descend with her to her palace to be king of the lakes.

And when I told her that I was in love with a mortal woman, she flew into an angry sulk, shed a few tears, let out a peal of laughter, then vanished in a sudden shower which streamed in pale rivulets down my blue window panes.

'Ondine'

Je croyais entendre
Une vague harmonie enchanter mon sommeil,
Et près de moi s'épandre un murmure pareil
Aux chants entrecoupés d'une voix triste et tendre.

Ch. Brugnot, *Les deux génies*

'Ecoute! – Ecoute! – C'est moi, c'est Ondine qui frôle de ces gouttes d'eau les losanges sonores de ta fenêtre illuminée par les mornes rayons de la lune; et voici, en robe de moire, la dame châtelaine qui contemple à son balcon la belle nuit étoilée et le beau lac endormi.

'Chaque flot est un ondin qui nage dans le courant, chaque courant est un sentier qui serpente vers mon palais, et mon palais est bâti fluide, au fond du lac, dans le triangle du feu, de la terre et de l'air.

'Écoute! – Écoute! – Mon père bat l'eau coassante d'une branche d'aulne verte, et mes sœurs caressent de leurs bras d'écume les fraîches îles d'herbes, de nénuphars et de glaïeuls, ou se moquent du saule caduc et barbu du pêche à la ligne.'

Sa chanson murmurée, elle me supplia de recevoir son anneau à mon doigt, pour être l'époux d'une Ondine, et de visiter avec elle son palais, pour être le roi des lacs.

Et comme je lui répondais que j'aimais une mortelle, boudeuse et dépitée, elle pleura quelques larmes, poussa un éclat de rire, et s'évanouit en giboulées qui ruisselèrent blanches le long de mes vitraux bleus.

'The Gibbet'

> *What is it that I see stirring around that gibbet?*
>
> Faust

Ah! And is that the north wind I hear, shrieking in the night, or is it the hanged man uttering a sigh from the gallows?

Could it be the singing cricket hidden in the moss and sterile ivy that clads the wooden struts out of pity?

Could it be a blowfly sounding its hunting horn around ears deaf to the bugle that signalled the kill?

Could it be a dung-beetle plucking, in its stumbling flight, a single bloody hair from the bald pate?

Or might it even be a spider embroidering a length of muslin as a scarf for that strangled neck?

It is the bell that sounds from the walls of a town beyond the horizon and the carcass of a hanged man reddening in the setting sun.

'Le gibet'

Que vois-je remuer autour de ce Gibet?

Faust

Ah! ce que j'entends, serait-ce la bise nocturne qui glapit, ou le pendu qui pousse un soupir sur la fourche patibulaire?

Serait-ce quelque grillon qui chante tapi dans la mousse et le lierre stérile dont par pitié se chausse le bois?

Serait-ce quelque mouche en chasse sonnant du cor autour de ces oreilles sourdes à la fanfare des hallali?

Serait-ce quelque escarbot qui cueille en son vol inégal un cheveu sanglant à son crâne chauve?

Ou bien serait-ce quelque araignée qui brode une demi aune de mousseline pour cravate à ce col étranglé?

C'est la cloche qui tinte aux murs d'une ville, sous l'horizon, et la carcasse d'un pendu que rougit le soleil couchant.

'Scarbo'

> *He looked under the bed, in the fireplace, in the cupboard – no one. He could not understand where it had got in, or how it had got out.*
>
> E. T. A. Hoffmann, *Night Stories*

Oh, how often have I heard him and seen him, Scarbo, at midnight when the moon shines in the sky like a silver shield set on an azure banner scattered with golden bees.

How often have I heard the buzz of his laughter in the shadows of my alcove, scraping his fingernail down the silk drapes around my bed.

How often have I seen him drop to the floor, pirouette on one foot and tumble around the room like the fallen spindle from a witch's distaff.

Did I think he had simply vanished? The dwarf would then rise up between myself and the moon, like the spire of a Gothic cathedral, with a little gold bell bobbing on his pointed hat.

But soon his body would take on a bluish tinge, diaphanous as candle wax, and his face would turn pale like the last glimmer of a candle-end – and suddenly he would snuff himself out.

'Scarbo'

Il regarda sous le lit, dans la cheminée, dans le bahut; –
personne. Il ne put comprendre par où il s'était introduit, par
où il s'était évadé.

E. T. A. Hoffmann, *Contes nocturnes*

Oh! que de fois je l'ai entendu et vu, Scarbo, lorsqu'à minuit la lune brille dans le ciel comme un écu d'argent sur une bannière d'azur semée d'abeilles d'or!

Que de fois j'ai entendu bourdonner son rire dans l'ombre de mon alcôve, et grincer son ongle sur la soie des courtines de mon lit!

Que de fois je l'ai vu descendre du plancher, pirouetter sur un pied et rouler par la chambre comme le fuseau tombe de la quenouille d'une sorcière!

Le croyais-je alors évanoui? le nain grandissait entre la lune et moi comme le clocher d'une cathédrale gothique, un grelot d'or en branle a son bonnet pointu!

Mais bientôt son corps bleuissait, diaphane comme la cire d'une bougie, son visage blêmissait comme la cire d'un lumignon, – et soudain il s'éteignait.

Henri de Régnier: From *La cité des eaux* (1902)

'FOUNTAIN'

The dolphin, the sea snail and the fat frog
Spangled with spume and with naked Leto's gold,
Sea goddess riding the turtle's back,
Laughing river god tickled by the water

The bowl overflowing, the soaking spray,
Surface shrinking, swelling, subsiding,
Wet particles render the statue iridescent
Turn its moss into pearls and brighten the rust.

The entire sparkling, watery celebration
of churning, chuckling, scattering and frothing
is stilled by evening in the enchanted park;
And in the silence, near the basin
returned to glassy stillness, now burst forth
Fountains of yew and jets of cypress.

'FÊTE D'EAU'

Le dauphin, le triton et l'obèse grenouille
Diamantant d'écume et d'or Latone nue,
Divinité marine au dos de la tortue,
Dieu fluvial riant de l'eau qui le chatouille;

La vasque qui retombe ou la gerbe qui mouille,
La nappe qui décroît, se gonfle ou diminue,

Et la poussière humide irisant la statue
Dont s'emperle la mousse ou s'avive la rouille;

Toute la fête d'eau, de cristal et de joie
Qui s'entrecroise, rit, s'éparpille et poudroie,
Dans le parc enchanté s'est tue avec le soir;

Et parmi le silence on voit jaillir, auprès
Du tranquille bassin redevenu miroir,
La fontaine de l'if et le jet du cyprès.

Notes

Translations from the French sources are my own unless otherwise stated.

Epigraphs

xv   *'I don't ask for my music'*: Ravel, in Henriette Faure, *Mon maître Maurice Ravel* (Paris: ATP, 1978), p. 70 ('Je ne demande pas qu'on interprète ma musique, mais qu'on la joue').

xv   *'If there is any trouble with interpretation'*: Ernest Krenek, *Exploring Music*, trans. Margaret Shenfield and Geoffrey Skelton (London: Caldar & Boyars, 1966), p. 180.

xv   *'There are no interpretations, only misinterpretations'*: Harold Bloom, *The Anxiety of Influence: A Theory of Poetry*, 2nd ed. (Oxford: Oxford University Press, 1997), p. 95.

xv   *'European music is founded on'*: Milan Kundera, *Encounter*, trans. Linda Asher (uncorrected proof) (New York: HarperCollins, 2009), p. 78.

Introduction

2   *Viñes . . . it might be argued*: see Elaine Brody, 'Viñes in Paris: New Light on Twentieth-Century Performance Practice', in *A Musical Offering: Essays in Honor of Martin Bernstein*, ed.

Edward H. Clinkscale and Claire Brook (New York: Pendragon Press, 1977), pp. 45–62.

2 *'The eye sees not itself'*: Ravel, in Arbie Orenstein (ed.), *Maurice Ravel: Lettres, écrits, entretiens* (Paris: Flammarion, 1989), p. 489. The quotation is from William Shakespeare, *Julius Caesar*, Act 1, Scene 2, lines 52–3.

3 *'the inmost essence of music itself'*: Krenek, p. 140.

4 *'The interpreter'*: ibid., p. 182.

4 *'I think and I feel'*: From Jules Renard, *Journal*, reproduced in Orenstein, *Maurice Ravel: Lettres, écrits, entretiens*, p. 489 n. 18. The full context is: '[I want] to say with music what you say with words, when, for example, you are standing before a tree. I think and I feel in music and I would like to think and feel the same things as you' ('Dire avec de la musique ce que vous dites avec des mots quand vous êtes devant un arbre, par exemple. Je pense et je sens en musique et je voudrais penser et sentir les mêmes choses que vous').

5 *'I don't have ideas'*: in Roger Nichols, *Ravel Remembered* (London: Faber, 1987), p. 55.

5 *'the mysterious, whether seen as inspiration'*: G. W. Hopkins, '(Joseph) Maurice Ravel', in *The New Grove Dictionary of Music and Musicians*, ed. Stanley Sadie (London and New York: Macmillan, 1980), 15:615.

6 *I have found her record*: Faure's book, *Mon maître Maurice Ravel*, has never been translated into English. Perlemuter's book is a transcript of a broadcast he did for French radio in 1950 along with a recording of the complete piano music: in the usual manner that survives to this day on *France musique*, the performances were accompanied by extensive interviews and discussion. The interviewer had been one of Ravel's closest friends, the violinist Hélène Jourdan-Morhange, who wove into the discussion extracts from her book of reminiscences *Ravel et nous* (1945).

6   *'Basic Principles of a New Theory'*: Krenek, pp. 129–49.

7   *'It is the thought's inherent need'*: ibid., p. 142.

7   *'there cannot be any doubt'*: ibid., p. 140.

7   *The musical thought is subordinate to the idea*: ibid., p. 141.

7   *'thought-gestalt'*: ibid. 'The musical *Gestalt* is the way the thought manifests itself in musical material. . . . The thought is identical with its Gestalt, each can replace the other.'

7   *Krenek insists that we are dealing*: ibid., pp. 138–9.

8   *'Your fountains are sad'*: Ravel, in Faure, p. 95 ('Vos Jeux d'eau ils sont tristes. On dirait que vous n'aviez pas lu le sous-titre d'Henri de Régnier'). Ravel did, however, also use the term 'epigraph.' See note for *'he wanted it published in the programme'*, chapter 2, p. 27.

8   *'Performers must not be slaves'*: in Marguerite Long, *At the Piano with Ravel*, trans. Olive Senior-Ellis (London: J. M. Dent, 1973), p. 59.

Chapter 1

11   *'Ravel's concern with perfecting'*: Léon-Paul Fargue, 'Autour de Ravel', in Colette et al., *Maurice Ravel par quelques-uns de ses familiers* (Paris: Éditions du Tambourinaire, 1939), p. 160.

11   *'In my childhood I had'*: Ravel, in Orenstein, *Maurice Ravel: Lettres, écrits, entretiens*, p. 355.

12   *'folk tunes of the usual Spanish-Arabian kind'*: Ravel, in Arbie Orenstein (ed.), *A Ravel Reader: Correspondence, Articles, Interviews* (New York: Columbia University Press, 1990), p. 477.

12   *'musico-sexual'*: Ravel, in Benjamin Ivry, *Maurice Ravel: A Life* (New York: Welcome Rain, 2000), p. 157.

12   *'a tiny man, delicate, with a matte complexion'*: André Suarès, in Nichols, *Ravel Remembered*, p. 29.

13   'shut himself up': Long, p. 118.

13   'Ravel exhibited a well-honed distinction': Steven Huebner, 'Maurice Ravel: Private Life, Public Works', in *Musical Biography: Towards New Paradigms*, ed. Jolanta T. Pekacz (Aldershot: Ashgate, 2006), p. 70.

13   'the emotional world of the subject': ibid.

13   'His music only occupied him': Roland-Manuel, *À la gloire de Ravel* (Paris: Nouvelle Revue Critique, 1938), p. 248.

14   'One of the most striking': Fargue, 'Autour de Ravel', p. 160.

14   'it would bore the public': Ravel, letter to Calvocoressi, 24 March 1922; in Orenstein, *Maurice Ravel: Lettres, écrits, entretiens*, p. 197.

14   'I don't ask for my music': Ravel, in Faure, p. 70.

14   'a complete indifference': Arthur Rubinstein, in Ivry, p. 41. For Ravel's friendship with Rubinstein see also Orenstein, *A Ravel Reader*, p. 585. To judge from his recordings, Rubinstein was a superb interpreter of Ravel, though he recorded only the Forlane from *Le tombeau*, *Valses nobles* and 'La vallée des cloches'.

14   'best friends could not help': Roland-Manuel, *À la gloire de Ravel*, p. 237.

15   'a curious discretion': Roland-Manuel, in Orenstein, *A Ravel Reader*, p. 271 n. 8.

16   *Manuel Rosenthal claimed that*: Marcel Marnat, *Maurice Ravel* (Paris: Fayard, 1986), pp. 464–5.

16   *as the critic Hans-Heinz Stuckenschmidt believed to be the case*: Hans-Heinz Stuckenschmidt, *Maurice Ravel: Variations on his Life and Work*, trans. S. R. Rosenbaum (London: Calder & Boyars, 1969), p. 105.

16   'Ravel was in a very gay, carefree mood': Marcelle Gerar, in Nichols, *Ravel Remembered*, p. 133.

16 *'He has in him a mixture'*: diary entry for 1 November 1896; Ricardo Viñes, 'La vie musicale à Paris entre 1887 et 1914 à travers le journal de R. Viñes', trans. and ed. Nina Gubisch, *Revue international de musique française* 1, no, 2 (June 1980), p. 191.

16 *'His complex, even contradictory character'*: Viñes, in Nichols, *Ravel Remembered*, p. 37.

16 *Ravel once observed*: Ravel, in Roland-Manuel, *À la gloire de Ravel*, p. 254. 'It's lucky I became a composer because I truly believe I would never have succeeded at anything else.'

17 *'lose himself in the anonymity'*: Louis Aubert, in Nichols, *Ravel Remembered*, p. 11.

17 *'Poetry is not a turning loose'*: T. S. Eliot, 'Tradition and the Individual Talent', in *T. S. Eliot: Selected Prose*, ed. John Hayward (London: Penguin Books, 1953), p. 30.

17 *'each one of you'*: Roland-Manuel, *À la gloire de Ravel*, p. 250.

17 *'a little thing [for] Ida Rubinstein'*: in Nichols, *Ravel Remembered*, p. 48.

17 *'Bravo Ravel, a triumph!'*: Ravel, in Madeleine Goss, *Bolero: The Life of Maurice Ravel* (New York: Holt, 1940), p. 239.

17 *'the more perfect the artist'*: Eliot, p. 27.

18 *'is obsessed by his creative work'*: Ravel, in Orenstein, *A Ravel Reader*, p. 17.

18 *'Everything must be done'*: Roland-Manuel, *À la gloire de Ravel*, p. 249.

18 *'But does the idea never occur'*: Ravel, in Michel Dmitri Calvocoressi, *Music and Ballet* (London: Faber, 1934), p. 51.

18 *'I know that a conscious artist'*: Ravel, in Orenstein, *A Ravel Reader*, p. 395.

19 *'trembled convulsively'*: diary entry for 1 November 1896; Viñes, p. 190.

19 *'The greatest of all dangers'*: Ravel, in Nichols, *Ravel Remembe-red*, p. 108.

19 *'technical perfection – I can strive'*: Ravel, in Orenstein, *Maurice Ravel: Lettres, écrits, entretiens*, p. 47.

19 *'The creation of a work of art'*: Eliot, letter to *The Athenaeum* (25 June 1920), cited in Bernard Bergonzi, *T. S. Eliot* (London: Macmillan, 1972), pp. 66–7.

Chapter 2

21 *'The butterfly wings of this piece'*: Claude Debussy, letter to Jacques Durand, 27 September 1917; in *Claude Debussy: Correspondance, 1872–1918*, ed. François Lesure and Denis Herlin, annot. François Lesure, Denis Herlin and Georges Liébert (Paris: Gallimard, 2005), p. 2151.

21 *'The man is prodigious'*: ibid.

22 *'from a* purely pianistic *point of view'*: Ravel, letter to Pierre Lalo, 5 February 1906; in Orenstein, *A Ravel Reader*, p. 79.

22 *'the origin of all the pianistic innovations'*: ibid., p. 44.

22 *'I very much want to write'*: Ravel, in Roland-Manuel, *À la gloire de Ravel*, p. 65 ('Je voudrais bien faire quelque chose qui me libérât des *Jeux d'eau*').

22 *'to hear* Jeux d'eau *well-played'*: Roger Nichols, *Ravel* (London: J. M. Dent, 1977), p. 19.

23 *'The Debussyan manner'*: Émile Vuillermoz, in Roland-Manuel, *À la gloire de Ravel*, pp. 218–19.

23 *So began the restrictive attitude*: Hence Hélène Jourdan-Morhange could call the great pianist Vlado Perlemuter (1904–2002) 'one of the keepers of the Ravel doctrine': Vlado Perlemuter and Hélène Jourdan-Morhange, *Ravel d'après Ra-*

vel: Les œuvres pour piano, les deux concertos, 5th edn (Lausanne: Éditions du Cervin, 1970), p. 8.

23 *'One cannot expect a pianist's confession'*: Roland-Manuel, *À la gloire de Ravel*, p. 219. Vuillermoz, on the other hand, diagnosed quite the opposite: 'For Ravel the piano held the key to a whole world of dreams. In communing with it the artist, I would suggest, is at confession, the piano is his instrument-confessor' ('Le clavier fut pour Ravel la clef de tout un mondes de rêves. Le piano est . . . ce qu'on appeler un instrument confesseur. C'est en tête à-tête aven lui qu'un artiste entre, si j'ose dire, dans la voie des aveux'). Émile Vuillermoz, 'L'œuvre de Maurice Ravel', in Colette et al., *Maurice Ravel par quelques-uns de ses familiers* (Paris: Éditions du Tambourinaire, 1939), p. 16.

23 *'One must not expect from Ravel'*: Roland-Manuel, *Maurice Ravel*, trans. Cynthia Jolly (London: Dobson, 1947), pp. 137–8. The French is even more purple in its expression ('Ce n'est pas à Ravel qu'il faut demander des oeuvres où le sentiment s'exagère sans cesse dans la véhémence de son expression. Ce n'est pas à Ravel qu'il faut demander de remuer le marais de la concupiscence [literally, 'the marshes of libidinous appetite'] ou d'ouvrir volontairement les abîmes de désespoir'). Roland-Manuel, *À la gloire de Ravel*, p. 256.

24 *We learn from Demuth*: Norman Demuth, *Ravel* (New York: Collier Books, 1962), p. 73.

24 *'worthy to rank with'*: ibid., p. 32.

24 *'In his own country'*: ibid., pp. 1 and 206.

24 *'vast frescoes and symphonies'*: ibid.

24 *'not very appealing musically'*: ibid. pp. 80–1.

25 *'is not an extra specialized one'*: ibid., p. 199–200.

25 *'it was the ways in which Ravel'*: Roger Nichols, 'Ravel and the Twentieth Century', in *The Cambridge Companion to Ravel*, ed.

Deborah Mawer (Cambridge: Cambridge University Press, 2000), p. 240.

25   *'Why, like Liszt of course'*: Ravel, in Nichols, *Ravel*, p. 16. Nichols does not give the origin of this remark, and I have not found it elsewhere.

27   *Régnier's* La cité des eaux *came out in 1902*: Régnier's contemporary, the psychologist and literary critic Havelock Ellis, made an inadvertently significant remark in relation to the poet's abiding interest in water imagery: 'All his life, one can well believe, the visionary music that has beckoned Henri de Régnier through the world is a creature of fountains and streams, a wayward and lovely Undine who has scarcely yet acquired a soul.' One wonders whether Ravel too divined this of Régnier – one of many paths to 'Ondine' – and whether at some level Ellis might have arrived at his image through connecting Régnier with Ravel. Henry Havelock Ellis, 'Henri de Régnier', *North American Review* 201, no. 712 (March 1915), p. 413.

27   *The quotation – which appears*: Roger Nichols, preface to Ravel, *Jeux d'eau*, Peters Urtext No. 7373, ed. Roger Nichols (London: Peters, 1994), p. 5.

27   *As Roger Nichols has pointed out*: ibid.

27   *he wanted it published in the programme*: The *Pavane* and *Jeux d'eau* were given their first public performance in early April 1902 by Ricardo Viñes. A few days before the concert Ravel wrote to his publisher, Eugène Demets, 'I would be most grateful, only however if there is still the time, if you would not omit from the program the epigraph to the second piece: *Dieu fluvial riant de l'eau qui le chatouille* (H. de Régnier).' Ravel, letter to Eugène Demets, 31 March 1902; in Orenstein, *Maurice Ravel: Lettres, écrits, entretiens*, p. 67.

30 *'who recommended using pedal'*: Viñes, in Hélène Jourdan-Morhange, *Ravel et nous: L'homme, l'ami, le musicien* (Geneva: Éditions du milieu du monde, 1945), p. 215.

32 *'One evening Maurice Ravel'*: Fargue, 'Autour de Ravel', p. 155.

32 *Roger Woodley has shown*: Roger Woodley, 'Performing Ravel: Style and Practice in the Early Recordings', in *The Cambridge Companion to Ravel*, p. 224.

32 *'His long, narrow, bony hands'*: Fargue, *Maurice Ravel*, p. 28.

32 *'never played it in his life'*: Ravel, in Demuth, p. 203.

33 *'The sense of an extended improvisation'*: Woodley, p. 226. The live 1960 recording of *Jeux d'eau* by Sviatoslav Richter (RCA #LSC-2611) is considerably faster than Cortot's.

33 *'the sound of water, the musical sounds'*: Ravel, in Orenstein, *Maurice Ravel: Lettres, écrits, entretiens*, p. 44.

34 *'I consider the music of Java'*: ibid., pp. 361–2.

35 *'their clanking and roaring'*: ibid., p. 355.

Chapter 3

37 *'We had more or less'*: Fargue, *Maurice Ravel*, p. 57.

38 *'I met Ravel in 1898'*: Jane Bathori, in Nichols, *Ravel Remembered*, p. 11.

38 *'To Maurice Ravel, in friendship'*: Debussy, *Correspondance, 1872–1918*, p. 2226.

38 *'Welcome home! my dear friend'*: Debussy, letter to Ravel, 17 June 1901, in ibid., p. 601.

39 *'Dear friend, I have just heard from Bardac'*: Debussy, letter to Ravel, 4 March 1904, in ibid., pp. 830–1.

39 *'In the name of the gods'*: Maurice Delage, 'Les premiers amis de Ravel', in Colette et al., *Maurice Ravel par quelques-uns de ses familiers* (Paris: Éditions du Tambourinaire, 1939), p. 100

('Au nom des dieux de la Musique et au mien, ne changez rien à votre quatuor').

39 *'Ravel was there, and we left together'*: diary entry for 30 November 1901; Viñes, p. 199.

40 *'Like Debussy, to whom'*: Manuel Rosenthal, in *Ravel: Souvenirs de Manuel Rosenthal*, ed. Marcel Marnat (Paris: Hazan, 1995), p. 36.

41 *'Debussy told him'*: Roland-Manuel, *À la gloire de Ravel*, p. 65.

41 *'admitted that the music'*: ibid.

41 *It was at this point*: ibid.

41 *Ravel later claimed this piece*: ibid., p. 66.

42 *'[When] a listener hears a succession'*: Calvocoressi, in Roland-Manuel, *À la gloire de Ravel*, p. 75.

42 *'At 3 in the afternoon'*: diary entry for 3 February 1906; Viñes, p. 229.

43 *'Ravel arrives one evening'*: Delage, pp. 102–3.

43 *'Ravel revealed his new piano piece'*: diary entry for 11 October 1904; Viñes, p. 203.

43 *'Only once in those early days'*: Calvocoressi, p. 66.

43 *'The title Miroirs, five piano pieces'*: Ravel, in Orenstein, *A Ravel Reader*, p. 35 n. 17.

44 *'impressionism, symbolism . . . useful terms of abuse'*: Claude Debussy, *Debussy on Music: The Critical Writings of the Great French Composer*, ed. François Lesure and R. Langham Smith, trans. R. Langham Smith (London: Secker & Warburg, 1977), p. 48. The terms 'impressionism' and 'symbolism' are largely interchangeable in relation to Debussy's and Ravel's descriptive music. Any attempt to distinguish them is fraught with difficulties, as in Jourdan-Morhange's assertion that in *Miroirs* 'each image is vividly and firmly drawn; straightforward painting that's a long way away from Debussyan symbolism' (Perlemuter and Jourdan-Morhange,

Ravel d'après Ravel, p. 22). While the descriptive music of these two composers is distinctly, even radically different, it is hard to see how this attempt to define the difference makes any headway. To say that Debussy 'symbolises' while Ravel 'draws' and 'paints' gets us nowhere at all. Jourdan-Morhange's terminology echoes Ravel's own in his lecture 'Contemporary Music': 'I myself have always followed a direction opposite to that of Debussy's symbolism' (Orenstein, *Ravel Reader*, p. 46), though in the same lecture he speaks of 'the symbolism of Debussy, his so-called impressionism.' I use the term 'impressionist' simply to refer to the descriptive intent of the music, though I am happier with the symbolist label because it is more historically accurate in the way it denotes the fecund symbolist milieu of the 1890s and the strong literary connections of both composers. This is Stephen Zank's position too, when he persists in calling *Miroirs* Ravel's 'symbolist' work, though he stirs the waters by quoting a recollection of Jacques Février's, to whom Ravel said: 'Do not play my music like Debussy. . . . The Impressionism of Debussy is one of fragrance, that of Ravel is visual.' Stephen Zank, *Irony and Sound: The Music of Maurice Ravel* (New York: University of Rochester Press, 2009), p. 257.

44 *'the universe is . . . a storehouse'*: Charles Baudelaire, *Baudelaire: Selected Writings on Art and Artists*, trans. P. E. Charvet (Cambridge: Cambridge University Press, 1972), p. 366.

45 *'new manner of writing'*: Pierre Lalo, in Orenstein, *A Ravel Reader*, 79–80 n. 1.

46 *'You dwell upon the fact'*: Ravel, letter to Pierre Lalo, 5 February 1906; Orenstein, *A Ravel Reader*, p. 79.

47 *'I was influenced by Debussy'*: ibid., p. 394.

48 *'The piano for us'*: Fargue, 'Autour de Ravel', p. 156.

48   *'through the imaginative influence'*: Émile Vuillermoz, in Louise Rypko Schub, *Léon-Paul Fargue* (Geneva: Librairie Droz, 1973), pp. 77–8.

48   *'I got to know Ravel'*: Fargue, *Maurice Ravel*, p. 52.

48   *'He was then known'*: Calvocoressi, p. 62.

49   *'melodies lurking in the air'*: Léon-Paul Fargue, 'Dans la rue qui monte au soleil', in *Poèmes; suivi de 'Pour la musique'* (Paris: Gallimard, 1919), p. 40.

49   *'a piano slowly ponders'*: ibid., p. 42. Peter Thomson, in his translation of Fargue's *Poèmes*, renders Fargue's line in the same way; Thomson, *An English Translation of Léon-Paul Fargue's Poèmes* (New York: Edwin Mellen Press, 2003), p. 27.

49   *'one of those friends'*: Jean Cocteau, in Schub, p. 157 n. 110 ('Il etait doux et féroce. Noctambule et lumineux').

49   *'The memory of one of his poems'*: Vuillermoz, p. 31.

49   *'La petite gare aux ombres courtes'*: Fargue, 'La petite gare aux ombres courtes', in *Poèmes*, p. 89.

50   *'With a few precise words'*: Vuillermoz, pp. 32–3.

50   *'weary at five o'clock'*: Fargue, 'La petite gare aux ombres courtes', in *Poèmes*, p. 89.

51   *A curious fact arises*: Schub, p. 88.

51   *'decided to avoid the horrors'*: ibid., pp. 88–9.

51   *'several friends, the dedicatees'*: ibid., p. 89.

52   *'We call for a moment's silence'*: Delage, p. 103.

52   *'flowers sprout out of chairs'*: Debussy, letter to Louis Laloy, 8 March 1907; in Debussy, *Correspondance, 1872–1918*, p. 999.

53   *'a raconteur . . . whose voice*: André Beucler, *Poet of Paris*, trans. Geoffrey Sainsbury (London: Chatto & Windus, 1955), p. 94.

54   *a precisely indicated decrescendo*: For an account of Ravel's characteristic dynamic inflections see the chapter 'Simple Sound: Ravel and "Crescendo"' in Zank, and especially his

identification of 'Ravel's rather peculiar reverse crescendo, p. 53.

55 *'straightforward painting'*: Jourdan-Morhange, in Perlemuter and Jourdan-Morhange, *Ravel d'après Ravel*, p. 22.

55 *'Everything stops and dreams'*: Fargue, 'La petite gare aux ombres courtes', in *Poèmes*, p. 89.

56 *'birds lost in the torpor'*: Ravel, in Orenstein, *Maurice Ravel: Lettres, écrits, entretiens*, p. 45.

56 *'One morning [he] was enchanted'*: Vuillermoz, p. 34.

57 *'A piano slowly ponders'*: Fargue, 'Dans la rue qui monte au soleil', in *Poèmes*, p. 42.

57 *'Fargue's every word carried authority'*: Vuillermoz, p. 32.

59 *The music tells us this without a doubt*: For Norman Demuth, however, the piece 'gives us a picture of a sunlit Mediterranean, in the afternoon; there is a breeze which ripples up the blue water. . . . The arpeggio writing smacks of the commonplace, but it comes off'; Demuth, p. 81.

59 *Henriette Faure misjudged*: Faure, p. 73.

59 *'a black gondola glides by'*: Aloysius Bertrand, 'Le soir sur l'eau', in *Gaspard de la nuit* (Paris: Le Livre de Poche, 2002), p. 218.

59 *'knowing from experience'*: Faure, pp. 23–4.

59 *'How seductive was this Paul Sordes!'*: Tristan Klingsor, 'L'époque Ravel', in Colette et al., *Maurice Ravel par quelques-uns de ses familiers* (Paris: Éditions du Tambourinaire, 1939), p. 128.

60 *'the inspirational Fargue'*: Vuillermoz, pp. 32–3.

60 *'he carried around everywhere'*: Marnat, *Maurice Ravel*, p. 181.

60 *'the reading [of scores] was done by Ravel'*: Calvocoressi, p. 55.

60 *'it was fun to inscribe'*: ibid., p. 66.

61 *'a cavalier and a lady'*: Bertrand, p. 218.

61 *'The stage is illuminated'*: Fargue, 'La rampe s'allume', in *Poèmes*, p. 80.

62 *'It begins to rain over the bay'*: Fargue, 'La mer phosphorescente perle entre les arbres', in *Poèmes*, pp. 97–8.

63 *'I understand your bafflement'*: Roger Nichols, preface to Ravel, *Miroirs*, Peters Urtext No. 7374, ed. Roger Nichols (London: Peters, 1995), p. 7.

64 *'Goya-like vision'*: Marnat, *Maurice Ravel*, p. 183. Marnat argues that Ravel, in turning Bertrand's *sérénade* into an *aubade*, was being characteristically mischievous.

64 *Faure remarked that*: Faure, p. 73.

64 *'the scalding rhythms of Castille'*: ibid., p. 74.

65 *'was a variant of the* bobo*'*: Enid Welsford, *The Fool: His Social and Literary History* (London: Faber, 1968), p. 279.

65 *Italian players travelled across Europe*: F. William Forbes, 'The 'Gracioso:'Toward a Functional Re-Evaluation', *Hispania*, Vol. 61, No. 1 (Mar., 1978), p. 79.

65 *'hold up a mirror to nature'*: Lope de Vega, *Two Plays by Lope de Vega: The Great Pretenders and The Gentleman from Olmedo*, trans. and adapted David Johnston, introd. Isabel Torres (Bath: Absolute Press), p. 10.

66 *'a subjectivist theory of art'*: Ravel, in Orenstein, *Maurice Ravel: Lettres, écrits, entretiens*, p. 489 n. 17.

66 *'a number of Ravel's friends'*: Ivry, p. 45.

66 *the* gracioso*'s role as a spoiler*: Janet Norden, 'Moreto's Polilla and the Spirit of Carnival', *Hispania* 68, no. 2 (May 1985), p. 237.

67 *'Polilla is a burlesque ruler'*: ibid., p. 239.

67 *'Polilla's play transcends fantasy'*: ibid., p. 240.

67 *'The mirrors which dominate'*: Torres, in Vega, pp. 11–12.

68 *'Art is the supreme imposture'*: Ravel, in Orenstein, *A Ravel Reader*, p. 395.

68 *'Good theatre'*: Torres, in Vega, p. 11.

69 *'the fascination of this music'*: Stuckenschmidt, p. 84.

70　*According to the pianist Robert Casadesus*: Marnat, *Maurice Ravel*, p. 184.

70　*We cannot know when*: I am indebted to Deborah Mawer's comments on Ravel's spatial awareness in her illuminating essay 'Musical Objects and Machines', in Mawer, *The Cambridge Companion to Ravel*, p. 50.

70　*The second of Schumann's* Drei Romanzen: John Worthen, *Robert Schumann: Life and Death of a Musician* (New Haven & London: Yale University Press, 2007), p. 179.

71　*'a new use of the piano'*: Stuckenschmidt, p. 85.

71　*'Though he was not a virtuoso'*: Faure, p. 80.

73　*'in one pour'*: Stuckenschmidt, p. 80.

Chapter 4

75　*'When I was working on "*Scarbo*"'*: Perlemuter and Jourdan-Morhange, *Ravel d'après Ravel*, p. 36.

75　*'A musician cannot move others'*: C. P. E. Bach, in Eva Badura-Skoda and Paul Badura-Skoda, *Interpreting Mozart on the Keyboard*, trans. Leo Black (London: Barrie & Rockliff, 1970), p. 1.

75　*'If an artist is to move others'*: Ferruccio Busoni, in ibid. Busoni is echoing a famous dictum of Diderot's concerning the objectivity of an actor on stage. Audiences, wrote Diderot in his *Paradoxe sur le comédien*, would be moved only if the actor remained unmoved, keeping 'a cool head, a profound judgement, [and] an exquisite taste – a matter for hard work, for long experience, for an uncommon tenacity of memory'; in Orenstein, *A Ravel Reader*, p. 455.

76　*'That flowing phrase!'*: Ravel, in Long, p. 41.

77   *'emotion recollected in tranquillity'*: William Wordsworth, 'Preface to Lyrical Ballads', in *William Wordsworth: Selected Poems*, ed. H. M. Margoliouth (London: Collins, 1966), p. 248.

78   *Faure tells us that Ravel expected*: Faure, p. 73.

79   *'It was while leafing through'*: Baudelaire, in John T. Wright, *Louis 'Aloysius' Bertrand's 'Gaspard de la nuit': Fantasies in the Manner of Rembrandt and Callot*, 2nd edn (Lanham, MD: University Press of America, 1994), n.p.

79   *Mallarmé related how*: Wright, n.p.

80   *'was extremely rare'*: diary entry for 12 November 1895; Viñes, p. 188.

80   *In his diary Viñes recorded*: diary entry for 10 August 1892; Viñes, p. 183.

80   *Viñes mentions the* Proses lyriques: diary entry for 24 September 1897; Viñes, p. 192.

80   *In September 1896 Viñes recorded*: diary entry for 25 September 1896; Viñes, p. 189.

80   *'He said he would bring it'*: diary entry for 19 December 1897; Viñes, p. 193.

80   *'take up Bertrand, for here is everything'*: Mallarmé, in Wright, n.p.

81   *'And when Maribas'*: Bertrand, 'Leaving for the Sabbath', in ibid., p. 31.

81   *'A deflated bagpipe whined'*: Bertrand, 'The Grand Companies', in ibid., p. 76.

82   *'Pity even the glow-worm'*: Bertrand, 'Rain', in ibid., p. 115.

82   *'The weathercocks cried'*: Bertrand, 'Roundelay Under the Bell', in ibid., p. 58.

82   *In fact there are two poems*: The first poem comes in 'La nuit et ses prestiges' (The Night and Its Marvels). It has the macabre qualities of 'Le gibet'. The first line runs: '"Whether you die absolved or damned," muttered Scarbo in my ear that night, "you will have a spider's web, for a shroud, and will bury the

spider with you!'" Bertrand, in ibid., p. 54. Bertrand had intended numerous illustrations for Gaspard, and his plans for these indicate that Scarbo is also the unnamed dwarf in the poem 'Le nain' (The Dwarf); Wright, p. 130.

82 *'one of those monstrous figures'*: 'Preface', in ibid., p. 9.

83 *'This manuscript will tell you'*: ibid., p. 11.

83 *'who communes with the spirits of beauty'*: ibid., p. 14.

84 *'Listen, listen!'*: 'Ondine', in Bertrand, p. 135.

84 *'plucking a single bloody hair'*: 'Le gibet', in ibid., p. 229.

85 *'Oh, how often have I'*: 'Scarbo', in ibid., p. 230.

86 *caricature romanticism*: Perlemuter and Jourdan-Morhange, *Ravel d'après Ravel*, p. 36.

86 *One wants to know about these things*: Not all opera librettos are, however, worthy of deep consideration. Claude Lévi-Strauss claims, 'There are few operas in which I feel the need to understand the words'; Claude Lévi-Strauss, *Look, Listen, Read*, trans. Brian C. J. Singer (New York: Harper Collins 1997), p. 117. His exceptions include *Carmen, Die Meistersinger* and *Pelléas*; and he is appalled by Colette's libretto of Ravel's *L'enfant et les sortilèges*.

86 *in* Gaspard de la nuit *Ravel's piano*: Charles Rosen, 'Where Ravel Ends and Debussy Begins', *Cahiers Debussy*, n.s. 3 (1979), p. 38. Rosen observes: 'Part of the pleasure in listening to Ravel is hearing an instrument sound unlike itself so effortlessly, and with such natural ease' (p. 37).

86 *Viñes tells us that Ravel wanted*: Jourdan-Morhange, *Ravel et nous*, p. 216.

87 *'murmurs her song'*: Bertrand, 'Ondine', p. 135.

87 *'bursts like a soap bubble'*: Vladimir Jankélévitch, *Ravel*, 2nd edn (Paris: Solfèges/Seuil, 1956), p. 82.

88 *leaving the sprite's voice*: Jankélévitch has suggested that such unadorned lines became characteristic of Ravel's later years,

after *Gaspard*, when he 'represses his taste for full, rich, vibrant sonorities' and so perpetuates 'this recitative of the soul, this solo song in the midst of silence'; Jankélévitch, *Ravel* (1956), pp. 52–3.

89 *He had an argument with Viñes over it*: Ravel, letter to Calvo-coressi, 24 March 1922; in Orenstein, *Maurice Ravel: Lettres, écrits, entretiens*, p. 197.

Chapter 5

91 *'It is at the piano that a poet of sound'*: Vuillermoz, p. 20.

91 *'I myself feel closer'*: Ravel, in Orenstein, *A Ravel Reader*, p. 488.

93 *though he performed in public*: The faults of Ravel's piano playing, especially in later life, are well attested, though it was not without its arresting qualities (see chapter 7). Stephen Zank has unearthed an amusing newspaper report of Ravel's visit to Chicago in 1928: 'Knowing the lovely, mystic, sensuous, glamorous music of his youth and his prime, it never would have occurred to me to discover anything sardonic in his nature had I not had the good fortune to hear him play piano. Only a supreme ironist would consent to play his own beautiful music in public as badly as Ravel plays it.' Glenn Dillard Gunn, in Norman V. Dunfee, Maurice Ravel in America – 1928', DMA diss., University of Missouri – Kansas City, 1980; quoted in Zank, p. 13.

94 *'Many people who would'*: Calvocoressi, p. 72.

94 *'favourable, or unfavourable'*: ibid., p. 70. Havelock Ellis, who knew well the milieu of 1890s Paris, diagnosed the characteristic Symbolist attitude towards the multitude in his assessment of Régnier: 'He has indeed no wish to thrust his vision of life upon us. He is the least insistent of fine artists, content to

assure us that he writes only to please himself.' Ellis, p. 420. This has considerable bearing on Ravel's aesthetic in *Valses nobles et sentimentales*, on the 'delicious pleasure' of his own 'useless occupation,' as well as on his apparent sang-froid in the face of criticism.

94 *'as many as possible'*: Ravel, letter to Émile Vuillermoz, 22 April 1910; in Orenstein, *Ravel Reader*, p. 113.

94 *'the protestations and boos'*: Ravel, in Orenstein, *Ravel Reader*, p. 31.

94 *'though stoic, he was'*: Vuillermoz, p. 45.

95 *it is significant that some*: Calvocoressi, p. 72.

95 *'the complicated harmonies'*: Roger Nichols, 'Early Reception of Ravel's Piano Music (1899–1939)', in *The Cambridge Companion to Ravel*, ed. Deborah Mawer (Cambridge: Cambridge University Press, 2000), p. 253.

95 *'a distinctly clearer writing'*: Ravel, in Orenstein, *Maurice Ravel: Lettres, écrits, entretiens*, p. 45 ('Une écriture nettement plus clarifiée, qui durcit l'harmonie et accuse les reliefs de la musique').

96 *'I learnt that there was not'*: Roland-Manuel, 'Des valses à *La valse* (1911–1921)', in Colette et al., *Maurice Ravel par quelques-uns de ses familiers* (Paris: Éditions du Tambourinaire, 1939), p. 144.

96 *'playing Debussy's Preludes again'*: Ravel, letter to Jean Marnold, 7 May 1910; in René Chalupt, *Ravel au miroirs de ses lettres* (Paris: Robert Laffont, 1956), p. 86.

96 *'I have received Debussy's Préludes'*: ibid., p. 88.

97 *'He was so insistent on precision'*: Perlemuter and Jourdan-Morhange, *Ravel d'après Ravel*, p. 42 ('Tellement il tenait à l'exactitude').

97 *'He was seated'*: Faure, p. 20. As for Ravel's own ability to master the waltz rhythms, Roland-Manuel relates a story about the first performance of the orchestral version of *Valses*

nobles (which Ravel cast as the ballet *Adélaïde*). Ravel's friends were alarmed when he decided to conduct it himself, as he had almost no conducting experience: "'It isn't difficult,' he declared the first evening, "It's always in three." And when we objected that the seventh waltz contained superimposed twos and threes, he willingly agreed that *did* make it difficult; "but when I get to that point I just go round and round."' Roland-Manuel, *À la gloire de Ravel*, pp. 108–9.

97 *'Despite the years that have passed'*: Perlemuter's original remark on interpretation and 'perfection of the letter' runs: 'Il y avait chez lui un tel désir d'être compris, de ne rien laisser passer non seulement dans son texte, mais dans l'interprétation de ce texte. Par le désir de perfection de la lettre, on rejoignait involontairement l'esprit.' Perlemuter and Jourdan-Morhange, *Ravel d'après Ravel*, p. 42.

99 *'his endless 1.2.3.'*: Faure, p. 20.

99 *'"lions" like Debussy and Ravel'*: Edwin Welte, in Orenstein, *Ravel Reader*, p. 532.

99 *'it is impossible to attain'*: Debussy, letter to Edwin Welte, 1 November 1913; in Debussy, *Correspondance, 1872–1918*, p. 1681.

100 *I am assured*: Roy Howat, *The Art of French Piano Music* (New Haven: Yale University Press, 2009), pp. 317–18.

101 *'incredibly schmaltzy'*: Angela Hewitt, liner notes for *Ravel: The Complete Solo Piano Music*, Angela Hewitt, piano (Hyperion, CDA67341/2, 2002), p. 10.

101 *'But what could this intense expression be'*: Jankélévitch, *Ravel* (French edn), p. 134.

102 *the ironic presence which gives*: For an illuminating account of Ravel and irony, in which Ravel, like Régnier, is firmly placed as a child of Symbolism, see Zank.

102 *'The delicious and ever novel pleasure'*: Henri de Régnier, *Les rencontres de M. de Bréot*, p. 9.

104 *'Nuances, accents and slur marks'*: Ravel, in Orenstein, *Ravel Reader*, p. 238. This is a note in Ravel's hand among papers at the Bibliothèque nationale: 'nuances accents points liaisons peuvent et doivent souvent être différents dans la transposition d'orchestre.'

104 *Ravel's wish for this*: Perlemuter and Jourdan-Morhange, *Ravel d'après Ravel*, p. 46. Roger Nichols's early monograph *Ravel* (London: J. M. Dent, 1977) published this version for the first time, though it was some years before it arrived in a published score: Maurice Hinson's 1988 edition of *Valses nobles* included the passage in an editorial note but not in the score; Hinson, foreword to *Ravel: Valses nobles et sentimentales* (Van Nuys, CA: Alfred, 1988), p. 11.

104 *'I see on my music'*: Perlemuter and Jourdan-Morhange, *Ravel d'après Ravel*, p. 46. In the radio programme, of which Perlemuter's book is a transcript (see note for *I have found her record*, chap. 1, p. 6.), he would have demonstrated this new reading at the piano. Unaccountably, the book fails to notate this new reading, despite printing many other of Perlemuter's musical examples. (My copy, the fifth French edition of 1970, even claims on the title page 'revisions and additions'; the English translation made from this edition also fails to rectify the omission.)

105 *Recordings by two other pianists*: see Ravel, *Valses nobles et sentimentales*, Peters Urtext No. 71000, ed. Roger Nichols (London: Peters, 2007), p. 27.

106 *'The paradox is that'*: Faure, pp. 42–3.

Chapter 6

107 *'I hear that Saint-Saëns'*: Ravel, letter to Jean Marnold, 7 October 1916; in Chalupt, p. 144.

108 *'As I felt I was going mad'*: Ravel, letter to Édouard Ravel, 8 August 1914; in Orenstein, *Maurice Ravel: Lettres, écrits, entretiens*, p. 141.

108 *'I will go (if they want me)'*: Ravel, letter to Cipa Godebski, 20 August 1914; in ibid.

108 *'would not have the slightest influence'*: ibid.

108 *'But Good God, Good God'*: Ravel, letter to Roland-Manuel, 1 October 1914; in ibid., p. 144.

108 *'In five weeks I have'*: Ravel, in Roland-Manuel, *À la gloire de Ravel*, p. 126.

109 *'After all, the fatherland'*: Ravel, letter to Maurice Delage, 4 August 1914; in ibid., p. 140.

109 *'And yet I am a peace-loving'*: Ravel, in Roland-Manuel, *À la gloire de Ravel*, pp. 129–30.

110 *'I saw something unimaginable'*: Ravel, letter to Jean Marnold, 4 April 1916; in Orenstein, *Maurice Ravel: Lettres, écrits, entretiens*, p. 151.

110 *'For now we've marched'*: Siegfried Sassoon, 'A Night Attack', in *The Penguin Book of First World War Poetry*, ed. and introd. Jon Silkin (London: Allen Lane, 1979), p. 119.

110 *'in the most lovely countryside'*: Ravel, in Roland-Manuel, *À la gloire de Ravel*, p. 130.

111 *'Beyond the German line'*: Sassoon, 'The Distant Song', in Jean Moorcroft Wilson, *The Making of a War Poet: A Biography, 1886–1918* (London: Duckworth, 1998), p. 315.

111 *'a moment completely quiet'*: Sebastien Faulks, *Birdsong* (London: Vintage Books, 1997), p. 181.

111 *'As a truck driver at Verdun'*: Hélène Jourdan-Morhange, 'Ravel à Monfort-l'Amaury', in Colette et al., *Maurice Ravel par quelques-uns de ses familiers* (Paris: Éditions du Tambourinaire, 1939), p. 166.

111   *'about which he spoke'*: Manuel Rosenthal, in Marnat, *Ravel: Souvenirs de Manuel Rosenthal*, p. 178.

111   *'quietly encapsulated in the Menuet'*: Howat, *The Art of French Piano Music*, p. 148.

112   *'posthumous tribute'*: ibid., p. 149.

112   *'mysterious influences'*: Roland-Manuel, *À la gloire de Ravel*, p. 125.

112   *'with little regret he would'*: ibid.

113   *'Coming from him'*: ibid., pp. 125–6.

113   *'the steep ascent of aircraft'*: Glenn Watkins, *Proof through the Night: Music and the Great War* (Berkeley and Los Angeles: University of California Press, 2003), p. 178.

114   *'What can possibly make us'*: Paul Valéry, quoted in Huebner, 'Maurice Ravel', p. 73 ('Qu'est-ce donc qui nous fera concevoir le veritable ouvrier d'un bel ouvrage? Mais il n'est positivement *personne*'). 'Au sujet d'Adonis,' in Paul Valéry, *Œuvres* (Paris: Gallimard, 1957–60), 1:483. I have used Huebner's translation.

114   *'simple pronouncement [that] music'*: Ravel, in Orenstein, *Maurice Ravel: Lettres, écrits, entretiens*, p. 47.

114   *'The fact is that'*: ibid. ('Le fait est que je me refuse simplement mais absolument à confondre la *conscience* de l'artiste, qui est une chose, avec sa *sincerité*, qui en est une autre'). For another angle on Ravel's argument see Huebner, 'Maurice Ravel', pp. 76–8.

115   *in French the word* conscience: *Conscience* can also mean 'self-awareness' and 'conscientiousness', so there is some variability in the translation of Ravel's credo at this point. However, it is clear he means to prioritize the artist's *technique* – the discipline required to bring art into being – over *feeling*. The artist's personal feelings are not the point, he is saying; there have to be impersonal forces at work otherwise 'sincerity' will amount to very little.

115   *Elsewhere he associates sincerity*: in Orenstein, *A Ravel Reader*, p. 395.

115   *'Art, without doubt'*: ibid., p. 47.

116   *for piano and orchestra*: Orenstein, *A Ravel Reader*, pp. 178–9 n. 3.

116   *or cello and orchestra*: Chalupt, p. 145.

116   *'pursued in the forests'*: Roland-Manuel, *À la gloire de Ravel*, p. 150.

116   *'the most poetic of our harpsichordists'*: Debussy, *Debussy on Music*, p. 273.

116   *'the entwined harmony'*: Michael Levey, *Rococo to Revolution: Major Trends in Eighteenth-Century Painting*, rev. edn (London: Thames & Hudson, 1977), p. 68.

116   *'nothing to do with the war'*: Ravel, letter to Lucien Garban, 8 October 1916; in Orenstein, *Maurice Ravel: Lettres, écrits, entretiens*, p. 163.

117   *'something of the inspired'*: Stuckenschmidt, p. 169.

117   *'that queen of the faculties'*: Baudelaire, p. 126.

118   *'Ah, what harm you've done'*: Alain-Fournier, *Le grand Meaulnes* (Paris: Fayard, 1971), p. 302.

118   *'He arrived at our house'*: ibid., p. 11.

118   *'sad beneath their fanciful disguises'*: Paul Verlaine, 'Clair de lune', in *Fêtes galantes*, in Brian Woleredge, Geoffrey Brereton and Anthony Hartley, eds., *The Penguin Book of French Verse* (Harmondsworth: Penguin, 1975), pp. 444–5. For a more detailed discussion of Watteau's *fêtes galantes* paintings and the *commedia dell'arte* see 'Watteau, Verlaine, and the *Fête Galante*', in Paul Roberts, *Images: The Piano Music of Claude Debussy* (Portland, OR: Amadeus Press, 1996), pp. 87–112.

119   *'not so much a tribute'*: Ravel, in Orenstein, *Maurice Ravel: Lettres, écrits, entretiens*, p. 46.

119 *Howat has admirably detailed*: Howat, *The Art of French Piano Music*, pp. 145–58.

119 *'was one of Ravel's favourite pieces'*: Wanda Landowska, in Ivry, p. 90.

119 *'the great poet'*: Edmond de Goncourt and Jules de Goncourt, *French Eighteenth-Century Painters* (Oxford: Phaidon 1981), p. 1.

119 *'In the recesses'*: ibid., p. 8.

119 *'The world of Watteau'*: ibid., p. 6.

119 *'robed allegories'*: ibid., p. 7.

120 *'The passage is a fine example'*: Wilfrid Mellers, *François Couperin and the French Classical Tradition*, rev. edn (London: Faber, 1987), p. 205.

121 *'left no documentary traces'*: Stuckenschmidt, p. 180.

122 *'like Debussy, to whom'*: Manuel Rosenthal, in Marnat, *Ravel: Souvenirs de Manuel Rosenthal*, p. 36.

122 *'Debussy's* L'isle joyeuse . . . La mer': Henri Sauguet, in Arbie Orenstein, *Ravel: Man and Musician* (New York: Dover, 1991), p. 127. Ravel told Sauguet, *'La mer* is poorly orchestrated. . . . If I had the time I would re-orchestrate *La mer'* (ibid.). But Manuel Rosenthal recalled Ravel's opinion slightly differently: 'One can't say his music is badly orchestrated, but it's written in such a way that nobody is able to learn anything from it.' Rosenthal, in Nichols, *Ravel Remembered*, p. 67.

122 *'the larger forms'*: Orenstein, *A Ravel Reader*, p. 421.

122 *'he achieved perfection'*: ibid.

122 *Ravel had little interest*: see Poulenc, *My Friends and Myself*, conversations assembled Stéphane Audel, trans. James Harding (London: Denis Dobson, 1978), p. 126. Poulenc also commented that as a young man he 'loathed' *Le tombeau de Couperin* 'violently.' Ibid., p. 127.

122 *'our incomparable Debussy'*: Ravel, in Orenstein, *A Ravel Reader*, p. 45.

Chapter 7

123 *'With music Debussy was'*: Hopkins, 15:614.

124 *'after the* Miroirs *I composed'*: Ravel, in Orenstein, *A Ravel Reader*, p. 30.

124 *we know that Ravel played*: Calvocoressi, in Roger Nichols, preface to Ravel, *Sonatine*, Peters Urtext No. 7375, ed. Roger Nichols (London: Peters, 1995), p. 4.

124 *'chaste artlessness'*: Jankélévitch, *Ravel* (French edn), p. 33.

124 *'The quiverings of melancholy'*: ibid., pp. 32–3.

125 *'It is the inner spirit'*: Faure, pp. 82–3.

125 *'rapidly slide the back'*: Vuillermoz, pp. 50–60.

125 *'It's almost always played too fast'*: Perlemuter and Jourdan-Morhange, *Ravel d'après Ravel*, p. 16.

126 *'imperceptible smile'*: Jankélévitch, *Ravel* (French edn), p. 33.

126 *'in a clumsy interpretation'*: Faure, p. 83.

126 *'Ravel asked me particularly'*: ibid.

126 *'Ravel loved playing'*: ibid., p. 84.

127 *'in the tempo of the minuet'*: Long, p. 84.

127 *'and not knowing where'*: Perlemuter, in Nichols, preface to Ravel, *Sonatine*, Peters Urtext No. 7375, ed. Roger Nichols (London: Peters, 1995), p. 4. See also note *though he performed in public*, chapter 5, p. 93.

127 *'startled by their objections'*: Ravel, letter to Léon Vallas, 8 April 1906; in Orenstein, *A Ravel Reader*, p. 81.

127 *'without prudence and without mercy'*: Faure, p. 86.

127 *'wanted it very fast but'*: Perlemuter and Jourdan-Morhange, *Ravel d'après Ravel*, p. 19.

127 *'presents no particular difficulties'*: Long, p. 84.

128 *'Mme de Saint-Marceaux has'*: Debussy, letter to Ernest Chaussson, 5 February 1894; in Debussy, *Correspondance, 1872–1918*, p. 191.

128 *Viñes, in his diary entry:* diary entry for 7 February 1902; Viñes, p. 199.

129 *'and made a face'*: Perlemuter and Jourdan-Morhange, *Ravel d'après Ravel*, p. 10.

129 *'with that somewhat testy air'*: Faure, p. 94.

129 *'very rapidly, as usual'*: ibid.

129 *'Ravel seemed only to recover'*: ibid., p. 95.

130 *'My first compositions'*: Ravel, in Orenstein, *Maurice Ravel: Lettres, écrits, entretiens*, p. 44.

130 *'In the afternoon the boy'*: diary entry for 22 November 1888; Viñes, p. 179.

130 *'We went for the first time'*: diary entry for 23 November 1888; Viñes, p 179.

130 *'In the evening to* le chevelure*'*: diary entry for 21 December 1888; Viñes, p. 179.

131 *'is dead with admiration'*: diary entry for 21 May 1898; Viñes, p. 195.

131 *'almost all the time at the piano'*: diary entry for 15 August 1892; Viñes, p. 183.

131 *'I went and browsed a bit'*: diary entry for 26 March 1895; Viñes, p. 188.

131 *'le Ravel Français d'origine Espagnole'*: Faure, p. 73.

131 *'The Spanish folk songs sung'*: Ravel, in Orenstein, *A Ravel Reader*, p. 477.

131 *'My mother used to lull me'*: ibid., p. 431.

131 *'the subtly genuine Spanishness'*: Manuel de Falla, *On Music and Musicians*, trans. David Urman and J. M. Thomson (London: Marion Boyars, 1979), pp. 94–5.

132 *'contains the germ'*: Ravel, in Orenstein, *Maurice Ravel: Lettres, écrits, entretiens*, p. 44.

132 *'I play ... Ravel's* Sites auriculaires*'*: diary entry for 5 March 1898; Viñes, p. 194.

132 *'suggesting a Latin American flavour'*: Roy Howat, 'Ravel and the Piano', in *The Cambridge Companion to Ravel*, ed. Deborah Mawer (Cambridge: Cambridge University Press, 2000), p. 75.

133 *'He disliked the whole concept'*: Brody, 'Viñes in Paris', p. 55.

133 *'Ravel told me that Debussy'*: diary entry for 31 October 1901; Viñes, p. 198.

133 *The pianist Maurice Dumesnil*: in Nichols, *Debussy Remembered*, pp. 160–1.

134 *'too dry'*: Debussy, in Roger Nichols, *Debussy Remembered* (London: Faber, 1992), p. 148.

134 *'À propos my new* Images*'*: Debussy, letter to Jean-Aubry, 10 April 1908; in Debussy, *Correspondance, 1872–1918*, p. 1083.

134 *'At one time or another'*: Klingsor, p. 135.

134 *'his irreproachable style'*: Brody, 'Viñes in Paris', p. 53.

134 *'who played and sight-read'*: Viñes, in Elaine Brody, *Paris: The Musical Kaleidoscope, 1870–1925* (London: Robson Books, 1988), p. 180.

134 *he mentions the crucially important*: Viñes's diary entry for 12 January 1895 reads: 'The piano is phenomenal, the latest model. It's very powerful and sings wonderfully, with a very easy action. What's more, it's got a third pedal, the invention of Pleyel [*sic*], in order to sustain whatever notes one wants.' I am grateful to Roy Howat for supplying me with this information.

134 *'for all of us his playing'*: Léon-Paul Fargue, *Portraits de famille* (Paris: J. B. Janin, 1947), p. 225.

134 *'Who could resist the image'*: ibid., pp. 221–2.

134   *'Viñes, alert and cheerful'*: Calvocoressi, p. 63.

135   *'I will not ask Ricardo'*: Ravel, letter to M. D. Calvocoressi, 24 March 1922; in Orenstein, *Maurice Ravel: Lettres, écrits, entretiens*, p. 197.

136   *'very painful to him'*: Elvira Viñes, David Korevaar and Laurie J. Sampsel, 'The Ricardo Viñes Piano Music Collection at the University of Colorado at Boulder', *Notes* 61, no. 2 (2004), p. 365.

136   *'I first got to know him'*: Fargue, *Portraits de famille*, p. 222. Fargue would almost certainly have heard Viñes perform *Jeux d'eau* in concert during this period, for Viñes performed the piece many times and was responsible for Ravel's becoming known as 'the composer of *Jeux d'eau*'. Viñes's copy of *Jeux d'eau* was inscribed by Ravel, 'To the keeper of the key to the waters' [Au gardien de la clé des eaux]. There is a reproduction of this inscription in *Le monde musicale* 12 (31 December 1935), p. 358; see Brody, 'Viñes in Paris', p. 50.

136   *'Everything he took up'*: ibid., p. 229.

137   *'the absence of vanity'*: Falla, p. 97.

137   *'His essential gift'*: Manuel Rosenthal, in Marnat, *Ravel: Souvenirs de Manuel Rosenthal*, p. 11.

138   *'evoke the naive, the unreal'*: Faure, p. 96.

138   *The epigraph relates*: The epigraph, printed in the original Durand edition, comes from Charles Perrault's *Histoires ou contes du temps passé avec des moralités* (Stories and Moral Tales of Olden Times), first published in 1697.

138   *'The difficulty of this piece confounded'*: ibid., p. 97.

138   *'She undressed and stepped into the bath'*: From Marie-Catherine, Comtesse d'Aulnoy, *Les contes de fées* (Fairy Stories) (1697).

139   *'after all, she is the empress'*: Faure, p. 97.

139   *'When I think of your kind heart'*: The tale comes from Marie Leprince de Beaumont, *Contes moraux* (Moral Tales) (1757).

139   *'You are the pretty one'*: Faure, p. 97.

139   *'This needs more reverence'*: ibid.

140   *'a torture that fifty years later'*: ibid., p. 20.

140   *'artistic directors, conductors'*: ibid., p. 32.

140   *'he had a horror'*: ibid.

140   *'the little Monsieur'*: ibid., p. 33.

140   *'Each time the ritual unfolded'*: ibid., pp. 23–4.

141   *'Ravel was a charming companion'*: ibid., p. 25.

142   *'he wanted the immediate realisation'*: ibid.

143   *'crowded with bibelots'*: quoted in Orenstein, *A Ravel Reader*, p. 506.

143   *'All over my score he wrote'*: Perlemuter and Jourdan-Morhange, *Ravel d'après Ravel*, p. 31.

144   *'Maurice Ravel demanded'*: Faure, p. 70.

144   *'Whenever I reached those places'*: ibid., p. 72.

144   *'I don't ask for my music'*: ibid., p. 70.

144   *The first concerns a recording*: Orenstein, *A Ravel Reader*, p. 536. Ravel could at times admit to inconsistency. Rosenthal, conducting a morning rehearsal of *La valse*, recalled an instance when Ravel had told him afterwards that it was very good, but in his opinion 'too fast.' At the evening concert Rosenthal took it slower. Ravel said: 'I was wrong to tell you that. It was much better this morning.' He then went on to suggest that metronome markings, which might appear to settle the matter, were only useful as 'safe-guards.' 'If I put 'quarter-note equals 92', then this means "not 120 and not 72 either"'. Marnat, *Ravel: Souvenirs de Manuel Rosenthal*, pp. 147–8.

145   *'play it as you want'*: Chalupt, p. 70.

145   *'the impression of playing'*: Orenstein, *A Ravel Reader*, p. 595.

146 *Any problems that might arise*: Krenek, p. 180.

146 *'and so all criticism is prose poetry'*: Bloom, p. 95.

Appendix A

147 *'at a livelier tempo'*: Faure, p. 95.

150 *'This music is very specifically descriptive'*: Viñes, in Jourdan-Morhange, *Ravel et nous*, p. 215.

151 *'was essentially concerned'*: Faure, pp. 71–2.

152 *'the character of an improvisation'*: ibid., p. 71.

153 *'must not be played strictly'*: Perlemuter and Jourdan-Morhange, *Ravel d'après Ravel*, p. 24.

153 *In her own account*: Faure, p. 71.

153 *'Look at those trees'*: in Jean-Jacques Eigeldinger, *Chopin: Pianist and Teacher*, ed. Roy Howat, trans. Naomi Shohet with Krysia Osostowicz and Roy Howat (Cambridge: Cambridge University Press, 1986), p. 51.

153 *'Even though Ravel loved exact interpretation'*: Viñes, in Jourdan-Morhange, *Ravel et nous*, p. 215.

153 *'weighed down by uniformity'*: Faure, p. 72.

154 *'not too fast, without dragging'*: Perlemuter and Jourdan-Morhange, *Ravel d'après Ravel*, p. 11.

154 *'slow but moving'*: ibid., p. 18.

154 *'very fast but not rushed'*: ibid., p. 19.

154 *'en général très marqué'*: Viñes, in Jourdan-Morhange, *Ravel et nous*, p. 216. On Ravel's characteristic crescendos, see 'Simple Sound: Ravel and "Crescendo"', in Zank, pp. 40–85.

155 *Ravel, as we have seen*: Ravel, letter to Calvocoressi, 24 March 1922; in Orenstein, *Maurice Ravel: Lettres, écrits, entretiens*, p. 197. See chapter 1, p. 14.

155 *'Whenever I opened my music'*: Faure, pp. 75–6.

156   *In those places*: ibid., p. 76.

156   *Ravel wanted me to play*: Perlemuter and Jourdan-Morhange, *Ravel d'après Ravel*, p. 29.

157   *oh, so slight!*: Faure, p. 76.

157   *une rumeur lointaine*: Perlemuter and Jourdan-Morhange, *Ravel d'après Ravel*, p. 29.

157   *a distant murmuring*: Vlado Perlemuter and Jourdan-Morhange, *Ravel According to Ravel*, ed. Harold Taylor, trans. Frances Tanner (London: Kahn & Averill, 1988), p. 26.

157   *eighth note = eighth note*: Perlemuter and Jourdan-Morhange, *Ravel d'après Ravel*, p. 29.

159   *correct the heaviness of her thumbs*: ibid., p. 57.

159   *no rhythmic weakness*: ibid.

159   *To Perlemuter he said*: Perlemuter and Jourdan-Morhange, *Ravel d'après Ravel*, p. 31.

159   *suggestive magic*: Faure, p. 57.

159   *a piece within a piece*: Perlemuter and Jourdan-Morhange, *Ravel d'après Ravel*, p. 32.

160   *In 'Le gibet' he insisted*: Faure, pp. 60–2.

160   *like Ricardo Viñes; an admirable artist*: ibid., p. 61.

160   *Above all Ravel was concerned*: ibid., pp. 64–5.

160   *'You might not see me'*: ibid., p. 31.

161   *not only where they are needed for expression*: Perlemuter and Jourdan-Morhange, *Ravel d'après Ravel*, p. 37.

161   *comme un tambour*: ibid.

161   *an orchestral transcription for piano*: ibid., p. 38.

161   *Most commentators (but not Perlemuter or Faure)*: See for example Roger Nichols, in Ravel, *Gaspard de la nuit*, Peters Urtext No. 7378 (London: Peters, 1991), p. 46.

161   *an enormous amount of pedal*: Perlemuter and Jourdan-Morhange, *Ravel d'après Ravel*, p. 38.

162   *weakness for Liszt*: ibid.

162 *'You know of my deep sympathy'*: Ravel, letter to Jean Marnold, 7 February 1906; in Orenstein, *Ravel Reader*, p. 80.

162 *'endless 1.2.3.'*: Faure, p. 20.

163 *'infinitely lonely lyricism'*: Paul Crossley, liner notes for *Ravel: The Complete Solo Piano Works, Vol. 1* (CRD, 1983).

163 *'shades of rubato'*: Faure, p. 39.

164 *'comme une révérence'*: Perlemuter and Jourdan-Morhange, *Ravel d'après Ravel*, p. 45.

164 *'so insistent on such details'*: ibid., p. 45 ('Ravel insistait tellement sur toute cette ponctuation!').

164 *Ravel gave Faure the title*: Faure, p. 40.

164 *'Ravel's fourth waltz is so close'*: Stuckenschmidt, p. 144.

165 *'Waltz 1830'*: Faure, p. 41.

165 *'In the spirit of a Schubert Waltz'*: Perlemuter and Jourdan-Morhange, *Ravel d'après Ravel*, p. 49.

165 *This is the one that Perlemuter said*: ibid., p. 50.

166 *This waltz put Faure in mind*: Faure, p. 41.

166 *'broken musical box'*: ibid., p. 42.

166 *'the most characteristic'*: Ravel, in Orenstein, *A Ravel Reader*, p. 31.

167 *'little touches of pedal'*: ibid., p. 63.

167 *These are imitative of baroque 'snaps'*: For more on Ravel's baroque imitation see Rosen: 'What Ravel aims at is not the early eighteenth-century style; it is the early eighteenth-century *sound*' (p. 33).

168 *the composer is no less Ravel*: In a lecture Ravel gave in Houston, Texas, in 1928, he made exactly the same point. Referring to his use of the blues he said, 'While I adopted this particular form of your music, I venture to say that nevertheless it is French music, Ravel's music, that I have written.' In Orenstein, *A Ravel Reader*, p. 46.

168 *'very much like a musical box'*: ibid., p. 68.

168 *Faure suggests using only finger weight*: Faure, p. 88.

169 *Perlemuter stresses the Fugue's intensely expressive nature*: Perlemuter and Jourdan-Morhange, *Ravel d'après Ravel*, p. 66.

170 *'like a curtsey'*: ibid., p. 45.

172 *'like a surprise'*: ibid., p. 73.

172 *'Play it as rapidly as possible'*: Ravel, in Orenstein, *A Ravel Reader*, p. 556.

173 *'Instrumentation is when'*: in Nichols, *Ravel Remembered*, pp. 67–8.

Appendix B

175 *On 16 January 1895*: See note for *he mentions the crucially important*, chapter 7, p. 134.

175 *Roy Howat, however, confirms*: Howat, *The Art of French Piano Music*, p. 288.

175 *Three pedals were standard*: ibid., p. 372 n. 17.

175 *The French piano makers*: ibid., p. 372 n. 15.

175 *Steinway had perfected its own system*: John Paul Williams, *The Piano* (London: Aurum, 2002), p. 26.

176 *pedal technique stretching back to Chopin*: see Eigeldinger, pp. 57–8 and 128–30. For pedalling in Ravel, see Howat, *The Art of French Piano Music*, pp. 279–81.

176 *'a kind of breathing'*: Ravel, letter to Jacques Durand, 1 September 1915; in Debussy, *Correspondance, 1872–1918*, p. 1927.

176 *(but not to Debussy)*: see chapter 7, p. 134.

176 *he had been a pupil of Viñes*: Poulenc studied piano with Viñes from 1914 to 1917. He relates how, beginning with just a thirty-minute lesson each week, 'imperceptibly, I began to spend my life with this Hidalgo with the face of a kindly inquisitor.' Francis Poulenc, in *Francis Poulenc: 'Echo and Source'; Selected*

Correspondence, 1915–1963, trans. and ed. Sidney Buckland (London: Victor Gollancz, 1991), p. 315.

176   *as much to do with the nature of Poulenc*: It is clear, however, that Poulenc was temperamentally in tune with Viñes's playing: '[To him] I owe EVERYTHING in my musical career,' he wrote to Viñes's niece, 'both as pianist and composer'; letter to Elvira Viñes Soto, 10 March 1949; ibid., p. 174. And Poulenc also recalls his pedalling: 'Nobody taught the art of pedalling better than Viñes. Thus he paradoxically managed to play clearly in a sea of pedal.' Quoted in Howat, *The Art of French Piano Music*, p. 371 n. 1. However, see chapter 7, p. 134.

176   *'from the self-evident necessity'*: Walter Gieseking, 'How Does One Perform Ravel's Piano Music', trans. Ronald E. Booth II, in Hinson, p. 14.

177   *that moment that Ravel loved*: see chapter 7, p. 126.

177   *'How do you manage not to blur'*: Perlemuter and Jourdan-Morhange, *Ravel d'apres Ravel*, pp. 18–19. Howat observes that Perlemuter's own piano was a model O with no sostenuto pedal. But this does not explain why he never recorded any remarks of Ravel's about the sostenuto (so we can only assume Ravel never made any). And Perlemuter would have repeatedly performed on Steinway Ds.

177   *'one of the keepers of the Ravel doctrine'*: ibid., p. 8. See also note to chapter 2, p. 23.

177   *'The phrases swam into each other'*: in Worthen, p. 69.

177   *'Ravel, in response to certain'*: Abram Chasins, in Hinson, p. 9.

178   *In* Valses nobles: Howat, *The Art of French Piano Music*, p. 289.

Selected Bibliography

Alain-Fournier. *Le grand Meaulnes*. Paris: Fayard, 1971.

———. *Le grand Meaulnes*. Translated by Frank Davison. London: Oxford University Press, 1970.

Badura-Skoda, Eva, and Paul Badura-Skoda. *Interpreting Mozart on the Keyboard*. Translated by Leo Black. London: Barrie & Rockliff, 1970.

Baudelaire, Charles. *Baudelaire: Selected Writings on Art and Artists*. Translated by P. E. Charvet. Cambridge: Cambridge University Press, 1972.

Bergonzi, Bernard. *T. S. Eliot*. London: Macmillan, 1972.

Bertrand, Aloysius. *Gaspard de la nuit*. Paris: Le Livre de Poche, 2002.

Beucler, André. *Poet of Paris*. Translated by Geoffrey Sainsbury. London: Chatto & Windus, 1955.

Bloom, Harold. *The Anxiety of Influence: A Theory of Poetry*. 2nd edn. Oxford: Oxford University Press, 1997.

Brody, Elaine. *Paris: The Musical Kaleidoscope, 1870–1925*. London: Robson Books, 1988.

———. 'Viñes in Paris: New Light on Twentieth-Century Performance Practice'. In *A Musical Offering: Essays in Honor of Martin Bernstein*, edited by Edward H. Clinkscale and Claire Brook, pp. 45–62. New York: Pendragon Press, 1977.

Calvocoressi, Michel Dmitri. *Music and Ballet*. London: Faber, 1934.

Chalupt, René. *Ravel au miroirs de ses lettres*. Paris: Robert Laffont, 1956.

Colette et al. *Maurice Ravel par quelques-uns de ses familiers*. Paris: Éditions du Tambourinaire, 1939.

Crossley, Paul. Liner notes to CRD Records 3383 (1983), *Ravel: The Complete Solo Piano Works, Vol. 1*, performed by Paul Crossley.

Debussy, Claude. *Claude Debussy: Piano Music 1888–1905*. Mineola, NY: Dover, 1974.

———. *Correspondance, 1872–1918*. Edited by François Lesure, Denis Herlin. Annotated by François Lesure, Denis Herlin and Georges Liébert. Paris: Gallimard, 2005.

———. *Debussy on Music: The Critical Writings of the Great French Composer*. Edited by François Lesure and R. Langham Smith. Translated by R. Langham Smith. London: Secker & Warburg, 1977.

Delage, Maurice. 'Les premiers amis de Ravel'. In Colette et al., *Maurice Ravel par quelques-uns de ses familiers*, pp. 97–113. Paris: Éditions du Tambourinaire, 1939.

Demuth, Norman. *Ravel*. New York: Collier Books, 1962.

Eigeldinger, Jean-Jacques. *Chopin: Pianist and Teacher*. Edited by Roy Howat. Translated by Naomi Shohet with Krysia Osostowicz and Roy Howat. Cambridge: Cambridge University Press, 1986.

Eliot, T. S. *T. S Eliot: Selected Prose*. Edited by John Hayward. London: Penguin Books, 1953.

Ellis, Henry Havelock. 'Henri de Régnier'. *North American Review*, 201, no. 712 (March 1915), pp. 412–22.

Falla, Manuel de. *On Music and Musicians*. Translated by David Urman and J. M. Thomson. London: Marion Boyars, 1979.

Fargue, Léon-Paul. *Maurice Ravel*. Fata Morgana, 2008.

———. *Portraits de famille*. Paris: J. B. Janin, 1947.

———. 'Autour de Ravel'. In Colette et al., *Maurice Ravel par quelques-uns de ses familiers*, pp. 153–61. Paris: Éditions du Tambourinaire, 1939.

———. *Poèmes; suivi de 'Pour la musique'*. Paris: Gallimard, 1919.

———. *An English Translation of Léon-Paul Fargue's 'Poèmes'*. Translated and with an introduction by Peter S. Thompson. New York: Edwin Mellen Press, 2003.

Faulks, Sebastien. *Birdsong*. London: Vintage Books, 1997.

Faure, Henriette. *Mon maître Maurice Ravel*. Paris: Éditions ATP, 1978.

Forbes, F. William. 'The "Gracioso": Toward a Functional Re-Evaluation'. *Hispania*, 61, no. 1 (March 1978), pp. 78–83.

Gibson, Robert. *The Land without a Name: Alain-Fournier and His World*. London: Elek Books, 1975.

Goncourt, Edmond de, and Jules de Goncourt. *French Eighteenth-Century Painters*. Oxford: Phaidon Press, 1981.

Goss, Madeleine. *Bolero: The Life of Maurice Ravel*. New York: Holt, 1940.

Goujon, Jean-Paul. *Léon-Paul Fargue: Poète et piéton de Paris*. Paris: Gallimard, 1997.

Hewitt, Angela. Liner notes to Hyperion Records CDA 67341/2 (2002), *Ravel: The Complete Solo Piano Music*, performed by Angela Hewitt.

Hinson, Maurice. Foreword to *Ravel: Valses nobles et sentimentales*. Van Nuys, CA: Alfred, 1988.

Hopkins, G. W. '(Joseph) Maurice Ravel'. In *The New Grove Dictionary of Music and Musicians*, edited by Stanley Sadie, 15:609–21. London and New York: Macmillan, 1980.

Howat, Roy. *The Art of French Piano Music*. New Haven: Yale University Press, 2009.

———. 'Ravel and the Piano'. In *The Cambridge Companion to Ravel*, edited by Deborah Mawer, pp. 71–96. Cambridge: Cambridge University Press, 2000.

Huebner, Steven. 'Maurice Ravel: Private Life, Public Works'. In *Musical Biography: Towards New Paradigms*, edited by Jolanta T. Pekacz, pp. 69–87. Aldershot: Ashgate, 2006.

———. 'Ravel's Poetics: Literary Currents, Classical Takes'. In *Unmasking Ravel: New Perspectives on the Music*, edited by Peter Kaminsky, pp. 9–40. Rochester: University of Rochester Press, 2011.

Ivry, Benjamin. *Maurice Ravel: A Life*. New York: Welcome Rain, 2000.

Jankélévitch, Vladimir. *Ravel*. 2nd edn. Paris: Solfèges/Seuil, 1956.

———. *Ravel*. London and New York: John Calder and Grove Press, 1959.

Jourdan-Morhange, Hélène. 'Ravel à Montfort-l'Amaury'. In Colette et al., *Maurice Ravel par quelques-uns de ses familiers*, pp. 163–9. Paris: Éditions du Tambourinaire, 1939.

———. *Ravel et nous: L'homme, l'ami, le musicien*. Geneva: Éditions du milieu du monde, 1945.

Klingsor, Tristan. 'L'époque Ravel'. In Colette et al., *Maurice Ravel par quelques-uns de ses familiers*, pp. 125–39. Paris: Éditions du Tambourinaire, 1939.

Korevaar, David, and Sampsel, Laurie J. 'The Ricardo Viñes Piano Music Collection at the University of Colorado at Boulder'. *Notes*, 61, no. 2 (2004), pp. 361–400.

Krenek, Ernst. *Exploring Music*. Translated by Margaret Shenfield and Geoffrey Skelton. London: Caldar & Boyars, 1966.

Kundera, Milan. *Encounter*. Translated by Linda Asher. New York: HarperCollins, 2009.

Levey, Michael. *Rococo to Revolution: Major Trends in Eighteenth-Century Painting*. Rev. edn. London: Thames & Hudson, 1977.

Lévi-Strauss, Claude. *Look, Listen, Read*. Translated by Brian C. J. Singer. New York: HarperCollins, 1997.

Liszt, Franz. *Musikalische Werke*. Ser. II vol. VI, *Années de pèlerinage*. Leipzig: Breitkopf and Härtel, 1916. Reprint, Farnborough, UK: Gregg Press, 1966.

Long, Marguerite. *At the Piano with Ravel*. Translated by Olive Senior-Ellis. London: J. M. Dent, 1973.

Marnat, Marcel. *Maurice Ravel*. Paris: Fayard, 1986.

———, ed. *Ravel: Souvenirs de Manuel Rosenthal*. Paris: Hazan, 1995.

Mawer, Deborah. 'Musical Objects and Machines'. In *The Cambridge Companion to Ravel*, edited by Deborah Mawer, pp. 47–67. Cambridge: Cambridge University Press, 2000.

Mellers, Wilfrid. *François Couperin and the French Classical Tradition*. Rev. edn. London: Faber, 1987.

Nichols, Roger. *Ravel*. London: J. M. Dent, 1977.

———. *Ravel Remembered*. London: Faber, 1987.

———. *Debussy Remembered*. London: Faber, 1992.

———. 'Early Reception of Ravel's Piano Music (1899–1939)'. In *The Cambridge Companion to Ravel*, edited by Deborah Mawer, pp. 251–66. Cambridge: Cambridge University Press, 2000.

———. *Ravel: A Life*. New Haven: Yale University Press, 2011.

———. 'Ravel and the Twentieth Century'. In *The Cambridge Companion to Ravel*, edited by Deborah Mawer, pp. 240–9. Cambridge: Cambridge University Press, 2000.

Norden, Janet. 'Moreto's Polilla and the Spirit of Carnival'. *Hispania*, 68, no. 2 (May 1985), pp. 236–41.

Orenstein, Arbie, ed. *Maurice Ravel: Lettres, écrits, entretiens*. Paris: Flammarion, 1989.

———. *A Ravel Reader: Correspondence, Articles, Interviews*. New York: Columbia University Press, 1990.

———. *Ravel: Man and Musician*. New York: Columbia University Press, 1991.

Palmer, Christopher. 'Debussy, Ravel and Alain-Fournier'. *Music and Letters*, 50, no. 2 (April 1969), pp. 267–72.

Perlemuter, Vlado, and Hélène Jourdan-Morhange. *Ravel d'après Ravel: Les œuvres pour piano, les deux concertos*. 5th edn. Lausanne: Éditions du Cervin, 1970.

———. *Ravel According to Ravel*. Edited by Harold Taylor. Translated by Frances Tanner. London: Kahn & Averill, 1988.

Poulenc, Francis. *Francis Poulenc: 'Echo and Source': Selected Corre-spondence, 1915–1963*. Translated and edited by Sidney Buckland. London: Victor Gollancz, 1991.

———. *My Friends and Myself.* Conversations assembled by Stéphane Audel. Translated by James Harding. London: Denis Dobson, 1978.

Ravel, Maurice. *Gaspard de la nuit*. Paris: Durand & Fils, 1905.

———. *Miroirs*. Paris: E. Demets, 1906.

———. *The Piano Masterpieces of Maurice Ravel*. Mineola, NY: Dover, 1986.

———. *Le Tombeau de Couperin and Other Works for Solo Piano*. Mineola, NY: Dover, 1997

Régnier, Henri de. *La cité des eaux*. Paris: Mercure de France, 1911.

———. *Les rencontres de M. de Bréot*. Paris: Mercure de France, 1946.

Roberts, Paul. *Images: The Piano Music of Claude Debussy*. Portland, OR: Amadeus Press, 1996.

———. *Debussy*. London: Phaidon Press, 2008.

Roland-Manuel. *À la gloire de Ravel*. Paris: Nouvelle Revue Cri-tique, 1938.

———. *Maurice Ravel*. Translated by Cynthia Jolly. London: Dobson, 1947.

———. 'Des valses à *La valse* (1911–1921)'. In Colette et al., *Maurice Ravel par quelques-uns de ses familiers*, pp. 141–51. Paris: Éditions du Tambourinaire, 1939.

Rosen, Charles. 'Where Ravel Ends and Debussy Begins'. In *Cahiers Debussy*, n.s., 3 (1979), pp. 31–8.

Schub, Louise Rypko. *Léon-Paul Fargue*. Geneva: Librairie Droz, 1973.

Silkin, Jon, ed. and introd. *The Penguin Book of First World War Poetry*. London: Allen Lane, 1979.

Stuckenschmidt, Hans-Heinz. *Maurice Ravel: Variations on His Life and Work*. Translated by S. R. Rosenbaum. London: Calder & Boyars, 1969.

Timbrell, Charles. *French Pianism: An Historical Perspective*. White Plains: Pro/Am Music Resources, 1992.

———. 'Ravel's *Miroirs*'. *International Piano Quarterly* (Spring 2001), pp. 52–61.

Vega, Lope de. *Two Plays by Lope de Vega: 'The Great Pretenders' and 'The Gentleman from Olmedo'*. Translated and adapted by David Johnston, with an introduction by Isabel Torres. Bath: Absolute Press, 1991.

Viñes, Ricardo. 'La vie musicale à Paris entre 1887 et 1914 à travers le journal de R. Viñes', translated and edited by Nina Gubisch, *Revue international de musique française, 1, no. 2* (June 1980), pp. 154–248.

Vuillermoz, Émile. 'L'œuvre de Maurice Ravel'. In Colette et al., *Maurice Ravel par quelques-uns de ses familiers*, pp. 1–95. Paris: Éditions du Tambourinaire, 1939.

Watkins, Glenn. *Proof through the Night: Music and the Great War*. Berkeley and Los Angeles: University of California Press, 2003.

Welsford, Enid. *The Fool: His Social and Literary History*. London: Faber, 1968.

Williams, John-Paul. *The Piano*. London: Aurum, 2002.

Wilson, Jean Moorcroft. *The Making of a War Poet: A Biography, 1886–1918*. London: Duckworth, 1998.

Woleredge, Brian, Geoffrey Brereton and Anthony Hartley, eds. *The Penguin Book of French Verse*. Harmondsworth: Penguin, 1975.

Woodley, Roger. 'Performing Ravel: Style and Practice in the Early Recordings'. In *The Cambridge Companion to Ravel*, edited by Deborah Mawer, pp. 213–19. Cambridge: Cambridge University Press, 2000.

Worthen, John. *Robert Schumann: Life and Death of a Musician*. New Haven & London: Yale University Press, 2007.

Wright, John T. *Louis 'Aloysius' Bertrand's 'Gaspard de la Nuit': Fantasies in the Manner of Rembrandt and Callot*. 2nd edn. Lanham, MD: University Press of America, 1994.

Zank, Stephen. *Irony and Sound: The Music of Maurice Ravel*. New York: University of Rochester Press, 2009.

Index

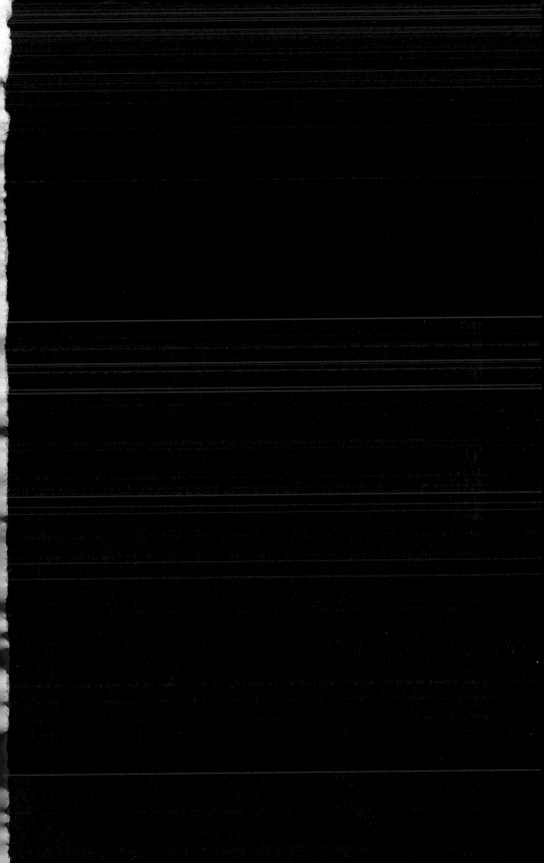